Date Due

DES PLAINES, ILLINOIS   60016

The
Five
Lives
of

Ben
Hecht

BEN HECHT

The
Five
Lives
of
Ben
Hecht

67955

Doug
Fetherling

Lester and Orpen Limited

Material from *A Child of the Century* by Ben Hecht, copyright © by Ben Hecht, reprinted by permission of SIMON & SCHUSTER, a Division of Gulf & Western Corporation.

Canadian Cataloguing in Publication Data

Fetherling, Doug, 1949—
    The five lives of Ben Hecht

Bibliography: p.
Filmography: p.
Includes index.
ISBN 0-919630-85-5

1. Hecht, Ben, 1894-1964
    Criticism and interpretation.
I. Title.

PS3515.E18Z62   812'.5'2   C77-001255-8

Printed in Canada

Designed and composed
at Dreadnaught
Toronto Canada
in VIP Pilgrim and
American Typewriter
and Antique #5

For
Dale
Singer
Fetherling

Contents

Foreword

This book is an introduction to Ben Hecht's work in various media and an attempt to sort out his reputation. It is not a biography. Nor is it a reworking of the abundant anecdotal material available from printed sources. Rather, it is what I believe must precede a biography by some other hand. The aim is to show those who know only Hecht's literary side that his work in film was not the sudden rebuke to art it was for so long presumed to be, but a continuation in other forms of his literary preoccupations. Similarly, I hope to demonstrate to the even greater numbers of people aware of his cinematic but not his other writing, that the origins of the screen-writer can be found in the newspaperman, the novelist and the playwright.

Accordingly, I have included little more than a running sketch of his life and only such anecdotes as I felt helped describe the parts of his personality being discussed. I have not tried to give the definitive forms of even those anecdotes and stories I have employed. It is in the nature of both literary and film people to leave behind them a tangle of different versions of the incidents, feuds and collisions which crowd their careers. Such versions as I have given are merely the commonest ones; for others the reader is referred to some of the books listed in Appendix Three.

This book's concern with the critical over biographical extends to the chapter dealing with Hecht's polemical writings; I have tried to discuss the manner and method of such works without dwelling on the apparent correctness or incorrectness of his political views.

The Five Lives of Ben Hecht

An exception to my bias in favour of the critical comes in part of the final chapter. There I have given a fuller account of Hecht's last years than might at first seem consistent with the rest of the book. I have done so because such material takes up where Hecht's various memoirs leave off and is not otherwise conveniently available.

My method in showing the origins and course of Hecht's writing has been to break his works and career into five "lives" or phases, which overlap and reinforce one another, and to discuss the seminal works under each heading. These writings, which include fiction and nonfiction books as well as work for the stage and the screen, will, I hope, illustrate the high-relief spots and turning points of his career, thus making some order from the confusing general picture of him now current. It is more within the province of this small study to recapitulate and categorize than to analyse in a serious way. My hope is that the literary people and the film people will be patient when I become fundamental in the course of arbitrating the claims of both groups.

I am indebted to many people for their help in this project. Ronald Evans and the Ontario Arts Council provided a grant in aid of research. Nancy Naglin interviewed Ralph Ingersoll in my stead, and Clyde Gilmour graciously allowed me to use notes he made during an interview with William Wellman, now deceased. Earle Birney provided the anecdote about the 1932 performance of *The Front Page* in Toronto, which he attended. Ross McLean of the Canadian Broadcasting Corporation arranged a screening of Hecht's television play, "Hello Charlie." Robertson Davies, Serrell Hillman and Fletcher Markle gave me the benefit of their reminiscences of Hecht; and George Jonas and David Lewis Stein offered valuable comments on Chapter Eight. Finally, I give thanks to Malcolm Lester, a patient editor, and to Margaret Wente, who also intercepted many of my stylistic crudities.

Doug Fetherling
April, 1977

1
The History of his Reputation

*Although I am known here and there as a writer
not without wit and fecundity, the information is
a bit spotty and I can rely little on reader snobbery.*
BH, *in* A Child of the Century

Ben Hecht was the kind of person to whom legends stuck like lint. Sometimes it seems that the stories about him, which he did little to deny and often embellished beyond credibility, have a wider audience than his works – the plays, novels, stories and screenplays he manufactured tirelessly till his death in 1964 at age seventy. He was the kind of man who impressed people, strongly and immediately, as being energetic, sardonic, kind-hearted or garrulous, a genius or a mountebank. The interpretation depended not so much upon his mood as upon the other person's receiving set.

Hecht was born February 28, 1894 on the Lower East Side of New York and attended Broome Steet grammar school in the ghetto. His parents were Jewish immigrants from Russia. Hecht himself chose to forget that he was a Jew, until the atrocities of World War Two and later the Palestine crisis brought his feelings to the surface with a wrath so intense it appeared to have been welling up for decades. Perhaps he would have been conscious of his heritage earlier had his family remained in New York. Writing in his late fifties of his return to New York from Chicago, he noted that he was surprised to encounter "Jews without accent, and not remotely connected

3

with tailoring – a novelty to me who had known only the Jewish voices and needle-ish activities of my family." But his parents did not remain in New York. They moved him at an early age to Wisconsin, where he enjoyed an outdoorsy childhood undistinguished except by precocious flings at performing later abandoned for the dream of the big city.

In young manhood Hecht cultivated a vaguely Latin appearance. He was a short, thin, broad-shouldered youth with a full head of dark hair and, by about 1912, a heavy black mustache that later wore grey and thin, like David Niven's. He was addicted to bowties and fedoras but that was nothing like his addiction to work. Usually he wrote in pencil, though in his younger days he had been quick-witted and agile enough to render Latin verses into rhyming quatrains on the typewriter as they were read to him aloud in rough English. In middle age he was inclined toward thickwaistedness, balding and an abundance of chins, but as one colleague remarked, he still looked tough and he was.

Although never really poor, he strove to be rich – for the hell of it, rather than out of fear or insecurity or thirst for power. In his time he made fortunes and spent them lavishly, mainly on travel and other luxuries, obtaining freedom from the film studios which at several periods in the 1930s paid him a thousand dollars a day. It was primarily with a view toward getting rich quick that he went to Hollywood. Making a fortune there, he disposed of it quickly to prove that he could do so uncaringly and earn another. But if he could make money and spend it, he could also turn away from it – at least in his salad years. During the Depression he told an interviewer that Samuel Goldwyn offered him a contract for $50,000 a year for two story ideas, only one of which had to be acceptable. Hecht tore up the contract for no other reason than that he felt like doing so.

The lifestyle needed capital to perpetuate itself, however, and Hecht later became trapped into supporting his habits. After the initial success of *The Front Page* in 1928, Hecht and his co-author Charles MacArthur purchased large neighbouring houses on the Hudson in Nyack, New York, MacArthur's boyhood home. Hecht lived there from the end of the 1920s onward at least six months of the year, writing books and plays. For the other six months he supported this luxury by writing scripts in California, for the longest period at a second home in Oceanside.

Hecht was a generous man but his generosity was peculiarly Hechtian. It seems to have benefited him not in material ways but with companionship and what MacArthur called "lively doings." At a time when the economic future of Hollywood's lesser writers, actors and technicians was bleak, Hecht got in the habit of treating them en masse to weekly feasts. The regularly scheduled banquets discharged his obligations neatly and allowed him more time for work. Once when the poet Maxwell Bodenheim, Hecht's Chicago collaborator and official antagonist, wrote imploringly for money, Hecht replied that he was enclosing an immediate $200, then deliberately failed to make the enclosure. Yet in the 1940s, perhaps that poet's darkest days, Hecht supported him by sending $35 a week in return for a weekly poem or piece of prose. Bodenheim's lifelong poverty came to an end in 1954 when he was brutally murdered in an eighty-five-cent-a-night room in the Bowery. Hecht made a big display of saving him from potter's field by paying for his funeral, though later research has revealed that Hecht contributed only $50 toward the burial.

Most of Hecht's friendships were with men and most were lasting. However, with peers who slighted him, he could be vindictive. He never forgave Heywood Broun, for instance, for some remark in Broun's column. Hecht also displayed a second kind of ingrained animosity, which probably would have existed even if no words had ever been exchanged. Hecht's hostility toward Ernest Hemingway, for example, outlasted even the more famous writer's death. Although Hemingway once said in a letter that he disliked "smart Jews" like Hecht, the reason for the essentially one-sided feud is not really known. Whatever the cause, it was in full swing for years before Hecht wrote the 1957 remake of *A Farewell to Arms*, which Hemingway disliked as he disliked all other screen adaptations of his work.

Hecht was twice married. His first wife was Marie Armstrong, a reporter whom he wed in 1918 and divorced in 1925. He hints in his memoirs that he married her to relieve his sexual frustrations; frustrations which only places like Madame Lil Hamilton's House of All Nations in Chicago had relieved. It seems his freewheeling

The Five Lives of Ben Hecht

newspaper existence brought him into constant contact with most everything except fornication. In his autobiographical writings, he mentions Marie and their daughter Edwina hardly at all. Aside from the fiction of *Erik Dorn*, his clearest statement on the marriage comes in *Charlie*, his memoir of MacArthur, when he discusses Carol Fink. She was a reporter MacArthur married early in apparently the same circumstances as Hecht's first marriage and whom he struggled to divorce in order to marry the actress Helen Hayes.

When legally free of his first wife, Hecht married Rose Caylor, a Russian-born former actress with whom he had moved to New York. She claimed descent from over a hundred rabbis, and was later to become a novelist, screenwriter and playwright. One of the plays she and Hecht wrote together, *All He Ever Loved*, was filmed in 1935 by Hecht and MacArthur as *The Scoundrel*. It was the best of the movies the two men wrote, directed and produced themselves in their brief attempt at beating Hollywood at its own game. By the second marriage Hecht had another daughter, Jenny, a child actress on whom he doted and on whose behalf he plunged into several of the nagging little controversies that punctuated his career. It was mainly in celebration of Jenny that Hecht occasionally composed doggerel long after the higher poetic ambitions of his youth had faded.

Hecht's career as a writer can be broken up into five phases or lives, each including work in more than one medium, each spilling over into a neighbouring phase in terms of chronology and content. First there was Hecht the Iconoclast, the apprentice rabblerouser of Chicago, the dabbler in Swinburnian verse and author of plays so daringly advance guard that they seemed once or twice to reach new heights of artistic unintelligibility. He was the nihilistic genius of the cityroom transformed by night into the writer of such porno-fantasies as *Fantazius Mallare* and *The Kingdom of Evil* or the corresponding elements of *Erik Dorn*, *Gargoyles* and the stories in *Broken Necks*. His style and ideas were largely German expressionist in origin, by way of H. L. Mencken and Mencken's precursors James Gibbons Huneker and Sadakichi Hartmann. These impulses and artistic leanings gained fresh impetus, then faded considerably, following his assignment in 1919 and 1920 as the Chicago *Daily*

6

The History of his Reputation

News correspondent in Berlin, where he met the German Dadaists and introduced their ideas, watered down, to Chicago. Some of this style, greatly diluted, can be seen in several Hecht films, notably *Crime Without Passion*.

Next came Hecht the Bohemian, the chronicler of the city wretched and reveller in urban excitement and decay. This persona burst forth in book form with *Erik Dorn*, a novel about a love triangle but also about the effects of urban life upon the triangle's three points. The tone was continued the following year with *Gargoyles* and 1001 *Afternoons in Chicago*, the second a collection of the sketches of city life he'd been contributing to the *Daily News*. In each of these books urban alienation was the preoccupation if not always the subject. It only became the subject, and reached its height of usefulness to Hecht as a writer, in 1926, with *Broken Necks*, a story collection. *Broken Necks* is a book of tales about disconsolate souls as he encountered them. It runs from a haunting mood piece about the pathetic existence of the Stockyards poor, to an attempt to reconcile the sunny side of society with a description of the hanging of two criminals in the Cook County Jail.

Hecht the Bohemian and Hecht the Iconoclast overlapped and fed each other. They both lived and wrote (as Upton Sinclair once remarked of Poe) to prove that art excludes morality, though the Iconoclast took this view deliberately and the Bohemian had it forced upon him. During this period both Hechts wrote for Margaret Anderson's *Little Review* and abided by the principles of that magazine as summarized in its motto, "No compromise with the public taste." The critic Harry Hansen spoke of both identities together when in 1923 he called Hecht "the Pagliacci of the Fire Escapes."

The third and longest-lived phase of Hecht's career had been forming in Chicago but surfaced fully only in New York and later Hollywood. This was Hecht the Sophisticate. He was a gay, shrewd fellow who, though no longer a newspaperman, looked upon life more than ever with a reporter's combination of cynicism and sentimentality. It was a duality Hecht continued living until, late in life, he grew sentimental about cynicism itself. During these years, roughly from his novel *Count Bruga*, in 1926, to his first polemical book *A Guide for the Bedevilled*, in 1944, Hecht did most (and practically all his best) writing for the screen. As a conse-

7

quence, he turned out fewer novels and stories. Those he did publish were mainly "smart" satires. Not a few found their way to the screen. They were supplemented by a number of original screenplays and by some adapted screenplays in which he exercised the sardonic outlook and racy dialogue that together became known as the Hecht touch.

It was also a time of great stage activity, but whereas in Chicago he had written quite definitely for the Theatre, he now wrote purposefully for Broadway. His plays of that period (as before, mostly in collaboration) included *The Front Page*, *Twentieth Century*, *The Great Magoo* and *To Quito and Back*. His novels and story collections included *A Jew in Love*, *The Champion from Far Away*, *A Book of Miracles* and the *Collected Stories*. The last one unfortunately was not a collected volume at all but simply a choice of his offbeat tales in the by then familiar uptown vein.

Hecht was the reverse of many of his contemporaries in that (as a Bohemian) he wrote proletarian fiction during the 1920s, when others were striving to be sophisticates and members of the smart set, and was the Sophisticate during the proletarian 1930s. The second half of this dichotomy had nothing to do with wanting to escape the Depression, which did not affect him, the best paid writer in Hollywood, and which is scarcely alluded to in his shelf of works. Rather, it was a continuation by other means of Hecht's attack on the single great conflict running throughout his life: the question of how to reconcile himself to his dislike and general fear of the middle class from which he, and everyone who surrounded him, had come.

As an artist and a personality, Hecht was at war with the ordinary. That is what had made him a good reporter, for only the extraordinary is news. If in his Chicago days he knew the rich and powerful – the gangsters, the officials under their thumbs, and the visiting dignitaries of every kind – he also knew the lowly whores, the petty thieves and their unfortunate victims. He was proud of his acquaintance with both sides of the track; it was his stock-in-trade. Their common element was that something highly unusual and colourful had happened to his characters voluntarily or otherwise. He had only contempt for the nameless and inconspicuous, and referred to them in one of his best-remembered phrases (from *Broken Necks*) as "the greedy little half-dead." Although later in life (in *A Child of the Century*), he mellowed enough to call them "the half-alive ones," the difference in nomenclature is not that great. Although he was equally at home writing of high society or low society, it was mainly the former that concerned him in his days as a Sophisticate. He was afraid to return to the latter, not because he envisioned loss of money or fame or the charmed companionship and salaries of Hollywood, but because he feared he might become one of them, a moderate in the non-political sense of the word; and Hecht was never a man to shy away from an extreme.

A casual consideration of the course of Hecht's career in the middle 1930s might have lead one to conclude that Hecht would have gone on chronicling the subcultures and supracultures of the two coasts while continuing to take exorbitant screenwriting fees from the middle-class gods, effecting thereby a sort of double revenge. It might have seemed that he would progress yet never really change, but that was not to be the case. The world war erupting in Europe was to affect him in a way that seemed all the greater alongside the almost total disinterest he had shown in World War One and the Depression. Life in New York and Hollywood and his unwilling slide into middle age had increased his sense of Jewishness. The exterminations by the Nazis changed what once had been his diffident defensiveness into an offensiveness that some people – more moderate Jews and liberal gentiles – likened in intensity to the Nazis' own propaganda pitches. This was the birth of Hecht the Propagandist.

In 1941 Rose Caylor Hecht arranged for her husband to write for $75 a week a daily column in *PM*, the experimental adless New York tabloid published by Ralph Ingersoll and staffed by such people as Louis Kronenberger (whom Mrs. Hecht once threatened to castrate for panning a Hecht play) and I. F. Stone. The columns, collected later that year in a book entitled *1001 Afternoons in New York*, lacked the Pagliacci-like quality of the earlier *1001 Afternoons in Chicago*. The differences in the two books, however, reflect the differences in the two Hechts who wrote them. Gone from the *PM* columnist was the prowler of the streets who delighted in their cosmopolitan whirl. Although in the New York column Hecht did try to recapture the old spirit – by writing a piece about the wretched life of his pal Bodenheim, for instance, or by writing about an unclaimed body in the morgue – it was with more will than joy and more nostalgia than excitement. Instead Hecht used the column both to decry the Nazi campaign of intimidation and terror and to lambaste American Jewry for its apathy. Hecht had been doing the same thing for some time in a more modest way. He was to grow more virulent later in his books *A Guide for the Bedevilled* and *Perfidy*, as preoccupation with the plight of Jews became a lasting part of his writing life.

It is ironic that the most moving column in 1001 *Afternoons in New York*, written just a few months before the United States entered World War Two, is a loud equation of Great Britain's position with the great struggles of human history and a poignant avowal that he will once again see the side of right prevail. It is ironic in that during the Palestine crisis, when Hecht's activity on behalf of the Jewish cause was at a peak and when the defection of friends and attacks upon him were most numerous, he was blacklisted in Hollywood as a result of action taken against him in Britain. Hecht had taken out newspaper ads in an attempt to rouse US Jews into doing something about the British occupation. "Everytime you blow up a British arsenal," he addressed the Irgun terrorists in one ad, "or wreck a British jail, or send a British railroad train sky-high, or rob a British bank, or let go with your guns and bombs at the British betrayers and invaders of your homeland, the Jews of America make a little holiday in their hearts."

It wasn't true of most other Jews, of course, as he quickly went on to say. Had it been the official position of Jews in the US the ad and later ones, and Hecht's other political activities, would have been redundant. As it was, the main effect was to stir up more domestic calumny against Hecht and to cause British cinema owners to refuse to show any picture with which he was associated. As a result, the unsympathetic Jews who ran the Hollywood studios, fearing the loss of the important British market, either refused to hire Hecht or else hired him without credit at a fraction of his previous prices. From then on Hecht wrote fewer films and more books.

In some ways this shift in priorities depended upon something other than politics and personal economics. Hecht's days as the foremost screenwriter had come to an end anyway through natural attrition. While he would continue to write scripts and write on scripts and doctor scripts almost to the day of his death, he had long ago surrendered to Hollywood in a war of taste in which he had been alternately hero and profiteer.

Hecht had now become Hecht the Memoirist and he consistently brought new life to what is often a stodgy literary form. Four of the books he wrote during the last period of his career were recollections. In reverse order of appearance, they are *Letters from Bohemia*, published posthumously in 1965; *Gaily, Gaily*, slightly fictionalized accounts of his reporter days; *Charlie*, a memoir of MacArthur; and *A Child of the Century*, his massive autobiography published in 1954 — in its wit and scope probably one of the greatest American literary autobiographies. While during that time he also published fiction and drama, it was nearly all melancholy in tone. It was in general a period of remembering and housekeeping, both mental and literary. Part of this second kind of housekeeping was the republication of *Erik Dorn*, his first success of nearly fifty years before.

When the book reappeared, it was with a preface by Nelson Algren, the writer since Hecht's time most closely identified with Chicago. It was inevitable that the preface should have led to controversy. Declining an invitation to the publication party, Hecht, now sometimes suspicious of younger writers, wrote that he had "no hankering to pose in your local festivities as a literary patsy," adding later of Algren: "I haven't the faintest idea of what he writes like. In this case [the preface] he stinks." Algren retorted that Hecht "hasn't done anything good since *Erik Dorn*," that he "made one or two good movies and some awful bad ones" and that he had refused "to take responsibility" for his talent. As a debate, it was fleeting and predictable. It is important now only in that Algren summed up one of the two patent opinions of Hecht (the other being that he sold out to Hollywood) more clearly than was usually done. In each accusation there is some truth (though less than in Hecht's assessment of Algren's preface). In reputation as in achievement Hecht could be slippery.

Hecht began writing shortly after his sixteenth birthday, as a reporter for the old Chicago *Journal*, moved later to the Chicago *Daily News*, and remained in the city until 1924, when he was thirty. He had arrived a wide-eyed teenager from Racine, Wisconsin, determined to get lost in the metropolis rather than go to university. When he left, he was an almost mythical figure whose name was as thoroughly associated with Chicago in some circles as Al Capone's was in others. On the day of his departure, Ashton Stevens, one of America's most influential drama critics and, according to Hecht, the kind of man "who smiled when he called you a son of a bitch," wrote a page one story in a rival newspaper. It suggested sincerely that the city's flags should be flown at half staff in recognition of the loss.

Hecht had already outgrown three careers by the time he arrived in Chicago. He had been an amateur magician, an acrobat in a small circus in which his uncle was the strongman, and a violinist who had given his first concert at age ten. But it was in Chicago that he gained wider recognition as a prodigy, becoming conspicuous in several fields simultaneously.

On the newspapers of the city (there were eight of them), he was early recognized as a master reporter. It was an age, particularly in Chicago, when the newspapers were livelier than ever before or since, when local scandal and crime took precedence over national and world affairs and responsibility meant the responsibility to scoop and be more sensational than the competition. Hecht was a fast and exiting writer. As Norman Mailer summed up sixty years later, Hecht was also never one "to tell the truth when a concoction could put life in his prose." This only made him more valuable to his employers, if maddening to later sifters through his life and career. It was an atmosphere he celebrated later, with MacArthur, in the play *The Front Page*, which, perhaps unjustly, has proved itself his most enduring work.

Hecht was the prime mover of the Chicago Renaissance of the late teens and early twenties, the star of a cast that included Sherwood Anderson, Margaret Anderson, Carl Sandburg, Maxwell Bodenheim, Floyd Dell, Burton Rascoe, Kenneth Rexroth and Vincent Starrett among the bellettrists, as well as a bevy of artists, critics, publishers, editors and lesser writers who enlivened the production and later peopled the literary stages of New York. Besides being the most important of the group, Hecht was also the most representative. The Renaissance (the dates and extent of the original birth are still a subject of debate) was in its origins journalistic, the only cohesive American literary movement to spring from the newsrooms; and Hecht remained very much a newspaperman of the old Chicago school to the day of his death, just as from the 1930s onward he was the personification of the Hollywood hack.

For one thing, his style was journalistic. It was nurtured under the watchful, celluloid-visored eyes of editors who cultivated the *mot juste*, the zappy adjective, the colourful metaphor. Hecht was able to satisfy their demands with an ease that became legendary. As his personality matured, as he delved into the sets of French and Russian masters sold by drummers who vied with Chicago's hookers and saloonkeepers for reporters' salaries, his mixture of newspaper English and the vernacular turned into something peculiarily his own. It became a blend of argot and the arcane with some debt at first to decadent writers such as Edgar Saltus, Arthur Machen, Remy de Gourmont and J-K Huysmans. Later, in his non-fiction books, all of them written in brief "takes" subheaded in the old newspaper style, the influence of his mentor H. L. Mencken was stronger. It was a style that strove for and frequently attained heights of a new kind of lyricism that was at once both hard-boiled and sentimental, just like the man himself.

But the larger part of Hecht's journalistic inheritance (and in turn the greater part of what he contributed to Hollywood) was his utter Chicago-ness. This was a quality incorporating great quantities of energetic self-confidence, a love of the picaresque and a contempt for the middle class he was never fully able to resolve. Equally important, perhaps, was a delight in the urban environment. In Hecht's case this last was so pronounced that he seemed to embrace St. Augustine's view that as long as society was decaying, at least it was still alive.

In those days, reporters were expected to know how to do most everything. Because this expectation brought to the surface a latent talent, Hecht was in fact able to do everything, or so it seemed to himself and a great many others. His success as a scenarist as well as playwright and author is attributable to the fact that he was, more than almost any other American writer, a professional storyteller. His whole newspaper career was predicated on his skill at distilling some current happening, always a human one and usually some crime or its aftermath, into a highly charged vignette or sketch. Usually, he had little time to do so. Often a lack of facts made necessary some elaborate invention. As his style grew under a variety of influences and experiments, he began to feel constrained in daily newspapering, work that encouraged the epigrammist but never quite tested the deft plot maker. So he turned to fiction and the stage.

To Hecht the shift in media was as natural as waking to a sleeper. Although at first he withstood urgings to become an author, just as he initially resisted the lure of Hollywood, he burst upon each medium with a vengence. In the latter case, the outbreak was a screenplay entitled *Underworld*, one of the most important early gangster films, for which he received the first Academy Award given for original screenwriting. (He later shared two other Oscars with Charles MacArthur for *Viva Villa!* and *The Scoundrel*.) In the publishing world the breakthrough was his novel *Erik Dorn*, published in 1921,which made him a national literary celebrity. It is his best book from the early Chicago period. That period so affected his later writing and thinking that, as one early commentator observed, whenever Hecht tried to imagine the Deity, he conceived of Him as some lustful amorphous energy somewhat resembling Col. Robert R. McCormick's Chicago Tribune Tower.

Many members of that fabulous generation of American writers who came to prominence in the 1920s (often midwesterners like Hecht) laboured at some point in newspapers. Hemingway, Theodore Dreiser and Sinclair Lewis are the most obvious examples. While not deluded into thinking that reporting would be mistaken for serious work, they acknowledged the effect it had upon their style and outlook. For this one broad generation of American writers, newspapering was an almost premeditated stage of their development, preceded by World War One and followed by bohemianism, expatriation, 1930s radicalism or any combination of them. If reporting was not always a stepping stone to literary activities, it was never a stumbling block; it was a little-remembered avenue that supported them and taught them skepticism and compassion.

Yet though the banquet years of American journalism and literature coincided, they were not interchangeable. Those news veterans who became important did so either in spite of their experience (except in the ways noted) or else because they had their

larger ambitions killed and sank to being "great" lifelong reporters who wrote several "classic" news stories — both words journalists toss about too easily. The one exception is Ben Hecht. He
is the only substantial American writer of the period whose
outlook, style and very spirit were intrinsically journalistic and
remained so for as long as he lived and in everything he wrote — in
forty-five books including novels, stories, plays, propaganda and
memoirs, and perhaps twice that number of movies.

One of Hecht's editors in Chicago was Henry Justin Smith of the
Daily News, a learned and kindly man who published two novels as
well as co-authoring a narrative precisely titled *Chicago: The History of Its Reputation*. With slight change of emphasis, Smith's subtitle is useful in discussing Hecht's posthumous career, for in a sense
he has no reputation, just a history of one. In assessments of his
worth as in summations of his life, misunderstanding has been
piled upon misunderstanding until at length no one is quite certain
who Hecht was — except that he was famous for being himself —
or knows quite what field he was in, only that he was important. It
is necessary to begin with his early notoriety and work forward.
  Hecht's initial reputation was local. Although bylines seldom
crowned news stories or features in his day, he quickly acquired
what passes in journalism for fame with his ability to write gaily of
that which was gruesome, macabre and exotic. Some of his early
accounts are fine examples of the kind of story cultivated by papers
in an era when the first obligation of the press was to be interesting.
Many of them are also examples of what newspaper editors think is
art. But with Hecht's introduction to artistic decadence in print
and in life, a curious thing happened. He found that he was able to
write in a way that was gruesome, macabre and exotic of that
which was newsy, instead of just the other way around. That led to
1001 Afternoons in Chicago, Erik Dorn and other morose yet somehow frenetic works. As a result Hecht became known outside of
journalistic circles. In fact he became something of a cult figure.
  Saul Bellow, in a wonderfully perceptive review of *A Child of the
Century*, confessed that for years after Hecht's departure for New
York and Hollywood there were legends about him in Chicago. To
the younger generation (Bellow was born in 1915) it was amazing

The Five Lives of Ben Hecht

"that the gloom of Halstead Street, the dismal sights of Back of the Yards and the speech of immigrants should be the materials of art." For using them as such, Bellow and his peers idolized Hecht; for that and for his excited style and extravagant metaphors.

No infatuation could be more normal. Bellow grew up in the bleak and culturally stagnant place Chicago was during the Depression. It was the time of the brave front of the 1933 world's fair, the Century of Progress, and only a shadow remained of Hecht's day when the South Side bohemians lived in claptrap buildings left over from the city's other world's fair, the Columbian Exposition of 1892. To Bellow and others like him it must have seemed ancient history and yet at the same time a *belle époque*. In a way, it was both. Hecht's youthful style carried his reputation into the next generation and brought about the first retrospective considerations of him as a writer.

When he wrote about "the scribble of rooftops across the sky" and the old lecher who thrust his hand up the woman's dress "like a surreptitious xylophone player," Hecht appealed to the young, bored with the dull nineteenth century, who wanted to return to the 1920s in much the same way Hecht longed to return to the 1890s. Although by that time Hecht was active in other fields, in other personas, he was, throughout the 1930s, at least a figure to be considered by younger writers. Nathanael West was just one who sought his criticism. Although Hecht's style was never successfully copied, the influence of his imagery turns up still in writers like John Collier and Peter De Vries and in the hard-boiled school of detective ficton.

Among theatre people, Hecht remains known for his most popular plays with MacArthur, *The Front Page* and *Twentieth Century*, which are regarded as durable period pieces. *The Front Page* still exerts a strong infuence on the public's idea of newspaper folkways. Hecht's interest in the theatre was somewhat transient and, as he half admitted, usually required a collaborator who would both bolster and complement him. The stage was a vehicle for playfulness or pathos, seldom for anything in between.

At the time of his first New York successes he was already a light in Hollywood, and it is difficult today to understand the harmful effect that had on his standing as a literary man. The common notion, that he had sold his creative soul to Hollywood, dates from

16

his early involvement in pictures. It remained unchallenged until the 1960s, when his books were nearly all out of print and forgotten. He was revived as a scenarist by writers who had discovered his cinematic importance in the course of archaeological surveys of popular culture. Hecht, in fact, was touted as the best screenwriter of the golden era and, in his attitude toward the movies, as the quintessential movie writer of the past. When critics wrote of his importance (Pauline Kael first and most persistently), other critics (Andrew Sarris for one) took exception. It was not so much a fight over custody of the corpse as it was a tug-of-war of ideologies. Today the question of Hecht's contribution to the movies ranks in stubbornness with the questions of exactly who wrote what in *Citizen Kane* and *Gone With the Wind*.

In the course of such debate the true importance of Hecht was lost sight of — that he was a man who flitted from one literary form to another, perhaps pollinating each as he went, but centrally concerned with expressing his gusto for life and individualism, and displaying them alongside the reactions of people in high and low places caught, by habit or fate, in extraordinary situtations.

That he was, over the long haul, the best screenwriter of his time may seem certain, but since so much of Hollywood history concerns ambition and promise rather than accomplishment, this is fainter praise than Hecht deserves. While it may be true that his wit, speed, irreverence and bank balance made him *the* Hollywood screenwriter, it is in large measure because he was first the very embodiment of the kind of reporter he immortalized in *The Front Page*.

The prevalent view of Hecht is that he was a screenwriter who also wrote other things; such a view is no more truthful than the complete reverse would be. He was a gifted writer with quite distinct ideas about ego, class, sex, and politics, which he put forward all his life in an attempt to clarify them to himself. He used whatever medium of expression was best suited or handiest at the moment. It is in such light that the five lives at first appear to be one. Only upon more careful inspection does each become distinct.

2
Our Man
in Gomorrah

If you did not believe in God, in the importance of marriage, in the United States government, in the sanity of politicians, in the necessity of education or in the wisdom of your elders, you automatically believed in art.
BH, *in* A Child of the Century

It was by chance that Hecht got into journalism. Having run away to Chicago, he was standing outside a burlesque theatre when spotted by one of his uncles. Hecht, fearing he would be turned over to his parents, told the older man that he was in the city to find a job. The relative led him to the office of John C. Eastman, publisher of the *Journal*, who put him to work writing obscene doggerel for a stag party. That is how he got started. Why he continued is explained if one substitutes the word "journalism" for the final word "art" in the above quotation.

In any other place but Chicago, Eastman would have been an extraordinary character. He had lost part of his left index finger, possibly in a shooting accident, and used the stub to stick in the faces of people he chose to intimidate. Once a reporter, he had become one of young William Randolph Hearst's front-line executives. At the time of his departure as president, treasurer and business manager of Hearst's Chicago *American*, he cabled Hearst that if he failed to respect him as an associate, he might come to respect him as a competitor. Eastman borrowed enough money from a

18

millionaire he had once interviewed to purchase the failing *Journal*. Founded in 1844, it was then the city's oldest newspaper in continuous publication. Eastman chose on the nameplate to call it the city's first, a distinction that belonged to the *American* (no relation to Hearst's), which had been founded in 1839.

Hecht was first assigned to picture-chasing, a hallowed tradition wherein one begs, bargains for or, if necessary, steals from atop the next of kin's piano, photographs of axe murder victims and other newsworthy persons. A certain cleverness was called for, and Hecht rose to the occasion. Soon he was living the frenetic life of a reporter. He would recall later how he "haunted streets, studios, whore houses, police stations, courtrooms, theatre stages, jails, saloons, slums, mad houses, fires, murders, riots, banquet halls and bookshops," adding: "I ran everywhere in the city like a fly buzzing in the works of a clock, tasted more than any fly belly could hold, learned not to sleep (an accomplishment that still clings to me) and buried myself in a tick-tock of whirling hours that still echo in me." That was one recollection in which his hyperbolic style well reflected the truth.

The armigerous visitors, the victims of tragedy and the gangsters elected or otherwise were colourful persons to the young news-man, but so were his colleagues. His mentor at the *Journal* was Sherman Reilly Duffy, a classics scholar with a Phi Beta Kappa key who languished as sports editor. In his Chicago days Hecht en-countered other reporters who used their jobs to support scholarly habits and at least one who used his as a cover for high-level criminal activity. In between was a motley collection of eccen-trics, including one man who aspired to an operatic career, another who was taking a correspondence course in embalming and still another who even in summer wore his hat, overcoat and muffler indoors. The man had been mistaken for one of the victims of the 1903 Iroquois Theatre fire and had been laid out with the other unfortunates. Corpses fetched from the rubble had been piled on top of him. The reporter woke with a chill of horror that per-sisted through the years.

The newspapers of Chicago were alive with literary ambitions. They also were hot with radical politics, though Hecht himself was not. To him, politics were part of the passing scene in which he revelled. A radical reporter was as odd to him as the one with operatic aspirations. He knew Big Bill Haywood, Emma Goldman and other prominent dissenters but was not much influenced by their ideas, only by their personalities. He saw radicals as separate from and more interesting than other politicians in the same way that gangsters were separate from other criminals. Gangsters were interesting as flamboyant outlaws from the established authority, as Hecht himself was to become an outlaw from the established artistic order.

Even thirty years later, while involved in the politics of the Jewish state, he still professed to see politics as demeaning and soul-destroying. He would, one likes to think, have been an anarchist had not anarchism been as political as Republicanism. The only established politician Hecht admired was Theodore Roosevelt, whom he saw in 1912 when the former President made a speech in Milwaukee with an assassin's bullet lodged in his stomach. For a while, Hecht confessed, his heroes were Roosevelt and H. L. Mencken. In his youth, he saw no incongruity in admiring two men who often stood for completely opposite ideals and in fact laboured to rid the Republic of each other's kind. He admired them for the same reason: their outspokenness and (at least so it seemed with Roosevelt at that time) total opposition to sham. In the case of the President, Hecht's liking was possibly a youthful indiscretion, though in his autobiography he feels no embarrassment in recalling exactly how he felt about him when young. As for Mencken, Hecht remained a lifelong admirer and lamented more than once that no statues of Mencken graced public parks. The Sage of Baltimore had a large, though changing, impact on Hecht's personality and writings.

Central to an understanding of Hecht's early career is the fact that he was performing an adult's job on the *Journal* while still a boy. Going from the relatively protected environment of his Wisconsin home to the environment that confirmed Chicago's reputation as the world's wickedest city brought him an exhileration he never lost. It also helped establish at the start of his writing life his natural, very rapid, working pace. He was thrust at once into a swirl of events and he wrote ever afterward as though that swirl was still going on.

He wrote that way because the style of reporting in which he was brought up tended to blur events in describing them rather than freeze them for analysis. "Trying to determine what is going on in the world by reading the newspapers," he wrote in the *Chicago Literary Times*, "is like trying to tell the time by watching the second hand of a clock;" and at least from his own experience, that was true enough.

For Hecht and his readers, Chicago seemed a prairie Gomorrah where homicide was the logical solution to arguments and chicanery a natural force in the administration of justice. Streets were torn down and new ones erected, gang bosses were murdered to be supplanted by their killers, a dozen railways brought an influx of immigrants never matched by the number of people heading out. The cities of the east seemed tame, lifeless and effete by comparison. The Midwest was still the New World and Chicago was its capital, and like the residents of all capitals, Hecht looked down on the poor provincials. It was a city powered by its own simultaneous construction and decomposition. Hecht's style was born of the need to describe this in prose. His short sentences, full of energy and stretching metaphor to the limit, captured his idea of the place. His rhythms were those of the train wheels, factory whistles, gunfire and later the jazz music of a city which was, just then, exactly what Sandburg said it was: hogbutcher, freight-handler, builder of railroads.

Chicago had a cultural life too. Hecht was thrown into it, or at least into the part of it concerned with literary culture, by reason once again of his employment. Chicago had not yet progressed to the point of being able to support a literary industry competitive with New York's, though it eventually would during the short-lived Renaissance. It supported instead a literary atmosphere dependent upon its newspapers.

Since the 1890s, when local reporters gathered at the White Chaple Club surrounded by human skulls and hangmen's nooses decorating the spot, the journalists engaged in an off-duty literary bohemianism and intellectualism as counterweight to the rowdyism and aboriginal instincts they dealt with daily and approvingly. A juicy murder-suicide was looked upon as excellent raw material necessitating a thank you to the gods. Blown up with prickly prose, replete with arcane adjectives, such a crime was a thing of beauty and a cause for rejoicing. It had been that way in the 1890s when such men as Gene Field and Richard Harding Davis were reporters. It was even more the case in Hecht's day. In the minds of its practitioners, journalism then was a division of literature, instead of the other way around. It is doubtful if anywhere else Hecht would have enjoyed quite the same opportunities to grow from typewriter jockey into serious writer.

It was natural that some of Hecht's first published literary endeavours should have taken a fictional form close to the stories from which he made his living. As Vincent Starrett, the least strident of the Renaissance autobiographers, pointed out, Hecht always had affection for the box office. It was in 1917 that Hecht, by that time on the *Daily News*, discovered that he was $3,000 in debt on a $40 per week salary. Enterprisingly, Hecht sat down that evening and wrote a short story which he sent to Mencken in New York, who was then editing the *Smart Set* with George Jean Nathan. Mencken bought the story at once, but paid only $45 rather than the $1,000 Hecht had somehow been expecting.

Mencken had translated Nietzsche into English as early as 1908 and set himself up as a Nietzschean superman who, from his position of eminence atop the journalistic tradition, tried to will away the common "booboisie." Hecht was happy to join him in such activity, at least with one hand. With his other he wrote at times almost maudlin appreciations of the little people he otherwise satirized.

Hecht was the ideal contributor and Mencken never turned down a story of Hecht's for publication. Even though he disliked most verse and verse drama, Mencken printed, in the August 1917 *Smart Set*, a play Hecht wrote with Maxwell Bodenheim, one of several collaborators Hecht exhausted in his early period of playwriting.

At the start of his purely literary writing, when he was about twenty-one, there was a division in Hecht's mind between plot and wordplay. The impulse toward the former usually had basis in his work as a reporter; the latter was brought on by the sheer joy of experimenting with language. In 1915, Margaret Anderson printed Hecht's "The Sermon in the Depths," the first of the intricate, almost ornamental sketches in the *Little Review*, which she had begun publishing the year before from a tiny office in the Fine Arts

Building. Hecht followed that with a series of sketches and stories influenced by Huysmans' *Against the Grain* and by other adjectival writers from the "mauve decade." Hecht's value as a contributor to that trend-conscious magazine reached its peak with "Broken Necks," later the title story of his important collection of shorter fiction.

Until he was able to merge the decorative story and the commercial story into a simple product distinctively his own, Hecht put much of his energy into plays. At first, these were also of two kinds: the one using language for language's sake, the other concentrating on plot and characterization. These two types came together and separated again according to the collaborator with whom he was working at any given time.

The first collaborator was Kenneth Sawyer Goodman, a lumber millionaire's son and Princeton graduate with socialist leanings. Hecht would often work with Goodman in the boardroom of the elder Goodman's corporation. Goodman wanted to write a stock of plays and use some of his father's money to build a theatre in the Maxwell Street slums where the poor might watch for free. The idea came to distorted fruition only after Goodman's death a few years later, when his family built in his memory an imposing granite theatre behind the equally imposing Art Institute on Michigan Avenue. While he lived, Goodman wrote perhaps a dozen plays with Hecht of a kind Hecht would later call "sane and practical little one-acts."

Goodman had been writing plays since about 1912. The collaboration with Hecht, one of several partners Goodman took on in his brief career, began sometime in 1914, and probably carried on intermittently until 1917, one of Hecht's busiest years. One of the interruptions came about when Hecht took time out to write with Sherwood Anderson a full-length play about Benvenuto Cellini. This collaboration resulted in an unfinished script with a running time of eight hours.

The abortive Cellini play remains interesting in that it speaks, albeit meekly, of Hecht's concern with Italian masque. That and the harlequinade were the forms of some of the Goodman-Hecht plays, the best known of which is "The Wonder Hat." It is a spirited, deliberately arcane piece in a mock-European vein which Hecht at that time probably considered the height of sophistication. Other plays, however, drawing on his reporting experience and even his family life, presaged his later writings. "An Idyll of the Shops," for example, concerns Jewish factory life. It is undoubtedly drawn from the experiences of Hecht's father, who moved to Chicago in 1917 after the failure of his clothing factory and retail store in Wisconsin.

There was also "The Hero of Santa Maria," which in 1920 became the first Goodman-Hecht play to be published. It was also the first issue of the Theatre Guild, and like a number of other plays performed and published by that Chicago company, was later performed by amateur groups in New York and elsewhere.

"The Hero of Santa Maria" centres on a patriarchal Civil War veteran who feels he has been unjustly denied his pension for service to the federal cause. News comes that his son, whom he considers worthless, has been killed fighting with the American expeditionary force in Mexico. He is the first US citizen thus honoured. The father will allow community leaders to mourn officially only if he finally gets his pension. The leaders and politicians agree to this; but unbeknownst to them and to the father, the supposedly dead son is hiding in the next room. In his wanderings, he has swapped identities with a stranger who is the real martyr to American independence. The father agrees to split the pension with the son in return for the latter's silence and immediate departure.

It is an unremarkable play, but it is important in that it is drawn from contemporary events. The Mexican adventure was news at the time. At least three of Hecht's friends – Charles MacArthur, Wallace Smith and Vincent Starrett – had taken part in one or the other of two US invasions of Mexico at about the time of World War One. The play shows Hecht turning his daily observations to good account in literary form, as he would do a few years later with *1001 Afternoons in Chicago*.

Another of Hecht's early collaborators was Maxwell Bodenheim, the poet. Two years older than Hecht, he had come to Chicago as a child from Mississippi where his father, a merchant from Alsace-Lorraine, had married a southern belle. The two men met in the offices of Harriet Monroe's *Poetry* magazine in 1912 and at once influenced each other. Bodenheim found in Hecht a partisan in the literary war against the philistines. Hecht, for his part,

24

discovered in this histrionic personality a writer with an insatiable appetite for wordslinging, a person of extravagant vocabularies.

While mainly a poet, Bodenheim was as subject to diversion as any other literary Chicagoan. By the early 1930s, he had published a dozen novels with such titles as *Replenishing Jessica* and *Naked on Roller Skates* containing enough hints at raciness to cause one or two of them to be banned in various parts of the country. In those early years he was interested in being a playwright as well. In 1917 he and Hecht collaborated on a number of small plays which fulfilled what Bodenheim's poems only promised at their worst: a jigsaw of flamboyant phraseology in which all trace of the original thought was purposely lost sight of. The best remembered of these is "The Master Poisoner," which appeared in Bodenheim's first collection of poetry, *Minna and Myself*, in 1918. Bodenheim called it "an exquisitely confusing work," a euphemism for incomprehensibility. Exotic phrases dropped from Hecht and Bodenheim's collective pen and bounced off the page like anarchic ping pong balls.

Bodenheim's word tapestries, little changed throughout his life, had their basis partly in the newspaper style Hecht taught him to love. Similarly, Hecht was influenced by the use the poet made of this style. Hecht's only appearance in *Poetry*, in February 1918, was with an execrable poem, "Snow Monotones," very much in Bodenheim's linguistic style yet in rhymed quatrains instead of the Imagistic form that helped make Bodenheim's work so fresh.

At this stage Hecht was just beginning to find a place for himself as a writer outside the cityrooms and could be subject to a different influence each week. As an unpaid researcher for a disciple of Krafft-Ebing, Hecht became interested in sexual pathology, or in what he thought was sexual pathology, as an extension of his work as a crime reporter. Then, of course, there was always Mencken, who showed him that all fields of human intelligence (or ignorance) were his beat and that the world was peopled mainly by dunderheads – both beliefs that Hecht's profession tended to confirm in spades.

Hecht read voraciously and was at that wonderful stage in which every new writer he picked up had something to say to him about writing. In one season Hecht rode the swells of George Moore, Dostoevsky and the lesser Russians, the full range of French

The Five Lives of Ben Hecht

decadents as well as Wyndham Lewis, or at least Wyndham Lewis of *Tarr*. He was still getting these and other writers out of his system when in 1918 something happened which, in retrospect, helped him develop a style and outlook more completely his own, one that he continued to shape and refine through most of his writing life.

Reporters who became too good at what they did (and Hecht's way with a crime story was the envy of both his peers and superiors) had to be dealt with − shipped off somewhere, promoted or demoted. Newspapers are not designed to give the news well but only quickly and at length. When a reporter's individuality became burdensome to management, he could be disposed of in several ways. Then as now, such people could be promoted to the rank of editor (they usually make poor editors) or exiled to the editorial board (where nothing matters but the publisher's feelings) or given credentials as foreign correspondents. The third fate is the one that befell Hecht. With scant knowledge of German and an ignorance of international affairs remarkable even for a Chicago reporter, he was sent to Berlin to report on the confusion following the war. He arrived on December 30, 1918 and stayed more than a year. He was twenty-four years old.

By the time Hecht left Chicago, his salary had risen to $75 per week, his total debt to $8,000. He spent his advance expense money clearing up the situation as best he could and arrived penniless in the war-ravaged capital. Germany was in turmoil. Humiliated by defeat, pressed by mounting economic problems and faced with a general strike, the Kaiser abdicated and was replaced by Spartakist leader Karl Liebknecht. Hecht reported how Liebknecht, entering the palace following the bloodless takeover, stripped to his underwear and jumped into the royal bed to symbolize the end of the old regime.

Hecht was able to buy some of his information. The favourable valuta of American dollars to marks was one of his great assets. But more of his information came from hopheads, high ranking military homosexuals, a friendly hotel waiter and a man he had met standing up all night on the train from Amsterdam to Berlin. The city was in chaos, but Hecht met his greatest reportorial challenge and cabled story after story to place the confusion in perspective, if not to actually explain and analyse it.

On one story he went against orders by hiring a plane. His pilot was an air ace who would later be a leader of the Luftwaffe. That fact is symbolic because Hecht was witnessing the political, economic and sociological conditions which proved favourable to the Nazis.

At first the events in Berlin seemed a burlesque, "a revolution in which anybody could do what he wanted." Trained in the politics of Cook County, Hecht chose to see the situation that way: as the greed of one group against the greed of another. But he knew too that it was something far more serious. His first dispatch, claiming that Liebknecht was but a slightly altered version of the deposed authoritarian Kaiser, gave broad hint of his cynicism. But even his cynicism, however, was inadequate for the events that followed. These included the execution (which he witnessed from a tree) of two thousand men, women and children at Moabit Prison and the bloody revolt at Munich that established for a brief time a communist state there.

Chicago, which came closer to a state of perpetual mayhem than any other place in the Americas, had not quite prepared him for what he found in Germany. Neither had Chicago's cultural atmosphere and his own expeditions into literature prepared him for the artistic life he found in Europe. If there was truly a revolution in which anybody could do exactly as he pleased it was the Dadaist revolt.

Hecht's introduction to this other revolution came through George Grosz, the painter whose later fame abroad was partly Hecht's doing. Grosz's depictions of fatty, evil Aryan war-mongers who had brought down Germany and thus made Dada necessary, reflected, not eloquently but cruelly, the shambles of central Europe. Through Grosz, Hecht met the apostles of the new movement and had a private box at the nihilistic events during which audiences were insulted, pistols discharged and troops summoned in unsuccessful attempts to restore order.

Dear to Hecht was the memory of Grosz's staging of a race between a woman operating a sewing machine and another woman operating a typewriter. The event was preceded by a poetry contest in which an audience which had paid twenty gold marks each listened to twelve compositions shouted simultaneously in one great noise. The race between the two machines was followed by a musical number consisting of women in leotards holding aloft

The Five Lives of Ben Hecht

large canvasses, each bearing the symbol of a different note. The whole festival ended as it was supposed to end, in a fiasco, with the audience in formal dress transformed into a mob and with Grosz and the others disappearing into the night with the gold. Grosz later married the woman who had held the F-sharp canvas in the musical number, fled to the United States in the early 1930s and prospered as an artist. Hecht embraced some of the zaniness of the Dadaists after his return to America, using it to good effect in Chicago and even Hollywood. One wonders whether he was harkening back to Berlin when years later he wrote for the Marx Brothers.

He took something else away from his immersion course in German artistic life. This was a feeling for German expressionism, the style that outlived the Dadaists and marked Berlin's cultural heyday through the 1920s and early 1930s, the period of Brecht and Kurt Weill paid homage to by Christopher Isherwood. It was a style that reflected a somewhat distorted view of the United States — one might almost say, of Chicago — as the land of Dionysian bootleggers, skyscrapers, free sex and even more gratuitous violence. It was an attitude more than a movement, and it manifested itself in a sort of raunchy impertinence in the face of total, irreversible disaster. It presupposed that the world was an urban one close to collapse. Its inhabitants were persons giddy from fatigue and serene from the insanity around them. The idea of expressionism, of the attitude and pose, was what Hecht needed to bring together the various fragments into which his writing had broken. Expressionism was the umbrella covering the sexual aberrations, crimes, and the dispossessed people who made up the huge, heartless city that was Chicago: a city good only to those who were bigger than its problems. He made of all that his own vision and used it in several books, most vividly in *1001 Afternoons in Chicago*. The vision would turn up in his films too, especially in *Crime Without Passion*. By then (1934) his expressionism was diluted, but seemed all the more in step with the fashion created by the German actors and directors who fled Hitler and ended up in Hollywood. But Hecht introduced it first in America and moulded it to fit a real rather than an imagined American style. It was this style that distinguished the emerging Chicago school, of which he was the epicentre, from its more strictly journalistic predecessor.

28

Our Man in Gomorrah

Carl Sandburg had joined the staff of the *Daily News* in 1917, coming from the *Day Book*, a socialist daily "about the size of a Pierre [*sic*] Marquette railway timetable." He had been hired at Hecht's suggestion, after Hecht had heard him read one of the verses which would make him famous when collected later as *Chicago Poems*. By the time Hecht returned from Europe, Sandburg was the paper's motion picture critic. In that capacity, in May 1921, he reviewed *The Cabinet of Dr. Caligari*, the classic of German expressionism directed by Robert Weine.

Sandburg once stated that he enjoyed the job mainly because it was relatively undemanding and allowed him to write poetry in cool, dark moviehouses. Nevertheless, he made a very astute judgement of the newly repatriated Hecht in his piece on *Caligari* by stating that the film "looks like a collaboration of Rube Goldberg, Ben Hecht, Charlie Chaplin and Edgar Allen Poe." The Goldberg and Chaplin elements were expressionist techniques, which Sandburg viewed as oddly slapstick. What he was ascribing to Poe and Hecht were the effects those techniques created: the heavy mood of destructive magic which Hecht had come upon in Germany and which he was employing in the *Daily News* in a column headed "1001 Afternoons in Chicago."

As usual, Hecht was financially troubled. After his return to Chicago, his debts had grown to $20,000. As always he tried to solve the problem with elaborate moneymaking schemes which were guerilla raids on the middle class. Usually such schemes meant that he had to leave the paper for a time. His incomparable energy and resourcefulness soon had matters under control and he began to long for the newsrooms which continued to sustain his imagination. In the spring of 1921, he offered his services for what he felt would be a new kind of feature, a daily column revealing the city as it really was, written with all the energy and skill he could muster.

Chicago had long had popular, respected columnists whose columns were not so much created as they were conducted. Such men as Bert Leston Taylor of the *Tribune* were essentially editors who assembled sketches, verse and anecdotes in the space allotted them. Even Eugene Field, once considered the doyen of columnists, wrote essentially light stories and comic tales. The column nearest to Hecht's premise was the "Stories of the Streets and of the Town" which George Ade had contributed in the 1890s to the *Record*, though Ade's work was a far cry from the type of realism Hecht had in mind.

"1001 Afternoons in Chicago," many of which were later published in a book of that title, lasted from June 21, 1921 to October 10, 1922. For the first five weeks Hecht used a legman to help ferret out baroque human interest stories and follow-up the tips which began pouring in almost immediately. The assistant was a college graduate Hecht's own age who dearly wanted a life in journalism. His name was Henry Luce, and within a few years he would co-found *Time* magazine. Hecht took him in at $16 a week after Henry Justin Smith had told Luce no work was available on the city side. After Hecht complained that Luce was naive and his research worthless, Smith finally reversed his decision and began paying Luce $20 from the city desk budget. Thirty-seven years later on his television show, Hecht said he didn't think at the time that Luce would amount to anything and he was correct in his assessment.

Hecht complained that Luce didn't know what "1001 Afternoons" was all about. What the column was about, in part, was preventive reporting, much like preventive medicine. Hecht wrote about anonymous individuals who, under ordinary circumstances, would never have got their names into print except by some quick and thoughtless crime – as either perpetrators or victims of the love slayings, card-game stabbings and heartless swindles Hecht had come to recognize as part of the city's energy. He understood that this violence was only one element of the collective life which included poverty, ignorance, greed and all manner of heartbreak. Hecht had sympathy for such people and even came to see them as the backbone of society. Yet he had a scientific interest in them as well. He dissected their apparently simple lives and found them much more complicated than he imagined, as complicated in fact as his own. In brooding, precise prose that daily grew more polished he reported his findings. Hecht caught the flavour of their speech, transcribing their half-finished sentences and slang; he set the scene and told the story in a style that was the first important flowering of the new wave of German expressionism in America. As in *Citizen Kane*, the final flowering, rooms seemed crowded without actually being so, shadows formed grotesque patterns on the walls and streets, and mysterious shafts of light arrived at unreal angles.

The entire populace was food for Hecht's columns. He wrote bittersweet investigations into the lives of shop-girls who, driven by the commercialization of love, purchased ten-cent wedding rings as part of a dream that the real thing would bring them happiness. He wrote of the shop-girl who kept writing and rewriting her own obituary. She carried it with her so that it might be published in the event of a fatal accident and thus immortalize, and somehow justify, her life. His head was filled with a hundred plots; and he would haunt the divorce courts and the domestic relations courts, witnessing there "a paragraph of tears."

Limited by space and hounded by a twenty-four hour deadline, Hecht had neither room nor time for digression, and so tried to pare his prose of all but the outlines of the story and the essentials of the mood. Sometimes he wrote himself into the columns as "the news-paperman," an emotionless observer whose task was to report not merely the events and actions but the atmosphere as well. Like a student in a Berlitz course, Hecht would immerse himself totally in the city, prowling the streets, haunting the speaks and riding the owl cars.

He knew that the secret to the success of the column was to have as much variety as possible without altering the framework. Sometimes he wrote mood pieces about Chinatown or other sections of the city, sometimes stories of individuals whose lives had no storylines or clever twists but depended solely upon the manner of telling. He even wrote one O.Henry-type story about a con man. But unlike O.Henry, who wrote of the metropolis as an exotic place, Hecht assumed his readers had a knowledge of the city almost as detailed as his own, although he neither possessed nor expected historical knowledge. Hecht, like Chicago, knew only what was (in Harry Hansen's phrase) *anno incendi*, or after the Great Fire of 1871. He was concerned with the city as it was.

Sandburg, in what was to become his stock poem for high school anthologies, had written of the fog "on little cat feet" that viewed the city "on silent haunches/and then moves on." Hecht altered the metaphor to suit his own ideology: the fog from Lake Michigan was "a great cat that comes slowly through the air and devours the city," leaving the people alone only after it "has eaten them up."

The Five Lives of Ben Hecht

The Chicago of his imagination was powerless in the grip of forces which sent the people off in confusion at best and, at worst, to their doom or damnation.

1001 Afternoons in Chicago is a work which gives rise to much that is essential or recurring in Hecht's later work. First there is the lemming-like relationship of the people to the city's cliffs, an idea explored more intensely in *Erik Dorn*, published the year before, but also in *Broken Necks*, four years later. Second, there is the column's whole style, which surfaced again in Hecht's early scriptwriting and later in the films he directed. A small part of this style is the constant appearance of the unnamed "newspaper-man," who is midway between a recording participant and a detached onlooker. Hecht wrote that Hechtian character into many of his screenplays, even into such a John Wayne vehicle as *Legend of the Lost*, in which, notwithstanding the total division between the actor and the character he portrays, Wayne becomes something like a watered-down version of Hecht's idea of himself.

Third and almost equally important *1001 Afternoons in Chicago* previews Hecht's life as a Memoirist and freewheeling autobiográpher. In these columns, he wrote about many subjects that he would later draw on in his memoirs. He wrote, for instance, of the Covici-McGhee bookshop, one of the focal points of the Renaissance that he would recall fondly, and of Bill Haywood, the one-eyed radical he met in a strip joint on the eve of Haywood's flight to Russia. He wrote about Tommy O'Connor, a condemned criminal he would use later in *Underworld* and *The Front Page*. Similarly, he created in one of his columns a character named Winkelberg, a pathetic yet proud rummy. Hecht would later apply the name to Bodenheim, who had always held a wino's position in Hecht's calendar of saints and came to fulfill it in reality as well.

The "Winkelberg" column is important, as is his one about a tattoo artist and those which wonderfully mimicked the sounds of jazz in speakeasies and blues in "mixed" cabarets. They illustrate how, more than anyone else previously, Hecht made the entire city, with its highlife and low, the subject of journalism, while at the same time blurring, with more skill than almost anyone since, the distinctions between journalism and fiction. These were accomplishments which generations of writers after him have tried to equal, while Hecht himself was moving on to other forms.

3
Tales of Chicago Streets

*Why should I return to that God-forsaken desert; there is only one
intelligent man in the whole United States to talk to — Ben Hecht.*
Ezra Pound, *in a letter*, 1918

Hecht was writing the way he was living — furiously, if sometimes
moodily. He portrayed himself accurately, with a certain amount
of wit, a sardonic intelligence and almost unflagging zeal. Even
when writing of the depressions and fits of emptiness which period-
ically overtook him, he was still zealous in his attempts to probe
and transcribe. Only one thing was lacking from the alternately
tortured and gleeful self-portraiture of his early work: an uncer-
tainty about his talent, which was prevalent in real life. From 1913
onward he banged away mercilessly at sketches that became vignettes, vignettes that became stories and stories that grew into
novels, yet his first published novel did not appear until 1921. That
was *Erik Dorn*. It was, however, not his first attempt.

While still on the *Journal*, Hecht wrote a novel (according to
Harry Hansen) entitled *Moisse*. No other details survive, though it
could be that Hecht borrowed for the title, if not for the subject, the
character of Lionel Moise, the reporter. Later he wrote another
novel, called *Grimaces*, about a blind man who falls in love with
an ugly woman whom he thinks is beautiful. He destroyed the
manuscript when Mencken, to whom he had sent it for criticism,
called it inferior work. The rejection probably took place sometime
around 1917. Hecht later told Hansen, in an interview for Hansen's
essay in *Midwest Portraits*, that elements from those two early

33

manuscripts were incorporated later (when, he doesn't say) in *Gargoyles*, which was published in 1922, the year after *Erik Dorn*. Thematic and stylistic evidence in *Gargoyles* does indeed suggest that that novel was conceived and at least partly written before either *Erik Dorn* or the 1924 novel *Humpty Dumpty*, since it treats in an embryonic way many of the concerns of the later books.

Set in 1900, *Gargoyles* is Hecht's attempt to imitate Theodore Dreiser (whom no one without Dreiser's precise gifts should try to emulate). It is an attack on the vacuousness of middle class lives and the corruptness of middle class institutions such as newspapers and courts. Hecht's knowledge of the latter was much greater than his understanding of the former, but he sought to cover his ignorance with indignant satire. The indignation rings hollow, however, partly because he lacked Dreiser's intimate knowledge of the turn-of-the-century city and partly because he displayed all too well Dreiser's somewhat wooden style. Throughout *Gargoyles* there is the sense that Hecht was holding back or covering up his own strange personality as it had been shaped by Nietzsche, Mencken and the city itself. The novel lacks for a pathological examination; it was not until *Erik Dorn* that Hecht became interested in full-scale biopsy.

It is common, indeed almost obligatory, for young novelists to write autobiographical revelations before venturing into imaginative society. Considering what is known about his early discarded work and the chronology of *Gargoyles*, it seems that, typically, Hecht reversed this order. *Gargoyles* was the work of a detached and sardonic observer, like the nameless newspaperman in *1001 Afternoons in Chicago*. *Erik Dorn*, a most remarkable novel, was about the same character in private life — private in more than the usual sense. Unlike *Gargoyles* and the later works of Hecht the Sophisticate, *Erik Dorn* was a book wrenched and distilled from great personal upheaval.

Hecht felt he was older than his years, and his alter ego, Erik Dorn, reflected this illusion in several ways, not the least of which is that Dorn is thirty-four years old, though Hecht, when he created him, was only twenty-seven. Also, Hecht, then a newspaperman for eleven years, made Dorn a veteran of sixteen years. Hecht explained that he borrowed the outward appearance of

Daily News editor Henry Justin Smith for Dorn. Still, it is important that Hecht made his character a married man of seven years' standing when he himself had been married then for only three. Such a ratio is revealing because *Erik Dorn* is the story of the breakdown of a marriage through inertia, brought about by the title character's disillusionment not only with married life but with life itself, especially as it is affected by the big city environment.

In *Literary Lights*, his 1923 collection of caricatures, Gene Markey, himself a literary light in Chicago and later Hollywood, reproduces a sketch captioned "Ben Hecht and some of the characters in *Erik Dorn*." The cartoon shows Hecht, seated, puffing a pipe and sneering. The cloud of tobacco smoke contains three miniatures of the same unmistakable face. The point was not lost on Hecht or anyone else. *Erik Dorn* was the story of Hecht's first marriage to Marie Armstrong told with, one imagines, little omitted that was painful and much included that was pleasant, including his relationship with his second wife, Rose Caylor, who is characterized in the novel as Rachel Laskin.

If written fifty years later about a woman rather than a man, *Erik Dorn* would have been hailed as an important feminist novel. If published in 1932 rather than 1922, and concerned with the life Hecht was then leading, it would have been the great Hollywood novel. The feminist genre Hecht ignored entirely, unlike Dreiser and Floyd Dell; and he wrote only one Hollywood novel, *I Hate Actors!*, a mystery published in 1944. The ingredients of both forms, however, are buried in *Dorn*.

Erik Dorn marked the first sustained appearance of Hechtian man, of whom hitherto only glimpses had been caught, notably in the "1001 Afternoons" column and the stories which had been appearing in the *Little Review* and elsewhere, later collected in *Broken Necks*. But now here he was straight from the brow of Zeus and the couch of Krafft-Ebing, shaped by some curious reading and even more by the two poles of his environmnet, which were not very far asunder: the cityroom and the city streets.

The title character is a Chicago newspaperman with more talent than he can handle, or at least more promise and certainly greater intelligence. But because of the nature of his existence — his hollow employment and his dull marriage to Anna, a woman who is his intellectual inferior — he finds his wit and vitality whittled down to a constant stream of mere epigram. It is a deterioration to which he succumbs; in fact, it is one he enjoys observing and chronicling with sardonic dispassion. Dorn is a man with more assets than the people around him — than even the city around him. Yet he cannot be ordinary even when he tries to be, or at least he likes to believe that he cannot. He is, in his own words, "the Don Quixote of disillusionment." He is also, of course, Ben Hecht under another equally euphonious name.

Dorn is a reporter who has risen to the level of an editor. It is a job he carries out mechanically and competently but not happily. Whereas formerly he stared wonderfully and uncomprehendingly at the whirl of the city, as someone else might stare at nature, Dorn now must contemplate instead a microcosmic version of Chicago, the editorial floor, which is memorably described. Dorn is still drawn to the city lights, hesitantly at times, eagerly at others, always with an almost atavistic urge that rises in his throat like phlegm. He is thoroughly urban. That fact, no less than his job, accounts for his disillusionment. "I'm what men will all be years later," he tells his wife Anna, "when their emotions are finally absorbed by the ingenious surfaces they've surrounded themselves with, and life lies forever buried beneath the inventions of engineers, scientists, and businessmen."

Erik Dorn sees the city from both an ant's- and a bird's-eye view instead of from the perspective of other six-foot mortals. To him, as to the newsman in the "1001 Afternoons" and *Broken Necks* pieces, it is an occasionally sentimental place otherwise incapable of any feelings at all. Through the years, and because of the strains on his personality, Dorn becomes exactly the same as the city. He turns into a psychotic who wears his psychosis on his sleeve.

Dorn is Hecht without Hecht's ambition as a writer. He is brilliant with no outlet for his brilliance. He is adept at "coining phrases for a profitless amusement." The minting of epigrams becomes a substitute for meeting his problems in a realistic way. The most pressing of these problems is the slow but steady decline of his marriage, which is complicated by the different kind of relationship he enjoys with Rachel, a magazine artist. His wife Anna comes to realize that the extraordinariness she earlier perceived in her husband is really a vocabulary unaccompanied by emotion or passion. Dorn meets his wife's silent charges with still more epigrams, coy paraphrases and shining generalizations, all the while aware that he is hastening the inevitable end. He is secure in his theatrical view of life as a game observed from afar. That same view, plus an honest, romantic attraction uncharacteristic of him, applies to his affair with Rachel as well. Rachel herself is torn between Dorn, whose theatricality she sometimes sees through but finds mysteriously attractive, and Hazlitt, a young, earnest − far too earnest − lawyer.

The character Hazlitt is all that Dorn is not. He is literal-minded, stable and forthright in his own idea of romance. He is everything Rachel was raised to think would be admirable in a mate were it only a mate she were looking for. "There was about Hazlitt's wooing of Rachel," Hecht writes, slipping into Dorn's own style, "the pathos which might distinguish the love affair of a Baptist angel and the hamadryad daughter of Babayaga."

Hazlitt is for Rachel what Anna must once have been for Dorn. The difference is that Dorn, for all his insouciant intelligence, is never so wise as Rachel. That fact annoys him; but rather than show his annoyance at Rachel, he vents it by making light of the seriousness of Lockwood, a local novelist, and older man, whose dedication to writing a secretly envious Dorn deceives himself into thinking is still another stall in the urban sideshow. Lockwood is clearly recognizable as Sherwood Anderson, the somewhat disdainful Anderson who in real life once warned Hecht, "You let Art alone . . . She's got enough guys sleeping with her."

Dorn's love of Rachel is largely the realization that here at last is a person who sees through his emptiness masquerading as worldweariness, but who truly cares about him. In the face of such concern, Dorn senses acutely the superficiality of his personality. Rachel, for her part, is torn between Dorn's sincere love for her, and her reticence about becoming involved with a man who is clearly unstable. Her common sense triumphs, and Rachel moves to New York. She leaves behind a Dorn who is almost, but not quite, disturbed enough to break out of his comfortable, static state. As it happens, it is Dorn's other mistress, "that blind old cat" the press, that causes the scene if not his make-up to change.

Like Hecht, Dorn is sent to Berlin as a foreign correspondent. But since the Dorn character is an almost satiric exaggeration of the part of Hecht's personality that is not a writer, he does not become involved with the German artistic radicals, only with the political ones. These people are a funny lot, and here Hecht's style — sentences austere in structure but ripe with exotic imagery — is at its most effective in dealing with the type of expressionism he concocted for himself. As he describes it, Berlin is a bizarre place charged with the kind of barely suppressed chaos common after holocausts. The style is that way as well.

In Berlin, Dorn reports the same sort of political confusion Hecht himself reported. He meets two disparate characters, each of whom eats away at the veneer of his cynicism. The first is a young German communist named Mathilde. She and Dorn fall in love more or less equally, though for different reasons. Mathilde is a woman passionately committed to a social cause, though not with the polemical brashness Dorn has always found distasteful because it reminds him of the forced flippancy of his own life.

The other Berliner he meets is Karl von Stinnes, an older man who was a double-agent in the war. He is a true cynic, unlike Dorn, who merely plays the role. Whereas Mathilde is dedicated to what she believes a noble ideal, von Stinnes is committed to harsh realities. He is aware that politics is futile, but he hopes, with the tiny part of him left unscarred by successive wars and revolutions, that he has made the correct move. Dorn sees his possible future in Mathilde but his probable one in von Stinnes. He prostitutes uncaringly his role as a newsman, as an untouchable without politics, by helping the pair of them smuggle money to Munich with which to buy arms for the insurrection.

In crazy, decadent Berlin, Dorn with his pathological posturing, is just another eccentric. This is both a great comfort and a great emotional burden to him. He realizes once more that he lives in only one dimension, and that ultimately such a state is soul destroying. The realization, however, is but another intellectual abstraction, and the old Dorn blunders on. "There are many ways of making love," he tells Mathilde in a typical moment. "Sorrowful phrases are the most entertaining, perhaps."

With von Stinnes, too, Dorn continues to be his acerbic self, possibly to the older man's sorrow. The two of them have a sardonic, masculine sort of relationship devoid of the sentiment which Dorn, in occasional lapses, lavishes on the woman. When Mathilde as much as calls von Stinnes a scoundrel, Dorn defends him and in doing so describes himself accurately. "He is merely a man without convictions and therefore free to follow the impulses of his employers. I thank God for von Stinnes. He has made Europe possible. A revolution would rival him in my affections."

Back in the States, Anna Dorn has been granted a divorce and has married Eddy Meredith, a nondescript surrogate for all the things she knew Dorn possessed but was so loath to reveal. Rachel meanwhile has taken up with a radical named Emil Telse, though not unequivocally. The idea of Erik Dorn, if not the reality of him, still plagues her from time to time. Unbeknownst to her, Hazlitt — Dorn's old rival for Rachel — is now an officer in the American army and looks up Dorn in Berlin. He is bitter, knowing that Rachel's idea of Dorn has cost him her love forever. When Hazlitt confronts the journalist, Dorn shoots him dead — not out of anger or passion, but because somewhere in the rear of his brilliant yet atrophied mind he wanted to prove to himself that he was capable of love or, if not love, then hatred. Even that terrible deed, however, fails to spring Dorn's emotions from their prison within a vocabulary and an attitude. Nor is he liberated when von Stinnes, who next to Rachel is the closest to a peer Dorn has ever known, takes his own life when the Munich revolt ends in failure.

Back in America, Dorn tries to look up Rachel and then does look up Anna, thereby committing, he thinks later, an emotional *faux pas*, the thought of which drives him back to the newspaper, the natural habitat of all such souls as Dorn.

According to conventional literary logic, *Erik Dorn* should be a flawed book because the main character remains exactly the same at the end of the novel as he was at the beginning. He is no wiser, no more or less committed to any idea or belief. Yet that very sameness is the key to *Erik Dorn* as the study of a peculiarly deviant, anti-utopian personality. Dorn is unchanged inwardly as well as outwardly. He is still capable of sentiment in moments of weakness, for which he hates himself. It is Hecht's best novel and also contains some of his best prose. It is a work he would come back to later from a somewhat different angle.

Had he lived, James Gibbon Huneker, who died in 1920, could have written a superb essay on Hechtian man. The New York critic, who was perhaps Mencken's greatest English-speaking influence, was, in his heyday before World War One, the important bridge between modernist European culture and the United States. Such an essay would have been the natural extension of those he did compose on Huysmans, Remy de Gourmont, Nietzsche and Shaw, among others. It is not illogical to suppose that Huneker would have viewed Hecht as the progeny of those men's ideas. Pursuing this line he could not have gone far wrong.

Hechtian man, as manifested in *Erik Dorn*, was a fellow with a moribund interest in life. He thought of himself as somehow ageless, though he was in fact very much a member of the intelligensia of his own narrow generation, consumed with interest (most of it misplaced) in the new pseudosciences of psychology and sociology. Havelock Ellis would be a more important figure to him than all the thinkers and politicians put together. If Hechtian man sometimes mangled ideas which were not always sound to begin with, well, that was all right, for the ideas fitted his view of his fellow humans and himself.

Hechtian man, or Hecht the Neo-Augustinean in Bohemian clothes, was at the crossroads of several literary currents. All of them are almost entirely assimilated into other forms today but then were very much the vanguard of a vanguard tradition. As Huneker pointed out in his essay on Shaw, "Swift's hatred of mankind was a species of inverted lyricism; so was Flaubert's, so may be Shaw's." And so too was Hecht's, but with two important differences.

The first was that Hecht was a closet sentimentalist whose work at this period was the result of a conflict between his sentimentality and his cynical view of his contemporaries. Swift, Flaubert possibly, and Shaw certainly, were pragmatists. They believed their fellow men unfortunate inferiors who had to be led down the road to fulfilment by whatever entertainment means necessary.

Hecht, by contrast, thought his fellow men were boobs. Everywhere he looked seemed to confirm that view. Far from leading them parentally, he made fun of them and also felt sorry for them. He pitied himself as well, fearing they might reduce him to their own level.

Why he felt as he did points up the second difference: that unlike those other authors, Hecht was a modern urban writer. He was the product of a wild and frightening environment created by the desire for the fast buck, left behind by the tide of politics. Chicago before 1930 was comparable to pre-1947 Shanghai or pre-1975 Saigon: a wildly furious place where everything was for sale. Hecht believed, mistakenly, that the spectacle which mesmerized him was the wave of the future. The city gave him proof of everything he had come to believe — that individually other people were scoundrels or ignoramuses, but that collectively they were (sometimes) a variant of himself, a mass-produced consciousness always in danger of being extinguished.

In an important sense, Hecht and the city of Chicago (as a place, rather than a population) were collaborators then and, by long distance, for decades afterward. But while similar in the ways already mentioned, he and the city were also very dissimilar. Chicago was anti-intellectual and vicious but too fast-paced to be calculating. It was the player with railroads. Hecht, conversely, was the player with ideas, a man almost Emersonian in his use of the notebook as a weapon in defense of individuality.

Chicago was a better collaborator for Hecht than even Charles MacArthur or Gene Fowler would become, since those writers were all so much alike in outlook. Not until his peak Hollywood days would Hecht find collaborators whose assistance, like Chicago's, would be both conflicting and complementary. One of these would be Howard Hawks, who shared Hecht's view of laissez-faire rough-and-tumble Chicago-ness but who lacked Hecht's urbaneness and urbanity. Another would be Alfred Hitchcock, who believed with Hecht that modern men are boobs lacking the hardihood to improve. Hitchcock, though, was interested in the plight of ordinary people in extraordinary circumstances as a dramatic situation. Hecht by then had come to be interested in just the reverse.

The Five Lives of Ben Hecht

In 1918, when Hecht's stories and sketches were appearing regularly in the *Little Review*, that keen talent-spotter Ezra Pound wrote to Margaret Anderson from Europe to compare Hecht favourably to Guy de Maupassant as a writer of *contes*, and otherwise to offer encouragement and praise. Later the same year he again wrote her to compare Hecht to the French master, this time unfavourably; Pound's contradiction reflected not so much his fickle politicking as Hecht's gourmandizing of influences and ideas. This gluttony was part of the process by which he was rapidly molding Hechtian man, a many-sided creature whose originality lay mainly in the whole rather than in a majority of the parts – parts which are clearly recognizable even outside the context of Chicago.

To begin with, Hecht owed stylistic debts. One was to Huysmans, whose writing, like the man himself, was somewhat dyspeptic. Another was to de Gourmont. In that writer's best work (as Huneker wisely said) the author's ideas are the heroes, whereas in young Hecht's best work (as Huneker might have said) the ideas are the hero's heroes.

But Hecht took more than a style and an approach from his favourite Continentals. He also took the pose of a decadent, meaning that he revelled in the decay around him. Unlike many other decadents, however, he was neither a reformer nor a poseur at heart. Or if he was, he was a Nietzschean poseur who was interested only in reforming himself through sheer Teutonic discipline. He also shared with Nietzsche a belief that morality was the outcome of tribal taboos. The tribe in this case was Hecht's own, the modern North American; his will was never quite strong enough to allow him to break free of the group's conventional attitudes and wisdom. Hechtian man was a sort of more fallible, more human Nietzsche, plunked down by some wry caprice in Chicago where votes generally sold for fifty cents and the price of a schooner of beer.

Hecht's coming of age was tied closely to his quitting the newspaper business, leaving the geographical Chicago and ultimately forsaking Hechtian man (though all these, in somewhat denatured form, remained with him to the end). As he digested completely the European writers he admired, as he began to involve himself with "real" people instead of only colleagues and news sources, and as he later became caught up in New York and Hollywood life, Hecht underwent a great change and so did his treatment of his subjects. He ceased to be Hecht the Iconoclast and Bohemian and became instead Hecht the Sophisticate. Hechtian man, however, kept cropping up, a little older than before, and with his disillusionment perhaps more justified. When embroiled in show business, writing things he did not want to write for huge sums of money he believed he needed, Hecht would resurrect his Frankenstein's monster as a kind of therapy, to once more make an honest man of himself as a writer.

In 1937, for instance, the creature turned up as Alexander Sterns in Hecht's play *To Quito and Back*. Sterns is an American newspaperman who elopes to the Ecuadorian capital with a woman he enjoys as the receptacle of his self-destructive magic. Like Erik Dorn, who as a journalist was "a man without conviction," Sterns is a newsman whose professed lack of politics carries over into his private life as a lack of morals. Like Dorn, he speaks mainly in epigrams, though in this case the edge of brilliance is gone, and the dialogue sounds like André Malraux made into musical comedy. Sterns' story also resembles Dorn's in that Sterns finds himself involved in a communist revolution — but this time one for which he gives his life in the same way he had lived it, melodramatically yet with heavy eyelids.

The play was produced in somewhat butchered fashion by the Theater Guild in New York and received attention in the *Partisan Review* from Mary McCarthy. She summed up, perhaps more succintly than anyone else before or since, the nature of the recurring Hechtian character.

The hero, who describes himself as "a second-hand Hamlet with a hollow heart and a woodpecker mind," for two acts engages in vacillation, amorous and political. He can love neither a woman nor a cause truly, no matter how desperately he desires to do so. In all branches of experience he is irrevocably a tourist, and his most poignant cry is "If I could only care!" His heroic death, which (to Mr. Hecht's mind) is his final salvation, is admittedly the product of a mood, whose impermanency he recognizes even while yielding to it.

The Five Lives of Ben Hecht

Erik Dorn for all its brilliance, or perhaps because of the flashiness of its brilliance, was very much in the familiar pattern of young men's novels. It was concerned with the odyssey of a man whose youthfulness is disguised by the author, who also conceals the fact that the character is an artist by writing of him as a mere newspaperman, and an editor at that. But in *Humpty Dumpty*, published three years later, Hecht recreated the character in a more mature light, telling a nearly identical story from a much different perspective. It was an unusual thing to do, possibly a deliberate attention-getting device designed to startle both the orthodox and the heterodox into reading both books when ordinarily they would have read one or the other, or neither.

In *Humpty Dumpty*, the protagonist is named Kent Savaron. Whereas Erik Dorn was a potential artist or artist *manqué* and Sterns possibly a failed artist as well as failed personality, Savaron recognizes early in himself the power to be a writer. He lives in a small city in a north central state (certainly based on Hecht's Racine, Wisconsin) with his widowed father, whom he deserts for the big city and a career. Savaron becomes the kind of writer Hecht was when writing *Erik Dorn* and other early decadent-impressionistic works. The reader of *Humpty Dumpty* has the eerie feeling that he is actually reading a rather condescending biography of the Hecht who wrote *Erik Dorn*. Hecht goes out of his way to criticize the way he had been only a few years before.

> Grinning with a precious excitement, he sat scribbling words. He was aware only of a fanatic intent to describe the things he knew, to invent phrases and images which in these things would become strangely enlarged. He avoided writing directly not because of a consciousness of symbolism. He wrote that the telegraph poles rising in the dark resemble music notes, that the night hovered over the roofs like a Madonna of the spaces, that the lamp-posts along the streets drifted out of sight like a string of expiring little balloons. He put down on paper the precise angle of smoke pillars leaning out of chimney mouths. He recorded the fact that the row of decrepit houses in a dirty street were like teeth in the mouth of an old man...He was cataloguing an inner world and his obsession permitted him no time to think, to relate, to select or to invest his writing with a sense of form or significance. The results of his labor were pages on pages of unfinished prose poems....

And so it goes on.

Hecht, not on balance a critical favourite, probably never received a worse review than that one he gave himself.

The most notable difference between the two novels, aside from the toning down of the style announcing the emergence of the Sophisticate, is that *Erik Dorn* psychoanalyzes the main character as an isolated specimen, whereas *Humpty Dumpty* investigates more rationally the nature of Savaron in terms of his literary time and place.

The second novel shares many of the elements of the first, including the husband and wife who think each other insensitive, and the mistress who this time is named Blanche Innes. But *Humpty Dumpty* is less infused with upper-case Writing and more interested in the hero's place in society. It is to some extent about love among the Babbitts, or potential love among them; it is not only a successful rewriting of *Erik Dorn* but another stab at *Gargoyles* as well. That fact, along with the presence of the enervated (for Hecht) style, announced a change in direction more important than it would seem at first.

Concurrent with all this novel-writing, Hecht was writing short stories at his customary fast pace. The stories fell into two categories. The first category included the impressionistic tales about Hechtian man or his view of his contemporaries, with all the accompanying contradictions. Actually such works were more frequently elaborate anecdotes, sketches and mood pieces than they were tales. Many of them appeared in the *Little Review* and later in *Broken Necks*.

The latter included the stories he was writing for Mencken, which not coincidentally resembled Mencken's own few early attempts at fiction. These were stories in which something happened. Usually some morally indigent Chicagoan was caught up by a twist of fate after the scene had been set in a rather smooth, sneering fashion. A great number of these stories were published or republished in seven of the Little Blue Books, the five-cent booklets of modern literature and social comment issued by Haldeman-Julius of Girard, Kansas, which did so much to educate the public of that time. To these booklets Hecht gave titles in imitation of the titles of cheap pulp stories, such as *Tales of Chicago Streets*, *The Sinister Sex* and *The Policewoman's Love-Hungry Daughter*. He grew biting in his satire to keep from becoming sentimental as he had occasionally been before. These wry stories, with their peep-show attitude toward the peccadilloes of the middle and upper classes, formed a respectable percentage of his work as a Sophisticate.

In his fiction Hecht had now become a social critic. Like many such critics, he began by being a literary commentator. Such literary comment goes back to *Humpty Dumpty*, in which he took swipes at the Society of Midland Authors and the society's foe, modernism; and dismissed (or in some cases, as with Mencken, lauded) the whole shelf of contemporary authors by name.

Unlike *Erik Dorn*, in which Hecht felt compelled to disguise Sherwood Anderson, *Humpty Dumpty* mentions by name two local aesthetes. These are Wallace Smith, a reporter who gained renown as a decadent artist, and Stanislaus Szukalski, a Polish emigré painter and sculptor who was recognized, in Chicago at least, as an internationally important artist. Both were figures of the then current Chicago Renaissance, a movement that brought Hecht, the closet sentimentalist, out of the closet, transforming him into a public iconoclast. It saw the one Hecht die away, and for a time made the next one – the one who was to become the Sophisticate – something of a force as a mover and shaker.

4
Backyard Athens

I once lived in a good world. I was young and somewhat indifferent to its charms. In fact, I sat up nights earning my spurs as an iconoclast. My youth was spent trying to convince a scattering of readers how stupid and cruel, how greedy and imperfect was that time of the Merry Widow Waltz *and the* St. Louis Blues.

BH, *in* 1001 Afternoons in New York

Although only a few of the famous participants remain alive, it is still possible to muster a respectable argument as to the true nature and dates of the Chicago Renaissance. The truth is that from the 1880s to perhaps as late as 1930, the city always seemed to be going through some sort of cultural birth or rebirth. The difficulty now lies mainly in determining where one robust period left off and another began. Most commentators, however, use the phrase Chicago Renaissance to refer to the period between the founding of Harriet Monroe's *Poetry: A Magazine of Verse* in 1912 and the dispersal of many Chicago writers approximately a decade later.

While everyone who discusses that era has his own prejudice as to the most important Renaissance figure, they virtually all agree that it was Hecht who provided the glamour, the publicity, the shenanigans and, ultimately, the awareness that, yes, this rebirth was much different, far more significant than earlier ones, even if this awareness came during the movement's last years.

As early as the 1860s, when Chicago was beginning to lose its image as a frontier town on the edge of the prairie, a naissance was sufficiently underway to warrant jibes in the city's press, obstreperous even then. The post-Civil War movement was dedicated largely to a romanticized concept of a bohemia that equated poverty with creative superiority. It included such native writers as Henry Blake Fuller and a notable import, George Gissing, author of *New Grub Street*, who fled to America after a term in an English prison. In the rebuilding of the city following the Great Fire of 1871, such bohemianism was put aside, at least for a time.

In the 1880s, Chicago was catching up to New York as a centre of trade and industry. It was a permanent boom town to which every ambitious midwesterner came to make good. These migrants included prospective authors and artists, and the decade between the early 1880s and the early 1890s saw Chicago alive with writers, musicians and scholars. Among the writers were Opie Read, George Ade and Finley Peter Dunne, as well as Herbert Stone, who published the *Chapbook*, the direct ancestor of the London *Yellow Book*.

Not coincidentally these men and scores of others with similar ambitions worked on the city's newspapers, labouring at witty tales and light verse compatible with the sheets that employed them. Through the 1880s, the 1890s and later, they came from Indiana, Iowa, Nebraska, Ohio, Wisconsin, Michigan, the entire Mississippi drainage, wanting to be writers but often settling for being reporters. One of them was Theodore Dreiser, who though more peripatetic than most, was certainly a part of the journalistic-artistic milieu, and went on to become the most important of the lot.

Chicago had its established, official culture as exemplified by the Art Institute and the University of Chicago, but it also had its unofficial one made up of newspapermen with pretentions to higher things. Hecht was a part of the latter. He at once became caught up in it and eventually changed it drastically. In his autobiography he never used the term Chicago Renaissance, for he was writing about himself alone. To a large extent the two creations were one and the same.

In 1892 and 1893, a world's fair, the Columbian Exposition, had confirmed the place of Chicago as a capital. Harriet Monroe, then eighteen years old, was the fair's poet laureate. She was to become one of the few native Chicagoans prominent in the Renaissance.

Backyard Athens

Most participants were migrants, and they naturally settled in two areas where the rents were cheap. The first was a section of the South Side inhabited primarily by immigrants. It was full of store fronts left over from the fair. Hecht from Wisconsin, Sandburg and Vachel Lindsay from downstate Illinois, Sherwood Anderson from Ohio and Floyd Dell from Iowa were only a few who lived in this bohemian residential area. Complementing it was the downtown of bohemia, an area called Towertown because of its proximity to a horror of gothic architecture known as the Chicago Water Tower. This neighbourhood was the home of the Radical Book Shop, the tearooms, the second-hand stalls and the garrets of bohemia, and also of such little theatres as the Jack and Jill Players, the Studio Playhouse and the Impertinent Players.

It was also the site of the Dill Pickle Club, located in narrow Tooker Alley, a few steps from Bughouse Square, where radicals, occultists and all manner of soap-boxers held forth in a noisy americanization of London's Hyde Park. The Dill Pickle was run by a former Wobbly named Jack Jones. It catered to students, newspapermen, artists and artisans of all kinds, and, later, after Prohibition began, to gangsters whom the newspapermen were naturally used to seeing in the course of their jobs. It was there that much experimental drama was produced, including Hecht and Bodenheim's "The Master Poisoner." It was there also that Hecht put on some solo efforts, including "Dregs," a one-acter some considered blasphemous as well as profane. The play concerned a wino caught in a blizzard who sees his own reflection in a store window and mistakes the experience for the Second Coming of Christ.

Like its counterpart on the South Side, the North Side artistic colony was only about a half-mile square. It was jammed between the vast rooming house section on the one extremity and the Gold Coast homes of the wealthy on the other. Housing conditions may have been primitive, but the place was alive with dancing, writing, acting and painting. Free love, blue jeans and long hair on men were the norms of unconventionality, but the area also boasted more original eccentrics. One, for instance, was a woman who would summon an audience to watch her take poison in the street, claiming the international record for unsuccessful suicide attempts.

Studio parties were in progress constantly. Not a few were held

49

The Five Lives of Ben Hecht

by Margery Currey, the first wife and former teacher of Floyd Dell, at her apartment in Cass Street, now Wabash Avenue. It was there that Sherwood Anderson is said to have written some of his early stories. It was certainly there that he read them aloud to a floating guest population that often included Hecht and Bodenheim.

Hecht had fallen quite naturally into such an atmosphere: it was inexpensive, Hecht was youthfully precocious and the nature of his work drew him there. On the *Journal* first, and later on the *Daily News*, it was expected that newsmen would also be literary stylists. The type of men hired quite understandably spent their free time, both in and outside the office, in a mixture of bohemian pedantry and bohemian revelry. It is not coincidence that, except for Sherwood Anderson, most of the important prose writers to come out of the Renaissance between about 1912 and 1925 were also newspapermen, nor that a number of the poets from Sandburg to Starrett were also reporters. It was the newspapermen's butt-end view of society that made them cynical and the rather gayer atmosphere of bohemia that made them literary.

The two outlooks were bonded together to create a writer who was a decadent naturalist, or impressionistic realist or, in any event, a sentimental tough guy. It is that kind of writer who is the mark of the Renaissance as it is remembered today. Hecht fitted that mould. He shaped and was in turn shaped by the artistic goings-on in the twin bohemias and the cityscape between them.

Between the residential and commercial bohemias was Schlogl's restaurant, a dark German eating-house dating from the Great Fire. It stood on Wells Street a short distance from the *Daily News* where Hecht, Hansen, Sandburg, Starrett, Smith and an entire wing of the Renaissance toiled. For years it had been a convenient watering place for newspapermen. As these writers gained renown it assumed almost legendary importance as the place where titans might be viewed in the flesh, often in the company of some visiting literary celebrity. Thus was born the reputation of Schlogl's Round Table, a victualing and pontificating place still talked about. Memories of the conversation (often with Hecht in the lead) have tended to overshadow memories of the equally exotic menu, which included not only venison and fowl, but eel and even owl.

Here one might pit his brilliance against others'. Here schemes were hatched and arguments waged. Damned or defended were the latest numbers of the local magazines, *Wave*, *Poetry*, *Little Review*, *Literary Review*; the local newspaper review sections edited at various times by Hansen, Henry Blackman Sell, Francis Hackett and Rascoe; and the products of the burgeoning indigenous publishing houses. Even after Hecht and later Hansen were sent to Berlin, and even after some of the participants had moved away for good, the conversation and the arguing continued.

Schlogl's, the Dill Pickle and perhaps a few other haunts helped to spread the reputation of Chicago as a literary centre and make a Renaissance out of what was otherwise a group of disparate writers sharing common excitements. It was all that which caused H.L. Mencken in Baltimore to write of Chicago as "the literary capital of the US" in 1920. He called it the "only genuinely civilized city in the New World [where] they take the fine arts seriously and get into such frets and excitements about them as are raised nowhere else save by baseball, murder, political treachery, foreign wars and romantic love . . . ." Hecht, writing more than thirty years later, in *Charlie*, would fondly speak of the scene as a "Backyard Athens."

The excitement Mencken remarked on was not limited to squabblings among the Renaissance men. Part of the friction was between those Chicagoans and society at large, as represented by censors and would-be censors. Chicago's authorities were not necessarily harsher than those in other cities. Compared with those of Boston, for instance, Chicago's reformers were absolute brigands. It was rather that some people in Chicago went out of their way to flaunt the standards and laws of the time. One who flaunted them in the name of art was Margaret Anderson, who was convicted of obscenity for publishing a fragment of James Joyce's *Ulysses* (the first piece of it to appear in America) in the *Little Review*. Most prominent, however, was Hecht, who thumbed his nose at censorship largely on principle, or just for the hell of it.

One can only guess at what scandal might have resulted from Hecht's discarded manuscripts. Probable difficulty with *Erik Dorn* was avoided by precensorship, though the novel as finally published was still regarded in some circles as immoral. In his memoirs, George Palmer Putnam, the publisher of *Erik Dorn*, relates that, at his company's suggestion, Hecht agreed to minor changes in the manuscript, such as altering a sentence about Rachel's breasts to read "breast," singular.

Such an uncharacteristic concession to propriety may be attributed to the fact that Hecht was, in terms of hard covers at least and certainly outside Chicago, a new writer. He was willing to make small compromises for the sake of making his name, especially with a New York publisher with whom he was dealing for the first time. This acquiescence did not necessarily indicate any lack of commitment to what was then a volatile cause across the country. The next year Hecht contributed an essay, "Literature and the Bastinado," to a collection of pieces Putnam published damning the censors and reformers. The book, which also contained articles by Alexander Woollcott and Heywood Broun and verse by Dorothy Parker, was perhaps the first such group rebuttal published by the liberal literary community. The community was then reeling in shock and disgust at such censorship and would later come out fighting even more fiercely.

For Hecht, who would endure censorship problems with many of his books and later with his filmscripts, 1922 was the height of his difficulties and defiance. The Rev. J. Franklin Chase, a former Methodist preacher and the author of a tract entitled *The "Dope" Evil*, had won a conviction against *Gargoyles* in Boston, where he headed the Watch and Ward Society. Chase was the New England counterpart of New York's notorious John Sumner, of the Society for the Suppression of Vice, who won similar convictions against works by Sherwood Anderson, Bodenheim, Aldous Huxley, Floyd Dell and John Dos Passos. He also succeeded in banning Boccaccio and Petronious as well as various well-intentioned marriage and hygiene manuals. A more significant event of 1922 was the publication of Hecht's *Fantazius Mallare*, which, no matter what its artistic failings, succeeded in its other purpose of testing the limits of the censors' wrath.

In the 1920s, the collecting, or in any event the publishing of limited, numbered editions was something of a fad. Often these were sold by advance subscription only, as had been the custom in England with works considered to be "naughty." Hecht persuaded two energetic Washington Street booksellers, a former priest, William P. McGee, and a book-lover, Pascal Covici, to follow that practice with one of his works. It was described in an unsigned prospectus, undoubtedly written by Hecht himself, as "without question the most daring psychological melodrama of modern writing...destined to arrest the cultural attention of the century that it mirrors." Such attention, however, was not arrested. The author was.

The book, subtitled "A Mysterious Oath," was published at ten dollars in an edition of 2,025 numbered copies and contained several interesting features. The text was a rather formless, repetitious babble of intricate and stylized prose, full of copulation and perversion both physical and mental, real and imagined, but the preface contained some remarkable writing. It was a long burst of contumely aimed at Hecht's and the book's imagined enemies, "The prim ones who fornicate apologetically (the Devil can-cans in their souls)...," and so on. It was a loud catcall laced with hard names and clever insults, woven in the rhythms of the synagogue cantors, with a dash of Walt Whitman and an overdose of Baudelaire. Decades later it influenced Allen Ginsberg's long poem "Howl."

The more important feature of the book, however, were the end pieces and six drawings by Wallace Smith, a Hearst reporter who drew in a style reminiscent of Beardsley though less ornately and concerned more with a nightmarish vision of sensuality than with myth and ancient literature. (Smith later confessed to Vincent Starrett, perhaps jokingly, that he had never heard of Beardsley.) The drawings were called diabolic; the most outrageous and powerful of them depicted a man locked in coital embrace with a leafless tree, whose limbs had outstretched to resemble those of a woman or a witch. The drawings were defended as phallic symbolism but, as Burton Rascoe remarked, were merely phallic.

As the book was for sale to subscribers only, Hecht and Smith were charged with a violation of federal law prohibiting the transport of "lewd, obscene and lascivious" literature through the US mails, rather than with violation of state or local statutes concerning the open sale of the same material. Hecht enlisted the support of Clarence Darrow, one of the many professional men with honoured observer status at the Renaissance, and Charles Erbstein, another famed trial lawyer. As Hecht describes him, Erbstein could well have been the inspiration for Sandburg's cynical verse, "Why does the hearse horse snicker/ Carrying the lawyer's bones?"

The Five Lives of Ben Hecht

The case became a *cause célèbre*, and for Hecht, something of a lesson. The lawyers had advised him to summon as many distinguished literary men as possible to speak of the book's artistic merits. Those he approached refused to testify because, as Hecht recalled with bitterness years later, they felt they would suffer "by coming out in the open and defending a book that had the word 'pissing' in it." Only Mencken, without being asked, offered to speak out, and to pay his own fare to Chicago as well.

After much publicity, and despite the case Darrow and his colleague put forward, Hecht and Smith were convicted and fined $1,000 each. Hecht somehow paid up but Smith lacked funds and so, with Putnam's help in New York, began writing slick magazine fiction. That led to work in Hollywood, and aside from a few frontispieces for Covici-McGee, Smith did practically no more work as an artist. His only brief flourish of later renown as an artist came in the 1960s, when the drawing of the man and the tree became a popular poster of the youth culture.

As a result of the *Fantazius Mallare* controversy, Hecht was fired from the *Daily News*. He published his final column October 10, 1922, and left the newspaper world. The parting more than ever committed him to the writing of books. In 1924, Covici, having parted company with McGee, published "A Continuation of the Journal of Fantazius Mallare" entitled *The Kingdom of Evil*, in an edition of 1,900 numbered subscription copies. But the text and the illustrations, by Anthony Angarola this time, were far inferior to those of the original, and the publication passed relatively unnoticed.

Meanwhile Hecht was supporting himself by publishing, and largely writing himself, a fortnightly newspaper called the *Chicago Literary Times*, which was probably the first underground newspaper in the United States as we understand the phrase today. Hecht ran serially a piece attacking the censors, written by himself and Bodenheim. When later published privately in what purported to be a limited edition, it was entitled *Cutie: A Warm Mama*. Hecht never saw fit to list it on any of his flyleaf bibliographies. Although this little known, slight comic work was dashed off as a satire on contemporary events, it is still useful today. It shows the direction his satire would take in such larger works as *Count Bruga*.

54

Backyard Athens

The cutie of the title is a twenty-one-year-old blonde who is, as the old phrase has it, a bit of all right. While a policeman is removing a splinter from her knee on a downtown streetcorner, she is noticed by a local book censor and reformer named Herman J. Pupick. (*Pupick* is Yiddish for navel and for the less appetizing parts of a chicken.) He is offended by the spectacle of the young woman's exposed knee, and drags her off to a nearby Methodist bookstore. He soon realizes that Cutie is not the innocent youth he took her for, and sends her on her way reprovingly.

Pupick cannot keep his thoughts from the image of this free spirit, even though she is the type of person who reads the books he spends his day suppressing. Nor can he find comfort in his equally devout wife Emmaline. At length he seeks help from a psychoanalyst. The doctor tries diagnosing Pupick's neuroses by noting his reactions to a series of lantern slides, including ones of Annette Kellerman, the swimming star, and other beauties of the period. The doctor recommends that Pupick shoot himself. Instead, the censor goes about his censorial activities with renewed vigour.

In disguise, he haunts the low speakeasies, until in one of them he meets Cutie. His reaction to her causes a small riot, and Cutie is forced to spirit him off to her apartment. Pupick convinces himself that he should convert Cutie and make her his partner-in-virtue. "He closed up all the dance halls by writing letters to the papers and caused the arrest of twenty-nine authors in Schlogl's restaurant, suppressed the *Chicago Literary Times*, and had all the abdominal belt displays taken out of all the drug store windows." But his liason with Cutie is finally discovered by Mrs. Pupick, who kills them both and then dies herself. It is low comedy of course, but also diffuse. In very few pages, Hecht and Bodenheim manage to assault the dignity of the censors and their supporters everywhere, psychiatry, the Chicago *Tribune* and themselves. *Cutie* is interesting mainly for its style. It is a fable in slang, in principle akin to George Ade's *Fables in Slang*, but with two differences.

First, the tale's blunt point emphasizes that the story is a plea for common sense rather than a statement of moral truth. Second, the slang is fresh and lively. The Chicago writers of the 1920s believed that the city had an argot all its own, and Hecht and Bodenheim did their best to prove this by inventing as they went. Cutie, for example, is described as "a Blue Ribbon roadster" with "a moth complex" who "gave St. Peter writer's cramp before she was eighteen. After she was eighteen St. Peter crossed her name out of the Judgement Book. Not taking any chances, he also threw away her telephone number." She was a warm mama, "the kind of a girl men forget, forty-nine years after their widows have collected the insurance." It was a new attitude toward language.

In *Cutie* it is difficult to determine which writer contributed what. Bodenheim more and more was aping the effects Hecht had learned from Mencken and others. In their personal relations too, the pair were growing closer, at least in a spirit of manic public antagonism that was no small part of the mood of the late Renaissance years. Their closeness continued until Hecht wrote his vicious satire on Bodenheim, *Count Bruga*, published in 1926 after both of them had moved to New York.

Hecht and Bodenheim were forever pulling stunts and pranks. One of Bodenheim's efforts was a barb aimed at the manifesto-making artists of Europe. He declared the existence of a new Monotheme school of poetry. The premise was that the world of verse was oversupplied with subjects and that poets should confine themselves to one topic per month. The topic, a broadsheet proclaimed, would be chosen by Monothemist René d'Or, who of course was Bodenheim himself. The ruse continued until Bodenheim gained, he thought, some notoriety under his alias. He hired a hotel room and notified the press that he would be available for interviews. The interviews never materialized, but the event is significant because in Hecht's novel *Count Bruga*, the title character, an unkempt, basically unprincipled poet named Jules Ganz, engages in much the same kind of sham. He installs himself in a hotel suite as a Polish count, awaiting representatives of the press. No one who knew Bodenheim even slightly could mistake the book-length caricature of him. Bodenheim's few friends were greatly upset by the portrait, as it sought to exploit Bodenheim's social shenanigans without treating seriously his sincere dedication as a writer.

Most of the evidence, however, indicates that Hecht did respect his friend as a poet, though the appreciation was not a subtle one. In *Count Bruga*, as in his later writing about Bodenheim, Hecht concedes that the man's talent was his saving grace. "Women who slapped his face grew frightened as if they had made some incredible mistake," Hecht wrote, "and sensitive gentlemen while punching his head were overcome with uneasy memories of the delicate and often beautiful words to which he signed his name as a poet."

Some of the absurd elements in Bodenheim's character were his own, though his association with Hecht increased his capacity for pranks and wild money-making schemes. Hecht was not fearful of getting carried away by his own pastiche of rumour, half-truth and self-concocted legend about Bodenheim's life and personality. Unlike his colleague, he felt that everything was a proper subject for ridicule in print, even his friends and even such mentors as Mencken. Bodenheim agreed with that philosophy outwardly, but inwardly he was badly stung by *Count Bruga*, primarily because for years afterwards the likeness would precede him in his travels.

Like many bohemians, Bodenheim felt his outrageous behaviour should not preclude him from being respectable. That curious duality of attitude caused him to make a real feud with Hecht from what till then had been a largely bogus one. Bodenheim took the whole episode more seriously than Hecht ever would, however, and in 1931 he was still sufficiently rankled to publish a comic novel entitled *Duke Herring*, lampooning Hecht.

Bodenheim's portrait of Arturo Herring is every bit as distorted as Hecht's of Hippolyt Bruga. It purported to prove that Hecht was a money-grubbing pornographer who at every opportunity tried unsuccessfully to cheat on his first wife with whoever came his way, including the wife of a thinly disguised Pascal Covici and a character who resembles Rose Caylor. As Herring is eventually divorced by his wife, the book is another depiction of Hecht's marriage to Marie Armstrong and its immediate aftermath. It is *Erik Dorn* and *Humpty Dumpty* told from another point of view, one from which to seek revenge on the man with "a thousand-and-one poses." But the book fails. Hecht's public image had changed drastically by 1931 and so the book seemed ancient history. Also, it was largely made up of private jokes and in comparison with *Count Bruga*, was so shot through with bitterness that it never touched the comic power of the book about the phony count Jules Ganz.

Count Bruga began with a description of the royal impersonator imbibing aphrodisiacs and continued in a ribald vein. It was less patently offensive than *Fantazius Mallare* and *The Kingdom of Evil* but inevitably was in some circles considered a pornographic work. Hecht's reputation for literary suggestiveness, if not obscenity, was eclipsing all others in the minds of people unfamiliar with his work as a whole. John Galsworthy, for example, when the subject of Hecht once arose in conversation, asked earnestly, "But isn't he rather an erotic writer?" And D.H. Lawrence, that at heart puritanical man whom Hecht had made light of in both *Fantazius Mallare* and the *Chicago Literary Times*, took violent, well-publicized exception to Hecht on moral grounds. To critics looking back from the late 1930s, it would seem that "Hecht was one of most frequently damned writers of the period." What was still more obvious both then and earlier was that he was gaining an extraliterary reputation as the epicentre of the cultural storms then playing havoc with Chicago.

The years between 1920, when he returned from Berlin, and 1924, when he would leave Chicago for good, were the most productive of Hecht's book-writing life. His adrenalin was flowing in such force that he wrote not only *Erik Dorn*, *Gargoyles*, *Humpty Dumpty* and a mass of stories, but several books blatantly displaying the cleverness, originality and impertinence that mark his contribution to the Renaissance.

George Putnam, for instance, relates that Hecht sent him an eighty-thousand word novel which he had dictated to three amanuenses in thirteen hours and twenty-five minutes and which he wanted to dedicate: "To Warren Gamaliel Harding, with the affectionate hope that its reading will afford him the keen diversion that the reading of his speeches has afforded the author." Putnam states the novel was never published, so it must be an entirely different work that was published in 1923 as *The Florentine Dagger*, a mystery novel which he also dictated. As Hecht tells the story, he made a $2,500 bet with Charles MacArthur's millionaire brother Alfred that in two days he could write a book that would be critically praised and sell more than twenty thousand copies. The dictation took thirty-six hours, he claims, and he won the wager.

Later in the 1920s Hecht would become involved in a notorious

Backyard Athens

Florida land development scheme. While still in Chicago, however, he helped promote such causes as J.P. Morgan's China
Famine Fund and Herbert Hoover's Far Eastern Relief, making a
great deal of money in the process. In his most outrageous scheme
he persuaded the Baptist synod to sponsor a contest for the best life
of Christ, with a cash prize of $5,000. Hecht wrote one of the
biographies under the name of an obscure Baptist minister, and
won the prize. Mencken would have been amused. Certainly
Hecht was.

Some of these stunts were in obvious imitation of the kind performed by artists Hecht met in Berlin. In fact Germany had taught
him a great deal. When he could, he went to pains to express his
obligations to the Berliners and other European writers, contemporary and otherwise. When he returned from Berlin he brought
with him some of George Grosz's drawings, which he captioned
with the words "fornication" and "fornicator" as frequently as possible, and displayed them in the window of Covici's bookshop. The
crowds pressed so closely that according to Hecht, they broke the
plate glass window. He must have felt paternal pride later when a
Danish anarchist printer named Steen Heindrikeson, who was publisher of *Wave*, a little magazine with an 1890s flavour edited by
Vincent Starrett, brought out the first Grosz book published in
America. No doubt he was similarly pleased when Covici much
later published works by Edgar Saltus with a preface by W.L.
George and a two-volume translation of de Gourmont by Richard
Aldington.

For ten years Covici was the quasi-official publisher of the
Chicago writers, and produced a list so eclectic and satisfying that
today one thinks of his Chicago shop as a hallowed place in the
history of literary publishing. Covici also published a number of
ephemeral books of Renaissance interest, such as a coffee table
volume of Stanislaus Szukalsi's art work and two newspaper novels
by Henry Justin Smith in which Hecht, Sandburg and others appear
under different guises. Hecht's prodding was responsible for the
appearance of some of these volumes. In one way Covici was the
backbone of the entire Chicago movement after about 1922, just as
Hecht was its principal press agent and hell-raiser; and it is only
natural that the publisher should have had a hand in Hecht's
Chicago Literary Times.

The Five Lives of Ben Hecht

The paper ran from March 1, 1923 to June 1 the following year and for the last three months was named *Ben Hecht's Chicago Literary Times.* It was operated on the Dadaist principle of attacking everything and everyone. Most conspicuous of all the targets was the establishment press and particularly the *Daily News.* The premier issue (the most normal in appearance; the others were printed on different coloured newsprint), set the policy of mocking the local and national literati in a parody of the *News'* headline style.

One of the spurious headings ran:

LOCAL INTELLIGENSIA
FACE ANOTHER CRISIS

Rollo Hemingway, Noted British Author, Cancels Lecture
at Orchestra Hall

—

"Carry On" Women's Club Slogan
for Culture-Blow

Another typical example was:

FORMER CHICAGOAN
UNDER FIRE FROM
EASTERN SAVANTS

—

Gotham Art-Kleagles De-
nounce Burt Rascoe

—

Backyard Athens

"Unjudicial [sic] and Eliotic" Hurl NY Ac-
cusers. Flayed Critic Mum.

Perhaps the height of the deskman's art was reached when
Bodenheim, who was associate editor at a small salary but often
had to take payment in room and board, reviewed epigrammati-
cally eleven volumes of contemporary verse by prominent poets
whom he disliked on principle. The head ran: BODENHEIM RUNS
AMUCK: SIX KILLED: FIVE INJURED.

The *Times* was bullish on epigrams and also, for some reason, on
headlines and stories in the Russian language. But other kinds of
material were allowed in its pages as well. For instance, Hecht
continued publishing some of his "1001 Afternoons in Chicago"
there after leaving the *Daily News*, and Starrett and many others
contributed from time to time. Bodenheim published as a serial his
memoirs, or what he liked to call his memoirs. Also, the paper
provided an outlet for Grosz, Herman Rosse, Wallace Smith,
Szukalsi and a few other remarkable Renaissance graphic artists,
most of whom, unfortunately, never survived elsewhere once the
Renaissance was dismantled. While it lasted, the *Times*, with a
circulation of less than ten thousand, was the object of considerable pride and derision, as well as income for its publisher. Hecht
claimed he kept the paper alive by charging merchants not to have
their businesses advertised. It is more than likely, however, that he
supplemented subscription revenues with funds from the saintly
Covici, who had first been told the paper would be his firm's house
organ, which in a curious way it was.

A caricature of Hecht by Gene Markey published in Alfred
Parry's *Garretts and Pretenders: A History of Bohemianism in
America*, shows the Hecht of the Renaissance wearing a fur-
collared overcoat, a top hat, striped trousers with spats, carrying a
walking stick, and the inevitable sneer. That is very much the
image he conveyed as Hecht the Bohemian, smacking of char-
latanism and failure on the one hand and considerable dedication
on the other. Hecht served as a rallying point for those whom either
the chicanery or the artistry was golden.

The Five Lives of Ben Hecht

The stories arising from the last Chicago years are legion, but a few representative anecdotes give the flavour of the others. Perhaps the best known concerns an invitation Hecht and Bodenheim received to speak before a pretentious literary society for a then considerable $100 honorarium. They let it be known that they would conduct a literary debate for the middle-class audience on a topic to be announced only after the event had begun.

When the evening arrived, Hecht walked to the foot of the stage and announced that the topic of debate would be – "Resolved: That people who attend literary debates are imbeciles." He scanned the audience in silence. At last he said, "I shall take the affirmative. The affirmative rests." He motioned to Bodenheim, who after an equally dramatic pause, intoned, "I guess you win." The pair beat their way out the back a hundred dollars richer.

Hecht adhered to the Dadaist ideal and took his Chicago-style nihilism to the streets whenever possible. To launch one of the city's small literary magazines, he suggested staging a parade with bands, and with poets, novelists and critics riding atop floats. Another scheme involved hawking a ballad on some contemporary event in the streets. He chose as the subject the scheduled execution of a local criminal. He printed strophes on the topic. He hired six men, wearing sandwich boards and dressed in mourning and with hangmen's nooses around their necks, to sell the narrative poem on the pavement, an installment at a time. When the criminal received stay after stay of execution, the idea petered out. The ballad became too long and the poem-butchers demanded to be paid for their services. And when the *Little Review* was evicted from its offices, because of Margaret Anderson's association with Emma Goldman, the anarchist, Hecht and Bodenheim snuck down to the lakefront, where the women were living temporarily in tents pitched on a sand dune, and coyishly pinned unsigned poems to the canvas flaps.

By dint of talent and circumstance Hecht had found himself a large fish in a small pond. As the pond began to swell, he sought to increase both its permanence as a navigable waterway and as a spawning bed for himself and others. It was a valiant effort, but in the end neither he nor Chicago could sustain their position of eminence in the face of fatigue and growing excitement elsewhere.

Backyard Athens

Once it was finished, many persons involved in it began speculating as to why the Chicago Renaissance had come about in the first place. To Burton Rascoe there was a medical explanation. He believed that since Chicagoans lived on the shore of Lake Michigan they absorbed iodine from the air. That fact resulted in a general hyperthyroid condition among the residents which took many forms, including artistic ones. As evidence he cited his observation that goiters were more common among young women in Chicago than in any other American city save Cleveland, another Great Lakes port. He did not explain why the literary manifestations of this epidemic were so relatively shortlived in Chicago or why, for that matter, they were not apparent in Cleveland.

To others who considered the question of the Renaissance more prosaically, the general collapse was the inevitable result of Margaret Anderson's decision to move the *Little Review* to New York in 1916, and then to Paris, where it folded in 1919. While the move was a blow to the local scene, it was more a concession to change than a herald of it. The true answer lies elsewhere, in a complex mixture of factors.

In that age before electronic media, regional attitudes and allegiances were stronger than they are today. For people between the densely populated eastern states and the still partly unsettled western ones, Chicago was the centre of commerce, industry, politics—and culture. To midwesterners it was the place to go to relieve tensions and monotony and also to seek one's fortune. To the writers, artists and intellectuals who began congregating there after the Civil War, Chicago offered escape from the provincial treatment they had received in smaller centres. It afforded them anonymity in which to work but also the promise of fame. It also offered the possibility of congenial employment – as journalists perhaps, or as artists' models or as clerks in bookstores or galleries – to subsidize their more serious endeavours. The intellectual community grew in proportion to the general boom in population. To keep from becoming too ingrown, too stable and too much like an enlightened version of all the Dubuques, Galesburgs, Cairos and Iowa Cities left behind, the community began to call attention to itself.

Such a desire for attention and change coincided with the general artistic upheaval taking place in other cities, in other countries and on other continents, as the old taboos on realism and experimentation were discredited. To average Chicago bohemians — and theirs was a full-blown community, with thousands of anonymous citizens for each star attraction — the city was their birthright as midwesterners, though some of the potential migrants had stayed home and created subsidiary bohemias, such as the one in Milwaukee. They would have no more thought of bombarding New York with their presence than of invading Paris or London. These like-minded people met one another in the newsrooms where they held their day jobs or in the speakeasies and theatres where they disdained those jobs. A Renaissance was born of demographic fact. It was in full swing when Mencken proclaimed its existence for a wider public.

Despite their similarity of background and general taste, these Chicagoans did not always share the same artistic bent. Some were radicals with artistic leanings. Others, believing the avant-garde was always more advanced on the other side of the fence, aligned themselves with either the Villagers of New York or the expatriates of Paris or both by turns. As Chicago gained in notoriety, it gained also in fakers, rubbernecks and thrill-seekers. That only increased the alacrity with which such persons as Samuel Putnam and Margaret Anderson fled. There were also those, such as Sherwood Anderson, Theodore Dreiser and eventually Ben Hecht, who established national reputations while in Chicago and so felt the call of the entire country, and moved on.

Bodenheim was one of the first important figures to leave. He began commuting to New York as early as 1915. Although he continued to enliven Chicago whenever he was in residence there, he grew increasingly attached to the East. New York always had more important poets than Chicago, despite the presence in the city of Sandburg and Edgar Lee Masters. Chicago was better as a home to versifiers than as a centre of the Imagists in whom Bodenheim was interested.

What Chicago did have was a great concentration of prose experimenters, since so many of the literary Chicagoans were newspapermen. It was mainly these people, the ones with permanent employment, who lingered on after much of the fun was over. Sandburg, for example, remained in Chicago until 1930. Starrett, aside from long sojourns in Peking and other farflung centres, stayed on through the Depression and World War Two to become book critic of the *Tribune* and ultimately "the dean of Chicago authors." Since his death there in 1973 at age eighty-seven, no one has remained in the city who might be called a principal figure of the Renaissance. Perhaps only one major writer from the Renaissance is still writing elsewhere in the nation: Kenneth Rexroth. He was a little known teenager in Chicago at the time, but has left a detailed account of the proceedings up to the time of his own departure for California at age twenty-two in protest over the execution of Sacco and Vanzetti.

With the writers beginning to trickle away, the support for them began to disappear as well. Pascal Covici went to New York in 1928. The next year he joined Donald Friede, late a partner of Hecht's other publishers, the Liveright firm, in founding Covici-Friede. That new imprint continued publishing Hecht and was firmly established as a major national house when it expired in the troubled times of the middle 1930s. Covici then moved to Viking Press where he was partly responsible for the reputation of, among others, John Steinbeck.

All that remained in Chicago was a hard core of bohemians and newspapermen who would remember the Renaissance as a gilded time and, in their persistent rationalizing and eulogizing, do much to establish it as a subject of historical interest. Rexroth contends that it was their newspaper training, with its sloppy sentimentalism and shock-value realism, that precluded Chicagoans such as Hecht, Samuel Putnam and Sandburg from becoming the writers he would have liked them to become. It was just such experience, however, that produced the Chicago Renaissance from what otherwise might have been a bohemian society jammed between the lake front and the open spaces of the near west. At least it was that fact and one other — Ben Hecht, who added the dash and verve and the awareness that something special was happening then in Chicago.

Hecht no longer had a newspaper job in Chicago. What he did have was a growing reputation, which he was eager to confront. On the eve of his departure for NewYork in late spring 1924, he was, quite fittingly, tendered a banquet at Schlogl's, and it was something of a last hurrah save one. That one was an article entitled

"Chicago: An Obituary" which Mencken persuaded Samuel Putnam to write for the August 1926 issue of the *American Mercury*.

When Margaret Anderson pulled the *Little Review* out of Chicago in 1916, Hecht uttered one of his more memorable quips. "Where," he asked longsufferingly and with mock despair, "is Athens now?" Decades later, when writing *A Child of the Century*, he penned another, equally theatrical and pithy statement on the Chicago days: "Would that our writing had been as fine as our lunches!".

5
The Front Page–
A Research

We were all fools to have left Chicago.
BH, *in* Charlie.

After try-outs in Atlantic City, Ben Hecht and Charles MacArthur's play *The Front Page* opened at the Times Square Theatre in New York, where it would run an impressive 276 performances. It was Tuesday, August 14, 1928, and almost from the first night, events conspired to make their play about Chicago newspaper life, the start of a notable collaboration, the best known work of either man or both.

In MacArthur's case, there is some justice in this judgement. He was a man whose lust for life betrayed a disconsolateness, put to rest with alcohol, that caused him to begin many more projects than he completed. Hecht was different. He had had another play, *The Egoist*, produced in New York in 1923. Although a more versatile writer than *The Front Page* or any other single isolated work would suggest, he is most widely remembered by this madcap comedy. One of the most frequently produced (and filmed) plays in American theatre, it is also, in its printed form, the only one of Hecht's books to continuously remain in print. The justice of that fact lies mainly in its being a good play of its kind, thus keeping his name alive for more serious inquirers; and in that it is also his most blatant evocation of the lifestyle which tinted almost everything else he wrote.

One reason *The Front Page* has remained alive is that it is the best known critique and cliché of American journalism, a work

67

which newspapermen have spent half a century trying to live down or up to. In our time, when most of the fun of being a newsman has been replaced by corporate blandness and notions of responsibility, it has caused a kind of ethical schizophrenia, whereby reporters and editors talk like cynical scoundrels while acting with the conscientiousness of chartered accountants. Editors enjoy behaving like the play's Walter Burns in front of their young reporters, who in turn delight in perpetuating Hildy Johnson for an audience of mere cilvilians. All of them know better, of course. They are constantly being reminded that those days are gone.

As early as 1934, Stanley Walker, a famous newspaper editor of the period, counselled young hopefuls to ignore what the play told them about journalism. In more recent years, both *Time* magazine and [*MORE*], a journal of media studies, have stated in their house advertisements that the *Front Page* tradition has been put behind. Yet lip service to the tradition persists. It is bolstered by the plays, films and novels about newspapering that entrench rather than debunk the stereotypes Hecht and MacArthur created. *The Front Page* and its progeny have created healthy suspicions about journalism and its servants in the minds of millions of people who otherwise have no real knowledge of either. In its effect on popular culture, *The Front Page* is one of the most powerful and lasting works in American literature.

What is all the more remarkable about *The Front Page* is that it is not truly a work of fiction but a *pièce à clef*. Not only are the names of some of the characters and institutions, situations, and some bits of dialogue taken from real life, but the play's whole flavour is that of a frantic age of American journalism which is gone now and which – because of unions, competing technology and a saner definition of news – can never return. Ignoring Hecht's and other people's often hyperbolic recollections and relying on historical evidence, it can be said that *The Front Page* was a pale reflection of the world it immortalized. For one thing, the language was toned down, only to be restored to something like its original crudity in Billy Wilder's 1974 film version, the third movie adaptation. More importantly, the eccentricity of the characters was considerably deemphasized in the paste-pot process by which the collaborators fashioned their finished product. As Hecht remarked, no one in the audience would have believed the literal truth.

The entire play takes place in the press room of the Cook County Criminal Courts Building, a seven-storey gothic structure erected in 1885, at Dearborn and Hubbard, where a posh gambling casino once stood, a site later occupied by the board of health. The building adjoined the Cook County Jail where the writers covered more than twenty hangings — Hecht for the *Journal* and later the *Daily News*, MacArthur first for the *Tribune* and then for the *Herald and Examiner*. The press room on the fourth floor was a dim slot-like space that Hecht remembered affectionately and that in photographs very much resembles sets for various productions of the play.

As the play opens, a group of reporters are playing cards and kibbitzing, passing time before the scheduled hanging of Earl Williams, a confused young radical who is to die for the killing of a black policeman. The scheming windbag mayor of the city and the inept Sheriff Hartman are using the execution as a political tool. It is an election year and the incumbents are running on a law and order platform. Hartman, claiming to see the slaying as the first sign of a Bolshevik revolution, coins the slogan, "Reform the Reds with a rope."

In the first act it develops that the *Herald and Examiner* managing editor, Walter Burns, is depending upon reporter Hildy Johnson to cover the hanging. Johnson, however, informs Burns that he is getting married and quitting the business for a New York advertising job. Those three fates — marriage, New York, advertising — were the ones most dreaded by subscribers to the florid Chicago tradition. Hecht once refused to speak to a colleague who told him of superior jobs in New York, a place inhabited, he thought, by wearers of bowlers hats. Reporters' views on marriage — Hecht's and MacArthur's no less than their co-workers' — were equally notorious. As for advertising, Hecht refused offers in that better paid field as a matter of course, though he later operated for a short time a screwball public relations agency at great profit.

Other reporters and visitors to the building are brought into focus, and Johnson soon faces an emergency of spirit. He is determined to leave town with his prospective bride and mother-in-law when gunshots and shouts indicate that Williams has escaped. Acting instinctively, he phones the story to Burns and, forgetting his wedding plans, discovers the killer hiding in the building. While the other newsmen are scrambling for details at the jail, Burns enters and takes charge of getting Williams away unnoticed so that, at the proper moment, the *Herald and Examiner* can print an exclusive interview and take credit for the recapture. It is precisely the sort of thing that used to go on.

Johnson's future marriage is several times in jeopardy as he and Burns struggle to keep the other reporters from learning of Williams' presence in the rolltop desk where they have hidden him. The desk belongs to *Tribune* reporter Bensinger, who uses an atomizer and resembles Felix Unger in Neil Simon's *The Odd Couple* in basic characterization. The mayor and the sheriff threaten the *Herald and Examiner* team with prison when they learn of this obstruction of justice. But Burns and Johnson use their trump card – their knowledge of the governor's reprieve, which the politicians have kept hidden in order to hang Williams for their own motives, even though the man's guilt is questionable on grounds of circumstance and sanity.

Throughout this ordeal and the various subplots – one involves a streetwalker who attempts suicide to keep the other reporters from learning where Williams is secreted – the audience feels that somehow Burns will keep his ace reporter Hildy from running off to New York and domesticity. Finally, when the night's excitement is over and the young couple are again about to catch their train, Burns pulls his long-awaited whammy. Summoning the full measure of his acting ability, he convincingly concedes defeat and makes the couple a wedding gift of his pocket watch, "a present from the Big Chief [William Randolph Hearst] himself." The watch is inscribed with Burns' name, "To the Best Newspaperman I Know." Hildy reluctantly accepts it, and the near-newlyweds depart.

Walter Burns is now alone on a completely dishevelled stage. His trusty subaltern Duffy back at the office has been patiently keeping the telephone line to the press room open. Burns picks up the receiver and tells him to contact the sheriff of La Porte, Indiana, just outside Chicago, to arrest Hildy Johnson and return him in custody. Says Burns, in a famous curtain-closer: "Wire him a full description. The son of a bitch stole my watch."

70

The Front Page - A Research

That final line (much more than the sprinkling of goddamns and such in the rest of the play) created a stir in the theatre world. The New York police wanted to arrest the cast. When the play first came to Toronto in 1932 the advance furor was so great that the orchestra had to be brought up during the last moments so that, though Burn's obscenity was actually spoken, it could not be heard over the music. As late as 1970, when the second Broadway revival was adapted for television, one critic commented: "This particular production marks a breakthrough for TV profanity because the play's classic last line, which is the essence of the character of Walter Burns, is intact." That line is only partly what Tennessee Williams was referring to, however, in his remark that *The Front Page* "uncorseted the American theatre."

By 1928 Hecht had begun his relationship with the film industry and was, like his friend MacArthur, already pining for the Chicago they had put behind them. As Hecht once observed, writers like to live in luxury and write as though they live in poverty, and the anomoly was plaguing him even then. He clearly missed the newspaper existence in which each day is written up and disposed of in the chaos of chronicling the next one. Also, he missed his Chicago friends as they once were, for though many of his cronies had joined him in New York, the old camaraderie was gone. What he missed, in short, was his youth, and he and MacArthur's long collaboration, on paper and in social situations through the years to come, was based principally on the way in which each reminded the other of his (in retrospect) carefree younger years.

Save for *The Egoist*, a work composed by the Bohemian, in 1923, *The Front Page* was Hecht's first full-length play to be produced commercially. It was also his first attempt at recapturing the spirit of Chicago. The attempt was successful but it was also plagiarizing from life. Much more was suitably rearranged than was created by the imaginations of the authors. By using biographers' and autobiographers' techniques Hecht and MacArthur concocted a kind of recent history, much as, individually and as a team, and as halves of other teams, they would later adapt literary classics for the screen. The difference here was that the history they were adapting was their own. By sticking closely to the actual characters they had known, it was reasoned, they could heighten immeasurably the mood they remembered. Sticking close to fact is what they did.

In his writings about Chicago Hecht usually changed the names of the less gangsterish politicians, and Sheriff Hartman of the play is undoubtedly an amalgamation of several whose administrations he observed first hand. Similarly, the unnamed mayor in *The Front Page* is also, a composite, though he likely owes his greatest debt to Hizzoner William Hale (Big Bill) Thompson Jr., who died in 1944 leaving more than $2 million in cash in safety deposit boxes. Mayor during the Capone years of the middle 1920s, Thompson made no bones about his buffoonery or dishonesty. He once charmed Irish voters by threatening to punch King George V in the nose and displayed his forthright nature by beginning campaign addresses with the words, "My fellow hoodlums."

Earl Williams, too, is a composite of various radicals, but his escape from the Cook County Jail on the eve of his slated hanging is pilfered from the case of Terrible Tommy O'Connor, a thirty-five year-old Irish immigrant convicted in 1921 of killing a night watchman during the robbery of the Illinois Central Railroad downtown station. He escaped days before he was sentenced to hang but, unlike Williams, was never recaptured. One rumour had it that he returned to Ireland and perished in the Black and Tan fighting. He was the last man sentenced to hang in Illinois, and to this day the gallows remain intact in the unlikely event that he should be caught. Hecht had used the O'Connor escape the year before *The Front Page* in his script for Josef von Sternberg's film *Underworld*.

The premise then – the escaped cop killer, the loss of a good reporter to pastures greener with dollar bills, the cut-throat newspaper rivalry in which both readers and accuracy were lost sight of – had its basis in the cumulative experience of the authors. The play's other characters are even more flagrantly lifted from memory. The character Bensinger, to whom at least latent homosexuality is imputed, seems to be based, in his fastidiousness, on a reporter called Spike Henessey in *Gaily, Gaily*, whose "germ philosophy" meant that he "sat at his fumigated desk, detached from our gossip and debate [and] studied real estate brochures and dreamed of migrating to Florida and spending his life in an orange grove." The character was real and so was the name. Hecht also recalled in print another old reporter, named in fact Roy C. Bensinger, who wore a glass eye which he would remove to frighten valuable information from elderly ladies.

In his history of Chicago journalism, *Deadlines & Monkeyshines*, John J. McPhaul cites the occasion when, during a lull in the press room card game, Buddy McHugh, a reporter for the City News Bureau, the local co-operative wire service, telephoned a woman to ask, "Is it true, Madam, you were the victim of a Peeping Tom?" His colleagues, McPhaul records, roared with laughter (you had to be there, one supposes) ; and the story became a classic of police stations and city rooms. Hecht and MacArthur had heard the story, and in their play a City News man named McCue asks the same question during a phone round-up, though without the resulting laughter. Other references in the play – such as the report of a doctor who's made a profitable sideline of stimulating middleaged females electrically – were taken from cases the young playwrights had detailed themselves in earlier times.

Vincent Starrett, the Canadian man of letters who knew Hecht and MacArthur when he worked on the Chicago dailies, recalled years later, "There was no newspaper slave in Chicago but swore he recognized every figure on the boards." Certainly the most obvious of the shanghai victims is the character Hildy Johnson. He is based on a Swedish immigrant named Hilding Johnson, who worked his way up from copy boy to top reporter.* "Poor Hildy!" wrote Starrett. "He died a few years after the play was produced [in 1931 at age 45] – I saw him laughing in his box opening night – and it was said that his determined effort to approximate his reckless counterpart on the stage had hastened his untimely end."

Johnson's death was surely swift, but his career had been not much different from that of the character who bears his name. Some of the cleverness and rascality of the stage Hildy was the natural

---

*Walter Burns's surname may have come from Walter Noble Burns, then a Chicago reporter and later a popular historian of the American West.

cleverness and rascality of the playwrights, and perhaps some part is traceable to other noted peers such as Lionel Moise, a famous tramp reporter who had been admired by Hemingway on the Kansas City *Star*. But part of the dramatic transmogrification was sparked by the man's actual career. The real Hildy Johnson, for instance, once broke into the jury room with a deadline pressing, learned of the verdict by going through old ballots in the waste basket and then left phony evidence for a competitor he knew would be breaking in later. Hildy Johnson of *The Front Page* was not entirely exaggerated; Walter Burns was, if anything, watered down in the transition from flesh and blood to greasepaint.

Burns is based on Walter Crawford Howey, for whom MacArthur had worked on both the *Tribune* and the *Herald and Examiner* and who was a legend in Chicago journalism. As a young man he had worked on the papers in his native Fort Dodge, Iowa. In 1903 he gravitated to Chicago, as most ambitious midwesterners did, and made the rounds of the newspaper offices with the usual discouraging results. One of the papers he applied to was the *Inter-Ocean*, a journal best summed up by its motto, "Republican is everything, independent is nothing."

Having exhausted all his potential employers, Howey was strolling unhappily down Randolph Street when confronted by a vision he attributed for a few seconds to fatigue and hunger. Before him, screaming as they emerged from a manhole or grating, were children dressed in brightly coloured costumes with gossamer wings. Howey's hesitiation was slight. Soon he pieced together what had happened and phoned the *Inter-Ocean*, telling them of the fairy chorus from *Mr. Bluebeard* forced to flee the burning Iroquois Theatre. The fire was one of the worst disasters in Chicago history, with more than 600 persons, mostly children, perishing. Howey was the first reporter on the scene and was hired on the spot. His stock went still higher when Mayor Fred Busse (according to notes in *The Front Page*, the original owner of Bensinger's rolltop desk) was driven from office by Howey's series of muckraking articles.

In 1910 Howey became city editor of the Chicago *Tribune* and there had a chance to put into practice the flamboyant style of news-gathering which made him a legend. He intimidated witnesses and officials, sent relief trains to disaster spots and discouraged matrimony among his staff; he would cut their salaries (already the lowest in the city) and even discharge those who sullied their affection for the paper with affection for their wives. (Howey himself was often married.)

The *Tribune* is a morning paper, and the day city editor, Howey's counterpart for the slack part of the day, was Frank Carson. It was from Carson that Howey learned some of his devious pranks or at least learned to polish them. Carson (who died in 1941) was said by a colleague to symbolize newspapering in the 1920s, when each big story was a melodrama. He claimed to know the name of nearly every cop in the city and the name of each member of his family. He also said he knew the location of every fire alarm box and the number of the nearest public telephone with the result that his reporters could interrogate onlookers as still others rushed to the scene. One of his later triumphs was staging a riot outside a police station so he could steal from the precinct safe a diary being held as evidence in a popular murder-suicide. The diary was printed serially in the paper, and the coroner had to postpone the inquest several times until all the salient facts had been read by a half million people. Carson was also a pioneer in developing methods of speeding up the dissemination of news. Some of that interest seems to have rubbed off on Howey, who in later years was principal owner of the patents for the telephonic transmission of news photos.

Even in the upper echelons, the *Tribune* was not known for its ideal working conditions. If Howey harassed his reporters into loving him, then he himself was under much the same pressure from his superiors. The paper's editor, John G. Keeley (called J. God Keeley), an austere authoritarian figure, quit the paper in a huff after Robert Rutherford McCormick became part-owner. He then purchased the *Record-Herald*, the product of a merger involving one of Hearst's rare "fire sales." But Keeley ran it into the ground, and in 1918 sold it to Hearst, who merged it with his own *Examiner* to create the *Herald and Examiner*, later called the *Herald-Examiner* and popularly known as the *Her-Ex*. Howey and Carson switched their allegiances to this new hybrid, and the paper became a fountainhead of colourful characters.

The Five Lives of Ben Hecht

One of these was Harry Romanoff, whose specialty was impersonating industrialists, senators, governors and even presidents over the telephone. Another was Dion O'Banion, the North Side gangster and friend of Hecht and MacArthur, who would be shot dead in 1924 in his flower shop (across from the Holy Name Cathedral, where he had been an acolyte) following his efforts to muscle in on Capone. O'Banion was the *Herald and Examiner's* circulation manager. His job was to use goons to force vendors to carry his paper in preference to the *Tribune*, and soon full-blown circulation wars developed. Howey had only one eye. Some said he lost his other one fighting in such wars, either in that particular set or more probably in the ones of 1907-1912. Others contended that he lost his eye in less noble pursuits by falling on a copy spike while sitting drunkenly at his desk. Whichever the case, Hecht is said to have remarked that he could tell the glass eye from the natural one because the glass eye looked warmer. That is the side of the man Hecht and MacArthur conjured up in their character Walter Burns.

The circumstances leading to Howey's leaving the *Tribune* for the *Herald and Examiner* are unclear. All that is known is that the departure was the result of a long intermittent quarrel with the paper's management. According to Burton Rascoe, the final straw was the reprimand Howey received for printing an interview with D.W. Griffith, who had offered Howey a job in pictures. The *Tribune* considered the interview thinly disguised public relations material. Howey had been earning $8,000 a year at the *Tribune*. When Hearst offered him $35,000 to be managing editor of his new paper, Howey quickly accepted, and used the *Her-Ex* to belittle the *Tribune* — a paper which, some liked to say, acted as though it had earned rather than coined its copyrighted motto, "World's Greatest Newspaper."

Howey's revenge was ruthless and knew no statute of limitations. His first act was to give a party for the man who had replaced him; he got him drunk enough to sign a contract making him *Herald and Examiner* city editor. One of his more public tricks came when he hired Eleanor (Cissy) Patterson, later owner of the Washington *Times-Herald*, to cover the 1920 Republican National Convention. Not unsubtly, he identified her in print as the cousin and sister respectively of McCormick and Joseph Medill Patterson, the proprietors of the arch-Republican *Tribune.* Howey also had his way with municipal, county and even state authorities. He dug up enough dirt to blackmail them into signing undated resignations which he kept locked in his desk for use in emergencies. It was this world, then, in which the future playwrights laboured and which they felt obliged to tone down on stage if their creation was to have an aura of plausibility.

The *Herald and Examiner* folded in 1939.* Howey died at age seventy-three in 1955, the year before MacArthur. An obit on his old boss called "Mister Front Page" for *Saga* magazine was MacArthur's last published writing. After editing Hearst's New York *Mirror*, a tabloid with a bright yellow tint, Howey ended up working as a Hearst troubleshooter and finally editing the Boston *American.* While there he broke his back, and MacArthur came to visit, giving him a watch engraved like the one in the play. When ambulatory again though still in a partial cast, Howey was struck by a derelict taxi which refractured his back and broke ten ribs. Pneumonia followed and his lungs filled.

By now Howey, a tired old man, had gone against his own long-standing dictum and had taken another bride. The shock of his new injuries was too much for his young wife, who was herself recovering from a delicate thyroid operation. He regained consciousness to learn that her funeral had taken place the day before. Again MacArthur called on the notorious editor and found him still showing people the watch and goodnaturedly deriding *The Front Page* and its perpetrators. He died there in a Boston hospital, the most infamous of Hearst's ruthless crew, one of the last of the old Chicago newspaper giants in whose honour, as much as for their own satisfaction, Hecht and MacArthur pieced together their permanent eulogy.

------

*The paper's assets were purchased by the *Tribune* which used them in publishing the Chicago *American.* Later, the name was changed to *Chicago Today*. The last remote vestige of the *Her-Ex*, it ceased publication in 1974.

The Five Lives of Ben Hecht

In a way, Hecht and MacArthur had been collaborating since they were teenagers. Stories which they covered together, Hecht for afternoon papers and MacArthur for his AM's, united their similar outlooks and personalities. Competition made obvious their gallows humour, their practical jokes, their prodigious work habits and their carnival vocabularies. It was with *The Front Page*, however, that they came together as co-workers rather than as friendly rivals and conspirators, and even that coming-together was a chance one.

Hecht met MacArthur on the street one day in New York, and they simply decided to work up a play about their old way of life. Most of the work was done in Hecht's Beekman Place apartment where distractions (to which MacArthur was overly sensitive) were few. Even so, MacArthur was a troubled man. His seven-year struggle to win a divorce from his first wife had just ended. She had been a *Herald and Examiner* reporter when they met, and he had taken a moonlighting job on a suburban paper to support them while she laboured on a novel which, like the marriage, never worked out. MacArthur was planning his second marriage to Helen Hayes when he encountered Hecht. She was appearing on Broadway in *Coquette*, produced by Jed Harris, who was to produce *The Front Page* as well. But MacArthur and Hayes were quarrelling at the time, and that, Hecht recalled in his memoir *Charlie*, "reduced the prospective groom to a hearse driver."

At least for MacArthur's immediate worries, as well as for both men's longterm homesickness for Chicago, the writing of *The Front Page* was therapy. They were writing "of people we loved, and of employment that had been like no other was ever to be," recalled Hecht, who added: "I remember of the collaboration chiefly the fact that I have never known since in anyone the inventiveness and certainty, the burst of creation, Charlie brought to *The Front Page*."

MacArthur would wander the room and otherwise busy himself while Hecht wrote in pencil on a lap desk. Each agreed to delete without argument any dialogue or development the other disliked. The same system would be employed later with success in such Hecht-MacArthur projects as the screen adaptations of *Gunga Din* and *Wuthering Heights*, the original screenplays *Crime Without*

Passion and *The Scoundrel* and the play and movie, *Twentieth Century*.

Because of their similarity of mind, temperment and experience, it is difficult, and perhaps even wrongheaded, to try to determine what is Hecht's contribution and what is MacArthur's. Still, it seems reasonable to suppose that the basic characterizations of Burns and Hildy began with MacArthur, who had worked with them in real life, and that Hecht added to them certain grotesqueries, as he had known them as enemies in the war for news. Other touches were clearly irrelevant to the nostalgia, but were products of the moment.

The date of the action, for instance, is deliberately imprecise. The authors left it that way to sum up an era rather than a particular month or year and also to make the play as up to date as possible. Although Hecht and MacArthur left Chicago in 1924, the play contains a reference to the Ruth Snyder murder trial, which took place in New York in 1927. Later, Hecht wrote that the casting and scenery of the first New York production were so good that seeing the play was like again being "in Chicago, 1917." The persecution of Williams the radical, however, would seem to suggest the Red Scare of 1919. On another occasion, writing in Martin Levin's Phoenix Nest column in the *Saturday Review*, Hecht reiterated that the play was no figment of their imagination but the product of an actual environment. The piece was headed "Chicago: Circa 1920," though this title may not have been Hecht's own. In making the 1974 film version, Billy Wilder wisely set the time as a spring day in 1929. That allowed him to bring in many realistic-sounding references to the 1920s, the era in which the play had its first success and with which it is associated, however much it is set, strictly speaking, in the previous decade.

Once when the writers were working on the play at MacArthur's home on Fortieth Street, they were bothered by Jed Harris. MacArthur, busily typing, failed to notice that the producer had come up behind him until Harris yanked the sheet from the carriage with a terse, "That's no good." MacArthur, not unskilled as a barroom brawler, went into a rage. Harris ran for the door and barely, Hecht remembered, was carnage averted. The incident was written into the play as the scene in which Burns, trying to dictate the Williams

The Five Lives of Ben Hecht

lead to Hildy, snatches away the copy paper. In the play, however, the action just causes a brief oath to be muttered and no one has to retreat. MacArthur and Harris tangled at least one other time, a year later by mail, and it is clear that Harris and Hecht also failed to get along subsequently. In *A Child of the Century* and again in *Charlie*, Hecht takes swipes at Harris, citing the fact that after success upon success he compounded failure upon failure.

At the time of the New York premiere, however, relations were better amongst all the principals. Hecht, who celebrated the success by giving away black Borsalino hats, wrote: "It is a rare thing for a writer to see his work so intimately revealed." He and MacArthur were delighted with Harris' work and with that of George S. Kaufman, who had agreed to direct the play, at first against his better judgment. They had worried about the casting and in particular about the choice of Osgood Perkins (father of Tony Perkins) for the Walter Burns role. The authors found the actor's off-stage appearance and manner all wrong, possibly because of their relative inexperience with actors; in rehearsals and afterward they recanted their opinion. Howey, after seeing the play, said mockingly that he had been so well portrayed he was going to have the authors executed. Everyone seemed pleased, and everyone — Kaufman, Lee Tracy as Hildy and others in the cast, and certainly the playwrights themselves — benefited from the association, even if some of them later were typecast as a result.

During the preparations the collaborators had to remove a character of whom they were fond and in fact considered vital. Alderman Willoughby was to appear at various points to represent still more ludicrous aspects of Chicago's political life. He was to be played by a black actor, but the man who got the part disappeared before the opening. The playwrights scoured Harlem in search of the man only to learn that he was in hiding, "kicking the gong," as Hecht put it — withdrawing from opium addiction.

The book version of the script (dedicated to Clark and Madison streets) was the major title on the first list of Covici-Friede. It sold through six printings the first year and was in fact the first American play to become anything like a bestseller between hard covers. It appeared the month the play opened and carried a brief foreword by Jed Harris which can be interpreted without much strain as condescending toward the authors.

The Front Page - A Research

Whether the preface was one reason for further discord can only be guessed. The preface does, however, shed some interesting light on the play. It states that in manuscript form the work carried almost no stage directions. It also gives Harris' views on writiers. Authors, he wrote, "are rarely as arresting as their plays. And I have learned from experience that a pretty good play can be written by an idiot. In fact, I can assure you that in a group of successful playwrights you are as likely to discover as distinguished a body of men as you might find at an Elks' outing."

About thirty years later Hecht admitted that playwrights as a class have little common sense, performers almost none. But a "dozen great directors," he concluded, " are worth less than half a good playwright. And a gross of producers doesn't equal one star."

The Front Page struck Broadway like a gale-force storm of fresh air and a look at the theatrical pages of the same time demonstrates why. Its competition were such shows as *This Year of Grace* with Bea Lillie, *Whoopee* with Eddie Cantor, *The Ziegfeld Follies* and *George White Scandals*. In such an atmosphere *The Front Page* was successful at once because it was different and true to life.

Of course there had been hits that pretended to be naturalistic, such as *What Price Glory?*, but they were tame both in language and morality. And there already had been plays about the newspaper business. As early as 1909, Broadway had seen the successful run of *The Fourth Estate*, co-authored by no less a personage than Joseph Medill Patterson of the Chicago *Tribune* Pattersons. *The Front Page*, however, stretched the acceptable standards of the time to their limit. It was a slick piece of work about very crude people who through constant traffic with corruption, had become ninety-nine per cent corrupt themselves. *The Front Page* made that moral predicament the subject of levity and ridicule. It was a groundbreaker for American theatre.

Although it would be difficult to name a more thoroughly American play, *The Front Page* depended upon more than just slang and parochial attitudes for its appeal and was a hit even when transplanted. A 1931 Viennese production entitled *Reporter* was one of the first successes of young Otto Preminger. In Australia the work enjoys periodic revival because, it is claimed, audiences there think it an accurate depiction of Australian journalism or at least of what Australian journalism believes itself to be. Great Britain, for its part, saw no version of the play for forty years because of its stricter stage censorship. Not until 1969 was it seen in London, but then it was produced by the prestigious National Theatre Company.

That same year there was a second New York revival, and Walter Kerr, in describing the play's durability, wrote of it as "a clock that laughed," a loud, excited farce the volume and excitement of which belied the smooth progression and perpetual movement cultivated in the 1920s. Those are the same qualities which have given it a long cinematic life.

In 1930, Hecht and MacArthur were writing for United Artists when the company bought film rights to *The Front Page*. It was a time when the studios were eagerly acquiring anything that could be exploited as a talkie, and the property was a natural. Its combination of manic action and rapid fire dialogue (a kind of dialogue which Hecht became famous for in pictures like *Nothing Sacred* and which was carried to absurdity in *His Girl Friday*) made it a good choice. So did its contemporaniety and the promise it gave of gunfire and other sound effects then being perfected.

In the first film version, released in 1931 and directed by Lewis Milestone, Pat O'Brien played Burns and Adolphe Menjou played Hildy. Edward Everett Horton appeared as Bensinger. The screenplay was by Bartlett Cormack, with additional dialogue by him, Charles Lederer and Hecht. The film was produced by Howard Hughes, for whom Hecht would work the next year writing *Scarface*. The script was little changed from the original except insofar as it was subservient to Hollywood's own moralistic punctilios. It was not so much an adaptation for the screen as an adjustment.

The adjusting, however, took some interesting forms. For instance, the setting is not Chicago; rather, as a title card indicates, "This story takes place in a Mythical Kingdom." A further attempt at disguise was the decision to avoid the names of actual newspapers, so that the *Examiner* was called the *Morning Post*. Perhaps this was in deference to William Randolph Hearst, whose retaliation to filmmakers knew few limits, as Orson Welles would learn after making *Citizen Kane*. Also, Milestone's version of *The Front Page* has Burns' final epithet drowned out by the noise of a typewriter carriage, which he has struck in mock anger.

Howard Hawks, the *Scarface* director, remade *The Front Page* in 1940 with a big difference. "I was going to prove to someone one night that *The Front Page* had the finest modern dialogue that had been written," Hawks contended in an interview, "and I asked a girl to read Hildy's part and I read the editor and I stopped and said, 'Hell, it's better between a girl and a man than between two men.'" The result was *His Girl Friday* in which Cary Grant as Burns and Rosalind Russell as Hildy are not only editor and reporter but also divorced husband and wife. Hawks reworked the play into one of the best 1930s-style zany romantic comedies, along the lines of *Nothing Sacred*. It is one of the most successful pictures of that type. While true to the basics of the play, it replaces the mood and texture of the original with a glib sophistication. The screenplay, by Lederer, is the kind Hecht himself would have written about five years earlier.

In 1946 MacArthur mounted a New York revival starring Arnold Moss and Lew Parker, and in 1949 there was a short-lived television series based on the play. The last revival in America came in 1969 with the formation the previous year of the Plumstead Playhouse Company for the purpose of performing again some of the best American drama. Named for one of the country's earliest theatres (founded in Philadelphia in 1749), the company presented Wilder's *Our Town* first and *The Front Page* second. The founding of the group was seen as a step toward the eventual establishment of a US national theatre. A version of their production, with the New York cast of Robert Ryan as Burns (he had already played a crusty editor in the 1958 film *Lonelyhearts*) and George Grizzard as Hildy, was televised in 1970 with an introduction by Helen Hayes MacArthur. There followed a road company with Ray Milland and de Veren Bookwalter.

All that while the revival of interest in Hecht was underway. Some of his books had come into print again, and Norman Jewison had made his well-intentioned but disastrous film of *Gaily, Gaily*. It was a time of much interest in Hollywood history and nostalgia for the 1920s and 1930s, and it seemed a logical moment for yet another remake of *The Front Page*. As the Watergate scandal brought about a new public awareness of journalistic tradition, even bad journalistic tradition, there were rumours that Elia Kazan was to undertake the project, but this came to nothing. Instead came Billy Wilder's version, scripted by himself and his usual co-author I.A.L. Diamond. It starred Walter Matthau as Burns and Jack Lemmon as Hildy Johnson.

Wilder's *The Front Page* appeared at Christmas 1974 and was in many ways a hymn to Hecht and the Chicago tradition. It was, one feels, what Hecht would have done had he still been alive, had he miraculously developed into a more modern screenwriter. At the time of the 1931 version, screenplays were just that, plays for the screen, as much theatrical as cinematic. Even *His Girl Friday* was firmly in the stage tradition that lingered on in light comedies about relations between the sexes. Wilder's film, though, was a movie rather than merely a talkie.

Although made with affection for the original, it bore the stamp of his own taste and the tastes of the generation for whom it was intended. It was an ideal blend of adherence to the original and fanciful departure. Wilder took the plot and extrapolated from it to include, for instance, a slapstick chase sequence. By giving a stronger part and ascribing new eccentricities to the escaped Earl Williams, he summed up by proxy Hecht's view of political animals as, at best, lovable imbeciles, much as Hecht did in his screenplay for *Comrade x* in 1940.

The Wilder-Diamond script was also the first to make a success of Jenny, the Criminal Courts cleaning woman; and while Lemmon was an acceptable Hildy, Matthau as Burns was the truest so far to the original Walter Howey. It was the part Matthau seemed to have been practising for his entire career: the conniving ham actor whose most unassailable characterisitic, his very sentimentality, has been perverted.

Wilder restored a part of the real Howey which Hecht and MacArthur felt compelled to play down. Wilder had Burns barking out imagined headlines as the story breaks. It was something which he probably did do and which is set down in record at least as being done by Charles Chapin, city editor of the New York *World* in the 1890s (who was later sentenced to life imprisonment in Sing Sing for murdering his wife). Indeed, the director made his version a virtual storehouse of newspaper lore, Chicago and otherwise. Part of Wilder and Diamond's story involves a small camera concealed on the ankle of the reporter, who hopes to use it to photograph Williams on the gallows. The incident has a factual basis; a New York *Daily News* photographer, Tom Howard, used such a device to photograph a criminal dying in the electric chair in 1928. The criminal was Ruth Snyder, mentioned in the original play.

His Girl Friday had been an adaptation with too little of the original's magic. The Wilder film was the opposite, an almost new work with the old spirit improved upon and updated in small ways. Hecht and MacArthur could no more than meekly suggest homosexuality in Bensinger. Wilder was more explicit. He had played with it in his earlier comedies such as *Some Like it Hot* and *The Private Life of Sherlock Holmes.* Now he made Bensinger decidedly gay, and reiterated the fact in the cameos at the end, in which he also stated (wishfully) that Burns finished his days lecturing at the University of Chicago on the ethics of journalism.

Wilder whipped up a peculiar blend of truism and anachronism which is wholly pleasing. His newsroom of the Chicago *Examiner* (as he called the paper) was one of the very few such sets ever to look like the real thing, and he placed the action (indicated by a wall calendar and by the dated front page of the paper) on Thursday, June 6, 1929, which was in fact a Thursday. The dating allowed him to refer to such celebrated news events of the period as the Leopold and Loeb case and the Scopes monkey trial. Wilder used Hildebrand instead of Hilding as the formal form of the reporter's name. He also had him leaving for Philadelphia rather than New York. He made no mention of the bride's mother, a superfluous character. More importantly, he restored the full thrust of the reporters' vulgarity of speech, a quality Hecht and MacArthur could only toy with and earlier films could merely hint at.

His Girl Friday contained a small inside joke that has become a cue for late show trivialists to lord over their less knowledgeable friends. Cary Grant as Walter Burns alludes at one point to a criminal named Archie Leach, which is of course Cary Grant's original name. In much the same spirit, Wilder had McHugh (he restored the correct spelling) refer to one of Burns' tricks. He has McHugh say that Burns had slipped a mickey into Ben Hecht's gin fizz in an unsuccessful attempt to keep him from taking the train to Hollywood, where he's currently composing dialogue for Rin Tin Tin.

The Five Lives of Ben Hecht

The greater tribute to Hecht and MacArthur in this most recent film version, however, came when Wilder and Diamond, in their carefree use of the original play, several times painted themselves into a corner in terms of plot. Whenever that happened, they reverted instinctively to the words of the playscript to get them out of difficulty. It always worked. While they were making a joke at Hecht's expense, they were also appealing to him in his grave at Oak Hill Cemetery in Nyack, New York, a grave which, incidentally, is only a few yards from that of Charles G. MacArthur.

6
1001 Afternoons in Hollywood

*[Jules] Furthman....has written about half of the
most entertaining movies to come out of Hollywood (Ben Hecht wrote most of the other half)...*
Pauline Kael, *in the* New Yorker, 1967

*We had no screenwriters in Europe as good as yours. Ben Hecht,
for example, is forgotten today, but in my opinion he invented
eighty per cent of what is used in American movies today.*
Jean-Luc Godard, *in* Take One, 1968

The fact is easily forgotten, but for a few years during and after
World War One Chicago had a brief glory as the film as well as
literary capital of the Midwest. It was the home of (to name two)
Essaynay Studios, which in 1916 made the first Sherlock Holmes
movie with William Gillette, and Argyle Studios, where dramas
and comedies were ground out, some of them with Ben Turpin. The
innovative *Daily News* not only boasted legitimate film critics
(W.K. Hollander first, Sandburg later), but had these men writing
weekly articles on the trade as well.

Local film production came to an end after such men as D.W.
Griffith, Cecil B. De Mille and Jesse Lasky realized the scenic
and climatic advantages of California over the rest of the country
and made a boom town of what had been a sleepy Los Angeles
suburb: Hollywood. But even then, Chicago always played host to

film stars and movie makers. Such people had to stop over there after leaving the Broadway Limited and the Twentieth Century at the La Salle Street or Illinois Central stations, before boarding the Super Chief or some other westbound train at the Union or Northwestern depots. Newspapers would fight with one another for the constant stream of interviews and gossip; Hecht perhaps more than most other Chicago writers was involved from early on in the allure of the film industry.

It was an industry which, from its infant days, drew heavily upon newspaper personnel for writing talent and other kinds of expertise. The wonder is not that Hecht, with his casual displays of prodigiousness, became involved in it, but that he became involved as late as he did. In 1915 Hecht received an offer from Theodore Dreiser, whom he had interviewed for the *Journal*, urging him to become a partner in a production company Dreiser was thinking of establishing. Dreiser was convinced that the cinema would virtually replace literature. Hecht showed the request to his editors, who entreated him to turn down the offer as the cinema was merely a passing fancy. "It was good advice though poor prophecy," Hecht would recall. Although that same year he sold his first story to the movies, more than a decade passed before he finally went to work in earnest in that medium.

He was in New York by then, broke as usual, when he received a fateful telegram from Herman J. Mankiewicz in Hollywood. The cable ran:

WILL YOU ACCEPT THREE HUNDRED PER WEEK TO WORK FOR PARAMOUNT PICTURES STOP ALL EXPENSES PAID STOP THE THREE HUNDRED IS PEANUTS STOP MILLIONS ARE TO BE GRABBED OUT HERE AND YOUR ONLY COMPETITION IS IDIOTS STOP DONT LET THIS GET AROUND STOP

Mankiewicz, who would go on to write *Citizen Kane*, was a former drama critic of the New York *Times*. When Hecht arrived out west, he went to work at once for, among others, B.P. Schulberg (father of the novelist Budd Schulberg), another old newspaperman. Indeed, the pattern of former reporters and editors working in the new film capital was already well established. Part of that pattern was the screenwriter's traditional bitterness at the system he felt exploited him while paying him exorbitant fees for mindless work. It was a combination of too much money, too easy work and too little respect that marked the screenwriter of the time, and Hecht became the archetypal example of this breed. That fact is only marginally less important than the claim that he was also, year for year, on large jobs and small, the best screenwriter of his day.

The studio bosses were petty businessmen who had operated nickelodeon parlours back east. They were joined by the actual filmmakers, not a few of whom had been adventurers of some sort. Then came the newspapermen, who were followed by the novelists, poets and dramatists. It seemed as though anyone who had ever won respect for anything he had written was being hired by the studios. The trains in and out of Los Angeles were as crowded with literary celebrities as the Chicago trains had been with actors and actresses.

For the writers, Hollywood was both a gold mine and a salt mine. The money was phenomenal, but the enforced mediocrity of the writing was harmful to both their serious work and their reputations. Many of the writers gave up Hollywood after a short time. Others, such as Scott Fitzgerald (who called Hecht one of the film industry's "spoiled" writers) proved unequal to the task. Still others somehow managed to maintain a delicate balance between the literary and the film worlds, allowing the one to support the other financially or intellectually. Such a person was Gene Fowler. Hecht was another. But given his personality, even while walking that narrow path (with more success than he and some of his critics realized), Hecht still managed to bring to both kinds of writing his characteristic gusto and style and also, inevitably, his satiric tongue.

George Bernard Shaw once said that the reason he could not write, as requested, for Samuel Goldwyn was because Goldwyn was interested only in art whereas he, Shaw, was interested only in money. As a Hollywood generalization that is less facetious than it would seem. It is especially useful as it regards Hecht, who found himself working two years on *Erik Dorn* for a total return of seven thousand dollars and working hardly at all on a scenario or original screen story for fifteen to twenty-five thousand dollars at first and later for easily double that amount. He himself likened the situation to the statement of his friend Chico Marx who, during the Broadway engagement of the Marx Brothers' *Animal Crackers*, said he would charge fifty dollars per hour for playing the bassoon and twice that amount for not playing it. If the former pants pressers who were running the studios were capable of bribing the screenwriters into abandoning their good works and possibly their good names, then the screenwriters were able at least to accept the money in a spirit of healthy extortion.

At first Hecht considered Hollywood a game, especially when his friends from Chicago and New York began accumulating on the Coast. Fowler, Wallace Smith, the publisher Horace Liveright, almost the full roster of boon companions, ended up in Hollywood sooner or later. There they mingled with a gaggle of new gay hearts such as the cinematographer Lee Garmes, the director and writer Charles Lederer and such actors as W.C. Fields and John Barrymore. They formed a colony in which private jokes and enthusiasms took some of the sting out of studio drudgery. But the longer they stayed, the greater their misery became and the dimmer the light at the end of the tunnel. As his natural talent adapted itself to the work at hand, Hecht was more and more in demand as a script doctor and adapter as well as a writer of originals. His income skyrocketed but so did his expenses. He was now maintaining a lavish home at Oceanside, down the coast from Los Angeles, as well as the house in Nyack and an apartment in New York City. Also, he was the periodic support of a large number of down-at-the-heels artist friends and a sucker for good causes of any size.

In his peak Hollywood years, to keep afloat financially, he needed an income of two hundred thousand dollars a year, though he sometimes made well over twice that amount. He found, however, that his overhead expanded to consume his revenue. There seemed little way out except to carry on, writing his books and plays between stints at the studios. Hecht still would have had to be the highest paid Hollywood writer even had he not been the best and best known. Fortunately, though, he found himself wearing all three crowns in the early 1930s. In 1929, already a veteran of the silents, he had written that talking pictures were a flash in the pan. Luckily for him that was another instance of wishful thinking and poor prophecy.

Although Hecht did not write a great number of silent pictures, those he did write taught him skills which stayed with him through the seventy-five or so talkies to come, or at least taught him how to retool his existing machinery for movie production. Telling a story visually, with as many and as clever plot turns as possible, was odd at first but not difficult for one used to writing plays or twisting the news a bit for his own purposes. Sometimes the screen stories were his own, at other times the premises were supplied him. Whichever the case, it was not so very different from writing stories to Mencken's plot suggestions, as he had done in the *Smart Set* years.

The principal difference was that no longer could he get away with depicting humanity as basically amoral, the way he had done in the past. A self-censorship was called for merely to prevent heavier censorship by other hands a little further along. If in Hollywood Hecht had to be his own H.L.Mencken, he also had to be his own Rev. J.Franklin Chase. At first, he merely enjoyed the opportunity to rewrite some of his Chicago experiences and impressions, carefully watering them down for a new audience. He was turning to good account what he had used before and would use many times again. He put both himself and Chicago blatantly into his scripts, as in a sense he would always continue to do, albeit more subtly.

The first film in which Hecht was heavily involved was *Underworld*, in 1927. He wrote an eighteen-page story from which Robert N. Lee created the screenplay. The film was directed by Josef von Sternberg, the Viennese emigré who would return briefly to Europe and make the 1930 classic *Blue Angel*, with Marlene Dietrich. It was from the start a curious team — for Hecht, whose influence on the final product was much greater than one would expect in the circumstances, was writing a desperately American story which von Sternberg realized in a decorative, romantic and decadent manner akin to Hecht's own in *Erik Dorn*.

It was a Chicago gangster story designed to capitalize on the public awareness of gangsters then still at its peak. While it has been called the first gangster picture, it was not a tale of bootleggers and organized criminals at all but of petty hoodlums with political pull. While the story fitted nicely within the criminal world familiar to Hecht, who had left Chicago before the gang wars we associate with that city were at their height, it was set in an atmosphere that predated even Hecht's first-hand experience.

Lee's script and von Sternberg's spontaneous bits of business embellished Hecht's original story but did not alter it in important ways. In the first scene, a wino stumbles past a bank just as a bomb inside blows the windows out into the street. The bank robber rushes outside with his loot and (through title cards) explains, "The great Bull Weed closes another bank account." The wino overhears this and is warned to keep silent. "Don't worry," he replies. "I'm a Rolls Royce for silence." In admiration as much as from caution, the bandit shoves the wino into his getaway flivver.

Later, Rolls Royce, as he has now come to be called, is working in a bar where Weed's rival, Buck Mulligan, attempts to intimidate him. Weed intervenes. Rolls, in gratitude, silently swears devotion to his rescuer and goes on to become his faithful lieutenant. Living by the sword, Rolls Royce comes under the threat of the sword, especially when he becomes enamoured of Weed's gun moll, Feathers McCoy; he betrays Weed with her while the gangster is away committing a jewel robbery. Still later, both Weed and Mulligan meet cinematic justice. The former is apprehended for the jewel theft, the latter gunned down in a flower shop.

That last touch Hecht based on the demise of his friend Dion O'Banion, one of the few true beer barons he had known (and, despite his name, an Italian rather than Irish one). Along with the film's depiction of hearses for carrying booze and bodies, a means of transport actually favoured by some Chicago bootleggers, this scene is one of the few touches liberated from the crime wars which *Underworld* is credited with portraying. Most of the rest of the film is based on a less dramatic, less famous and older underworld which Hecht had known in fact since 1910 and from long before in legend.

The fact that *Underworld* is concerned with essentially small-time robbers and footpads, rather than the imperial Capones and Morans, is one indication of this. Another is the underworld revel scene, which is the heart of the film. The event was based on the

First Ward balls held annually in Chicago from approximately 1880 until 1908, two years before Hecht arrived in the city. Sponsored by Aldermen Hinky Dink Kenna and Bathhouse John Coughlin, the affairs were held at Christmas ostensibly to raise funds for the Democratic party, though the two sponsors managed to siphon off much of the take for themselves. The Chicago *Tribune* had once commented that "if a great disaster had fallen upon the Coliseum Ballroom there would not have been a second story worker, a dip or a pug ugly, porch climber, dope fiend, or scarlet woman remaining in Chicago."

Hecht then, while drawing on what he had not witnessed himself as well as on what he had, was trying to tell a realistic story. Von Sternberg, in the way European directors have continued to do, was lessening the realism by transforming the script into an American romantic myth. He shot the film in an expressionist manner and also embellished the story in ways Hecht found alarming. One of the changes consisted of having Weed, leaving the scene of a robbery, pause to give a dollar to a street beggar. Hecht was appalled and demanded that his name be removed from the credits. The request was denied, and he felt no qualms the next year about accepting the first Academy Award for an original story.

In many ways, *Underworld* was a film ahead of its time as well as one perfectly in touch with the demands of the day. It was not really the first gangster film. Rather, it was in the line of descent from Griffith's *Musketeers of Pig Alley*, made in 1912. But as it was set in Chicago, the city which during Prohibition had more than five hundred gangland killings and, in retaliation, two arrests and no convictions, it was welcomed by the public. Its success rather than its trueness to life, sparked a series of similar films which had more to do with actual types and events in the news — films such as *Little Caesar*, *Public Enemy*, and *Scarface*. It began a tradition that still flourishes today.

Underworld was also one of the first American-made films (albeit directed by a European) to exist in the expressionist atmosphere which Hecht and so many others had long ago imported in print and with which Hecht would continue to experiment long after the commercial appeal of such a style had waned. *Underworld* was the film that saved von Sternberg's career, which was dangling precariously following a string of box office failures. More importantly, it was the one that taught Hecht that he could write for the cinema by bringing to bear his experience as a reporter — bringing it to bear both as it involved practical matters of writing quickly, cleverly and dramatically and as it involved writing about Hechtian man and later, writing from the standpoint of Hecht the Sophisticate.

If Hecht did not actually invent the modern gangster film but allowed it to be invented, he at least originated some of the concepts which were to become his great hallmarks as a screenwriter. The cynical but sometimes sentimental character who was the victim of wry, irresponsible caprice and who became an anti-hero in spite of himself, was his creation. This, along with the style of dialogue he would develop in later sound films, would be his principal legacy to the cinema.

Equally important, *Underworld* taught him the intricacies of the special kind of collaboration Hollywood demanded. *Underworld* was the result of tensions between Hecht and von Sternberg working at cross purposes. Although Hecht never worked with the director again, he learned the necessity of treating moviemaking as a kind of temporary marriage in which the lesser partner (the writer) must choose his dominant mate carefully, to anticipate the other's moods and generally to strive for an atmosphere in which those elements common to both personalities result in issue. Such knowledge is not entirely what made him a different screenwriter from the others. But it is what helped him become more successful than most of the others, both artistically and financially. It stood him in good stead for nearly forty years.

Hecht faced many problems as a movie writer. The most important, aside from the one of literary morale, was that writing for the movies forced him to be a writer of parts rather than a whole. That fact overshadowed even a sorrier one — that he was forced into writing many things in which he had no particular interest and for which he had no special skill. Hollywood work tended to dilute his various selves — the Bohemian and the Sophisticate, for example — and to show them one at a time rather than in force, all together.

The effect was destructive except when it involved him with

directors who complemented him and he them. These were generally either action directors, who appealed to Hecht's Chicago cynicism and toughness, or European ones, who were more sardonic than cynical and used the side of him that was the Sophisticate. The most important director of the first kind was certainly Howard Hawks.

Hawks was an intelligent tough guy who liked to play up that part of his intelligence that was rugged and practical. He was a pragmatist. His direction reached its height as a mirror of his own ideas — for instance, in the way he used Humphrey Bogart in *To Have and Have Not* or *The Big Sleep*: as a thoroughly professional fellow who gets a difficult job done without ostentation, who thinks he knows something about women, especially when they are independent types like himself but with the violence taken away, and who enjoys above all the companionship of fellow pros, whatever their sex. That crossing of sexual lines, often ignored by critics, is interesting if one considers that it was Hawks' idea to use a female Hildy Johnson in *His Girl Friday*.

Such an outlook on professionalism and comradeship was a small part of Hecht, but the greater part of his affinity with Hawks. Another bond between them, and one loosely related to the first, was that both men dreaded nothing so much as the prospect of being labelled tame and middle class. They fought against that fate (Hawks rather more blindly than Hecht) by associating themselves in life and in their work with loners, outcasts, outlaws and all manner of anti-authoritarian figures. These similar attitudes, combined with the fact that both were at the height of their Hollywood success, made their working together somehow natural. When such a collaboration came about in 1931, a year in which Hollywood produced fifty-one gangster features, it was only logical that their first project should be a film on the Chicago crime wars.

The picture was *Scarface*, which the Hays office would force them to subtitle "Shame of a Nation" and otherwise lace with phony moralistic canards. The film was produced by Howard Hughes, whom Hawks would work for again in 1943 on the famous Jane Russell sex-western *The Outlaw*, for which Hecht would co-author the script without credit. At the time of *Scarface*, Hughes was merely a multimillionaire, not the supposed billionaire he became later. Fearing Hughes might go bankrupt at any moment,

The Five Lives of Ben Hecht

Hecht demanded payment of one thousand dollars each writing day, in cash. In that way, he stood to lose only a day's work if Hughes should suddenly go belly up.

Hughes had purchased the rights to *Scarface*, a rather incredible novel by the young pulp writer, Armitage Trail. In the end only the title of the book was retained. Hecht's script was an original in more than even the usual sense. Although he was writing of Chicago again, he was now writing, in the light of *Public Enemy* and *Little Caesar*, of a criminal lifestyle that had run rampant after his departure.

Both Hecht and Hawks have said that the film was an attempt to superimpose the story of Al Capone on the story of the Borgias. While the film has as much of the Borgian incest element as they could slip past the censors, it is clearly more relevant to contemporary news than to Renaissance Europe. It is the story of the ruthless rise of Tony Camonte (Paul Muni) to the top of the gangster heap and of his ultimate capture and death. Although Capone's biography had little to do with the story, the title of the film and Muni's facial scars left no doubt in the audience's minds of the intent.

The scars were in the shape of xs. Part of the renown of the film is the way Hecht and Hawks made the x a running symbol, just as newspaper photographs of the day used the device to denote the spot where bodies lay. The opening credits roll over an x. A fallen gangster flays his arms in an x. There are many more instances. Perhaps the most famous occurs in the scene in which a gangster is gunned down in a bowling alley. The ball, which he has let loose of just as the bullets strike him, leaves two pins standing for a moment. But then they totter and finally collapse, in the shape of an x.

Scarface would have an effect on actual gangsters much as *The Front Page* had on newspapermen. Four years after the film was released, gangsters in Chicago, inspired by *Scarface*, gunned down a rival in a bowling alley. The victim was Machine Gun Jack McGurn (another Italian with an Irish *nom de guerre*) who had engineered the St. Valentine's Day Massacre in 1929, an event caricatured in Hecht's script.

Just as the stage production of *The Front Page* had done, *Scarface* established the careers of many persons involved in it, for better or for worse. Its success prompted Muni to forsake the theatre for films, most notably for a long series of biographical pictures. George Raft, who played Muni's bodyguard and was seen tossing a coin in the air repeatedly, went on to make a long list of gangster films. His coin-tossing became a favourite bit of business for impressionists and, ultimately, a sad bit of self-parody for the actor himself. Hawks would grow professionally over the decades to become the great American action director, with his tough western, detective and war films. Hecht, for his part, would strive for a happy compromise with Hollywood by working with people who could best realize on film the Chicago anti-hero side of his personality.

The action directors were by nature adventurers, either physically or vicariously. For example, Raoul Walsh (with whom Hecht never worked, it seems) had been a seaman and a cowboy before going to work for Griffith, who sent him to film the Mexican Revolution. Others, such as John Ford, Henry Hathaway and William Wellman possessed much the same free spirit and anti-middle class attitudes. With each of them, however, the stance took a different form. Thus Hecht's writing for each also took a different form and resulted in a different kind of script.

Ford, for instance, was the most serious of the lot. Like the others he had a remarkably pronounced sense of history. He would harken back to a time of what he imagined were clear-cut moral codes and clear distinctions between good and evil. He put that concept into play by sometimes representing history as Nature and pitting against it the ruggedest type of individual. Hecht wrote only one film for him, the John Hall-Dorothy Lamour vehicle, *The Hurricane*, in which exactly this idea is played out against a South Seas background.

For Hathaway, who was sort of a lesser, more muddled Hawks, Hecht wrote four diverse films. They illustrate Hathaway's scattergun work and Hecht's failure with such a director to produce anything more than a good script well-filmed, rather than a collaboration between writer and director. The films were *China Girl* (1942), a farfetched World War Two adventure; *Kiss of Death* (1947), a gangster film resting on the power of the script and perhaps the last first-rate piece of film writing Hecht did; *Legend of the Lost* (1957), another adventure, set in North Africa and likewise more interesting for the Hecht touches; and *Circus World*

(1964), the last Hecht film released before his death and interesting hardly at all.

On most of these films Hecht was left pretty much alone. That is, he was left to write, at best, merely a good script in the abstract, without the magic which might otherwise have resulted between the script and the camera. Such a situation, however, allows one to trace the evolution of certain recurring elements in Hecht's screenwriting and his writing generally. *Kiss of Death*, for example, is, like *Underworld*, a film about a thief masquerading as a more glamourous kind of criminal. This time the masquerade is Hecht's doing, not the director's. The thief, Victor Mature, is apprehended as the logical result of the storyline, not as a concession to the censors. Once captured, he squeals on his colleagues. There is no romanticizing of his virtues or failings as there had been in *Underworld* and to a lesser extent in *Scarface*. The essential integrity of the story differs from Hecht's *Underworld* story (as distinct from Robert Lee's finished script) by being the work of a much more mature writer.

Legend of the Lost is another example of a change in Hecht as he grew older. The Hechtian man of such works from the 1920s as *1001 Afternoons in Chicago*, *Broken Necks* and *Erik Dorn* was bitter about his own failure to find a place in a stupid world. Now the same character has grown older and more tolerant of himself and others. He is also perhaps (as in *To Quito and Back* from the late 1930s) somewhat more desperate. In *Legend of the Lost*, he is, in the unlikely person of John Wayne, a tired soldier of fortune in Timbuctoo hired by Sophia Loren to help find a hidden treasure. Eventually they stumble upon the deserted Holy City of Opher, once a Roman outpost, and in a typically Hechtian piece of irony, discover the jewels while digging for water needed to remain alive.

The Wayne character is a man who knows human nature and doesn't like it. He remains largely silent whereas once he would have been noisy and iconoclastic. Loren, however, thinks he is a bit of a rogue, and tells him, "Every place you go is a barroom." Actually he is no rogue at all but spiritually a newspaperman. He is an older, wearier version of the nameless diarist of *1001 Afternoons in Chicago*, who in this film has substituted his reporter's fedora for the garb of a tough but half-hearted fortune-seeker.

This multifarious character at first appears to be one of Hecht's cinematic inventions. Actually, he is a much older Hecht stock figure brought to Hollywood from his own books and his own life and disguised a bit along the way. The same is true of that character's kindred spirit, the screen newspaperman who is really a younger Hecht recycled again and again, generally for comic effect. He turns up as a reporter in the person of Fredric March in Wellman's *Nothing Sacred* and as a former reporter turned press agent (Roscoe Karns) in Hawks' version of *Twentieth Century*. He is also the bumbling but cuddly foreign correspondent (Stuart Irwin) in Hecht's Oscar-winning script for *Viva Villa!*, with Wallace Beery in the title role.

Many former newspapermen who became screenwriters used that character, of course. The creature was generally shown as a wisecracking nuisance who never took off his hat. (Frank McHugh of the Warner stable must have played the part dozens of times.) Including the character was a way of adding to the mayhem of 1930s comedies. It owes most of its existence to the originals of *The Front Page*, for this Hecht-Hollywood "invention" was actually born in Hecht's pre-Hollywood days.

The fact that Hawks would direct three comedies propelled by such characters — *Twentieth Century*, *His Girl Friday*, and, to a lesser extent, *Viva Villa!* — is a good indication of why the Hecht-Hawks collaboration was the most successful writer-director match either of them ever knew. Hawks taught Hecht a great deal about how to put both power and subtlety into films, knowledge Hecht employed when he became a director himself. Hecht in turn encouraged Hawks to develop the quality most notably absent in the films he made with other people: a sense of humour. Coming from Hecht it was a backhanded, epigrammatic and rapid-fire sense of humour, but it added a great deal to their relationship. It nearly succeeded for a time in making Hawks a more European, less American director. It almost made him a Sophisticate: almost but not quite.

The Five Lives of Ben Hecht

Hecht and MacArthur were under some pressure to repeat their success on Broadway once *The Front Page* had made them a famous and prosperous team. Their response was *Twentieth Century*, which enjoyed a long run in 1932 and, like the earlier work, would enjoy periodical revivals, notably the one by Jose Ferrer in 1951. The play was a noisy farce making fun of New York theatrical types in a rather crueller manner than *The Front Page* had made fun of Chicago journalists and politicians. They adapted it for the screen in 1934, and, directed by Hawks, it became one of the best and most influential of the screwball comedies so popular during the Depression.

The story, which was altered little in the transition to the screen, involved passengers aboard the New York to Chicago express train, the Twentieth Century Limited, though the title also refers to the century the authors were ridiculing. The passengers are Oscar Jaffe, a down-on-his-luck theatrical producer (who bears a resemblance to David Belasco but who is part Count Bruga) and the famous actress Lily Garland (whose real name in the movie is Mildred Plotker). The change of name had come three years earlier, when Jaffe discovered her and made her a star. John Barrymore played Jaffe, a role in which he excelled, being much like the character in temperament and carriage. Lily Garland was portrayed by Carole Lombard. She went from that film to many other wacky comedies, including, three years later, Hecht's *Nothing Sacred*.

Declaring that she is no Trilby, the actress has broken away from Jaffe's tutelage, which included long hours of listening to him describe his own genius. She is giving up the theatre for a career in films and is heading westward on the train, unaware that Jaffe, his own career dashed without her, is also aboard, fleeing his creditors. Just as in *The Front Page*, when the suspense led to Burns luring Hildy back to the newspaper, here it leads to the moment when Jaffe will lure Garland into his new dramatic production, which happens to be a bastardization of the Passion Play.

Indeed, the similarities between the two plays are striking. Both Burns and Jaffe are the type of scoundrel Hecht and MacArthur loved creating, who will commit any crime, perpetrate any outrage, in the name of personal glory and the passion ruling that glory, be it a scoop or Broadway hit. Garland in a way predates

100

Hawks' female Hildy of *His Girl Friday* by already being a strong-willed, younger female character who has been strung along for years and is now determined to be the dupe no longer. Like Hildy, she regresses in the end, in the name of the higher calling (journalism over advertising, the stage over Hollywood) and in the name of a peculiar camaraderie.

Even the supporting characters of *Twentieth Century* resemble those in *The Front Page*, at least as types. Mac Jacobs, Jaffe's rival producer, who is also on the train courting Garland, is the equivalent of Hildy's fiancée. He also represents the *Tribune* in that he is a threat and uses pranks to serious ends. Just as the newspaper play made light of radicals and rightists, in the person of Earl Williams and the sheriff, so here the authors include two mad Bolsheviks, and for good measure a gentleman named Mr. Clark. He is an insignificant little worm with evangelical delusions. He also believes that he is wealthy and backs Jaffe's religious epic with what turns out to be nonexistent capital.

In the end, of course, Jaffe and Garland manage to reconcile their differences and, presumably, actually bring the story of Mary Magdalen to the stage once more. The film is interesting because, although another example of the uneven collaboration between director and writer, it is at least an example in which the writer dominates and the director goes along playfully, enjoying the exercise, as caught up in the rapid pace as the audience. The effect was one Hawks would try and fail to recreate later in *Bringing Up Baby*.

The film *Twentieth Century*, like the play, was a statement of the authors' basic theatrical ideas and of their social ideas as well. But while the techniques were as of old, their attitude toward them had changed somewhat. Still under the influence of Mencken, Hecht was centrally concerned with debunking (a favourite Mencken word). He was debunking the boobosie, the middle class, and also the people the middle class feared (the reds) and revered (the politicians, the glamorous show business folk). He did not debunk by tearing down the beliefs and pretentions a brick at a time with his logic. He did it by purblind mockery, as exemplified by the natty dialogue which ridiculed middle class sentiments and fears of failure.

Upon first being rejected by Lombard, Barrymore collapses like a card table with mock-plaintive cries of "Oblivion! Oblivion!" Later, in a sentimental moment, he says in reference to his protégé: "When I love a woman, I'm an Oriental. It never goes. It never dies." It was a case of the silly made gauche by magnification, and audiences of the 1930s thrived on it, thinking it was meant to make fun of the fortunate whom the hard times had not affected, rather than themselves.

Twentieth Century was not the first of the screwball comedies. It was, however, one of the first adapted from a stage work, and one of the funniest. Nor was it original in design. Still, by its success, it helped set the pattern for what were not just screwball comedies but screwball comedies about relations between the sexes. The way it treated sexual mores, as a sort of prolonged and inevitable misunderstanding at once both important and a diversion from more serious matters, became in time a mark of great sophistication. The script is useful as a gauge of the way Hecht worked with other directors who held ideas on personal relations either more or less solemn than his own.

There is a sense in which one's attitudes toward sex in America, rather than toward money, are often the better indicator of class. Certainly this rule applied to Hollywood. In the geographical and social Hollywood there was no upper class in the Continental sense, only a middle class with upper class wealth, a sort of aristocracy based on demand for services (mistakenly termed talent) and then on the income and privilege resulting from such demand. As regards the films Hollywood produced and the ethical codes they created and maintained, there is quite a different, more varied story. Each director tended to promote the view of sex he adhered to by reason of the class to which he belonged or aspired. Hecht worked for a number of directors with different ideas on the subject. Taken in retrospect, such work tends to surgically separate his own views on class and thereby give a clearer picture of the whole.

Generally, Hecht's poorest scripts were those he wrote for the great exploiters of Hollywood, the Otto Premingers and Billy Roses to whom sex was part of the spectacle and box office appeal. In other words, for those who thought themselves above class distinctions and exemplars of the high tone, but who were really somewhat tacky, like their products. He wrote much better for persons who, taken together, were like himself. That is, for Hawks, who was an ardent masculinist; for David O. Selznick and Ernst Lubitsch, who despite different backgrounds considered sex a minor theatrical form, like comic opera; and for Alfred Hitchcock, who finds both sexes treacherous and amusing. It was with the last two that Hecht had most in common. With those men and with William Wellman, a director of little originality but, like Hawks, a possible convert to Hecht's way of doing things, the Sophisticate in Hecht rose to the level of actual sophistication, Hollywood variety.

Hecht wrote two films for Wild Bill Wellman. The second, in 1942, was *Roxie Hart*, a comedy in the by now archaic 1920s debunking style, which was actually set in the 1920s. It told of a publicity-hungry murderess, Ginger Rogers, and her lawyer, Adolphe Menjou. It was another of those stories written less from Hecht's actual newspaper experience than from the viewpoint of a former newsman to whom all later exploits belonged by inheritance. The other Wellman film was *Nothing Sacred*, which Selznick produced in 1937. The title was appropriate enough since the script consisted of Hecht debunking the society that had supported him, with all stops out. Here, because of Wellman's acquiescence to his writer, Hecht was not just a collaborator showing only the part of himself which seemed comfortable and combustible to Wellman. Here he stood alone even to the extent of satirizing that which had been most dear to him, the newspaper life. Earlier works had treated the subject kindly by comparison, as would the later works of Hecht the Memoirist. In *Nothing Sacred*, however, his satire was rooted in truth and previewed a rude awakening.

The story concerns Hazel Flagg (Carole Lombard once again), a native of a small Vermont town. She is smitten with a strange disease which her doctor wrongly diagnoses as radium poisoning. At the suggestion of his Howeyesque editor, a reporter named Wallace Cook (Fredric March) sets out to make the fatal case into a big city *cause célèbre*, utilizing his newspaper's considerable skill at ballyhoo. What develops, of course, is that Lombard learns the prognosis was mistaken. For quite a while she strings along the press and the sympathetic public, feeling that it is better to be allegedly dying in Manhattan, where Cook has brought her, to a heroine's welcome, than to be pathetically alive in Vermont. It is a patent 1930s romantic farce. In fact, it is one of the last examples of the species. The characters speak almost as quickly as auctioneers. Every excruciating plot device is called into service. The whole product is distinguished by devilish bits of business.

For all that, *Nothing Sacred* is much different from other comedies, mainly by being much different from Hecht's other contributions to the form. Here the newspaperman is a sadder figure: a fact not hindered by the choice of March for the part. Here he is hated, ridiculed and tricked by the semi-rural New Englanders and deceived by the news source he is trying to exploit. The comedy is less wacky at base than previous Hecht works. Sex is less a laughing matter than a subject for confused speculation shrouded in a sardonic blanket. The changes in environment and medium, and the amelioration of his youthful flippancy and posturing, had brought on another Hecht – the Sophisticate.

Hecht the Bohemian and Hecht the Iconoclast were essentially newspapermen moonlighting as artists. They endured the old reporter's overexposure to stupidity, mindless greed and violence which they covered up with gallows humour. For them, the mark of sophistication, small "s", was to ponder the immorality around them and turn it into upper case Art. The later Hecht, the one who fled Hollywood each year to produce a stream of novels and stories and wallow in the luxury of honest work, was different. For him the mark of art was to observe a different type of immorality, a different kind of decadence, and to turn it into classiness. This new creature was Hecht the Sophisticate, a confused and confounding man. He was no longer attacking an older generation but his own, to which, against his better judgement, he sometimes felt a curious loyalty. The loyalty sparked a confusion of the spirit, a loss of identity and a political awakening, all of which he would try to work out in a spate of literary works and works for the screen.

7
Cynic's Night Out

Ah, the smell of art — the lovely smell of art!
Pollikoff, *in* BH's Spectre of the Rose

In the 1930s when he was stuck, so to speak, at the top of the Hollywood heap, Hecht went through a profound change as a writer. He discovered that he truly was what he had been posing as through the years — a cynic. Not a man who was cynical to keep from becoming sentimental, as he had been, but a cynic who needed all his literary self-control to keep from lapsing into bitterness. The change was a response to his new life in the studio script mills and his anticipation of many more years of the same existence. In the sense that it extended a line of his career to date, the change was a progression. In another way, however, it was a deterioration. It was, there is no mistaking it, a great stylistic upheaval, the roots of which were planted in Chicago.

Reporters in his day constantly saw a great deal of the unappetizing side of human nature; more of it in fact than many of them could bear emotionally. In order to cover their disgust and their various methods of escape, such as alcohol, they carefully cultivated a cynical air. They also cultivated a gallows humour. It would allow them to place bets (as Hecht is said to have done) as to which step of the scaffold a condemned man would pretend to trip over in his pitiful stalling for time. To be too deeply moved by such spectacles was to be considered somehow unmanly, unworthy and green. Most reporters secreted thin layers of cynicism which at times seemed real. Certainly Hecht behaved that way, though the fact he was an artist made him somewhat different from the others.

His early writings gave him an opportunity to let down his defenses and to feel sympathy for his subjects, all the while using his reporting experiences, and the mental attitudes they produced, as grist for the mill. On the plus side, that method resulted in a curious combination of sympathy and detachment which is quite unusual in such an extreme. On the minus, it led him to approach his serious writing in a way that tended, as in *1001 Afternoons in Chicago*, to make both his literary and his service writing complement one another, if not actually to make them interchangeable. Thus to Hecht, and to the majority of other writers of the Renaissance, art became a form of journalism disguised as art, or journalism with nearly all the pins removed. Art, in Chicago, was journalism carried to the nth degree, well beyond what the newspapers would let one get away with in print.

After Hecht moved to New York he "lived for years in a shower of anecdotes" rather than in a welter of crimes and other events. At first the change seemed not to affect his writing, for he spent several years just catching up on his left-over experiences and characters. After *Count Bruga* and *The Front Page*, however, he looked around him and saw fatuous writers, such as the Algonquin Round Table group he generally disliked, making a literature from one another's literature instead of from life. He felt, quite rightly, that he had cut himself off from his roots and source of inspiration, that he had lain down with a group of mere wits, anecdotists and versifiers who either ignored people unlike themselves or led lives of such rarified literary conformity that they refused to dig deeply into their surroundings for fear of digging too deeply into themselves.

The situation was only aggravated when he became embroiled in Hollywood life amongst people shallower and more vain than those on Broadway. In Chicago, art was something which had been torn from daily contact with an almost barbaric society. In New York it was something one undertook to become successful. In Hollywood it hardly existed. Chicago had been a place of action, New York a place of anecdote and Hollywood a place of

—gossip, innuendo, drudgery. Hecht looked around him and did not like what he saw. It made him bitter. The stupidity of the studio bosses, the callowness of the entire society in which he travelled, now gave him something to be cynical about which was unfounded in fancy and pretense. His cynicism was less ostentatious than before but even more necessary. He fashioned from that predicament something like a new form and a new life.

Hecht the Sophisticate was not a sophisticate like those on Broadway whom one can recall today in a score of old musicals: the slick-haired men always in tailcoats, the coiffed women always in gowns, who lived manicured lives, who considered the prank and the well-told anecdote the marks of talent in repose, and who never seemed to do anything for a living. While Hecht was the thinking-man part of that crowd, he was also separate from it. He examined it like a heavily biased sociologist and ultimately made it the target of his satire. In the process, of course, he quite consciously examined himself and sometimes found himself wanting, not in emotion but in passion, much as he had done in *Erik Dorn*. As he was now dividing his time between Hollywood writers' buildings and his own desk, he made his discoveries in both scripts and books.

Of course the former could accomodate only a fraction of his ideas and prejudices, and then only in a form acceptable to the mass esthetic, which leaned toward a type of formula escapism. As for books, the short duration of the furloughs from Hollywood meant that he had to confine himself to short stories, many of which could be composed in his six-month vacations, rather than novels, which required long periods free of interruptions. He also worked in the novella form, a compromise procedure. In these years, he published but one novel, *A Jew in Love*, a work that had been in progress for some time before the demand for his movie services became so great.

Until *Erik Dorn*, Hecht's reputation had been local and literary, confined to the readers of little magazines in Chicago, New York and, to some extent, Europe. It was *Erik Dorn* that made his name familiar to a broader public. He did not become truly popular with the larger audience, however, until *Gargoyles*, with what was then considered its racy tone and its notoriety resulting from censorship cases. Even so, Hecht's fiction was never in the first

The Five Lives of Ben Hecht

rank of popularity. Such appeal as it did hold waned in the 1930s after his production of stories and novels had peaked. By that time his Hollywood connections had reduced his standing among serious observers and critics to an ignoble place from which it has never recovered.

Although less appealing in many ways than previous incarnations, Hecht the Sophisticate was in other ways a better writer or at least a better-intentioned one. The Sophisticate wrote with less artifice than his predecessors and to clearer purpose. Where once he was concerned with elaborate stylistic feats, Hecht was now content to polish a style of which he was very proud and which was more bitter than bittersweet. Where once his cynicism had been an offensive posturing, displaying stylistic finery that could serve for full-dress artistic occasions, now it was a defensive action. He was not coming near to solving the conflicts of class which dogged him but at least he was addressing them more directly. That made him a less derivative writer, if also a less impressive stylist.

When writing about daily events in Chicago, he had been one of the few to address the problems of the poor and nameless in a way which in some measure was perhaps a characteristic of the Renaissance. He wrote about the poor with less enjoyment but more seriousness than he wrote about the rich, who were flamboyant figures described by the press as "politicians" and "wealthy sportsmen," which meant ward grafters and gangsters respectively. His concern for the poor was sometimes clouded by his expressionism and often cheapened by his avarice for good copy, but it was there, underneath, and it was compassionate.

He never became sufficiently intimate with New York that he could see such people in that city with the same clarity or write about them with the same familiarity. Instead what he found were Broadway wags and rips who frightened and disgusted him because they were much closer to the middle class. No doubt Bodenheim's remorseless examination of Hecht's middle class attitudes in *Duke Herring* (of which his attitude toward the rich was part) rankled him severely, and he became determined to show himself superior to his rightful peers. Whether he liked it or not, Hecht resembled the New York and Hollywood young bloods he despised for their sheer mediocrity. He resolved to make himself as distinct professionally from these contemporaries as possible, even while he basked in the company of some of them socially. So he satirized them in reams of stories, novellas and even screenplays. He believed that by his vitality, talent and craft he would make himself different from such people. He might have succeeded had not one of those three qualities been drastically altered.

Hecht's vitality — his "fecundity and wit," as he would later term it — was unchanged by the basics of life in California. If anything, it was all the more amazing in view of the pressures of hack work he had to tolerate. His talent, too, that combination of high spirits and penetration applied to upperworlds and underworlds, remained substantially unaltered throughout the 1930s. It was his ideas about craft and art which changed. In Chicago art was something made in rebellion against a morally indigent and violent society. In New York art was what made one a fortune without forcing one out of character. In Hollywood, however, for Hecht and an entire generation of screenwriters examined today with such critical affection, art was something else again. Art, in Hollywood, was what one did not write for money. Indeed, it was what one used his money to be able to write, to regain a measure of self-respect.

Hecht published three story and novella collections during the 1930s. These were *The Champion From Far Away* in 1931, *Actor's Blood* in 1936 and *A Book of Miracles* in 1939. The fact that they were written by someone who was now more a screenwriter than man-of-letters made them very different from his earlier fiction. The new pieces were not necessarily the result of work undertaken for money — unlike *Broken Necks* and others, which had come out of his reporting. Because they were escapism from his cinema drudgery, their style was different from that of earlier work.

For one thing, the short fictions of Hecht the Sophisticate were longer. Many can be called novellas if only on the basis of length; and generally they took longer to get where they were going than earlier ones. They were not so tightly structured as older stories. Also, they approximated "pure" stories, with plots, narrative progressions and clever twists at the end, rather than experiments in mood. They were in fact more conservatively constructed stories except that in most cases they were macabre and bizarre in taste and alternately ridiculing or melancholy in approach. The ridicule was heaviest when the stories concerned Hollywood, the Hollywood that was looking over the author's shoulder as he wrote. Even those, however, fit into the old pattern since they deal with immigrants or persons in the slums of show business or people who have slid from the top of their calling to the bottom. The overriding theme in these books is that spiritual collapse is attendant upon a deterioration in materialistic trappings. The materialistic world is often symbolized by the phony glamour of the entertainment industry.

The people in *The Champion From Far Away*, which was published on the heels of *A Jew in Love*, are freaks. Hecht doesn't know whether to make fun of them or pity them. Usually he chooses the former course. Most of the stories are just that – stories – ones he had left over from his earlier experiences or ones told to him, which he then passes along like a marketplace entertainer. In "A Wistful Blackguard," for instance, he recounts straightforwardly, from all evidence, an encounter he had in Europe during his war correspondent days. It is the story of a member of the mysterious Irish Brigade which fought with the Germans against the British during the Great War. Another, "An American Kangaroo," sketches the character of a passively demented real estate promoter during the Florida land boom of the 1920s. Hecht had worked for one such person. The style is less bombastic than before, as it would be in nearly all that he wrote from the 1930s on.

His experience as a crime reporter (in Chicago, all reporters were crime reporters) left him with a life-long interest in murder and related subjects. He believed, but never quite articulated, a theory of pop criminology whereby the crime's aftermath, rather than its commission, revealed human nature at its rawest and most fascinating. In the title story of the book, a central European who fought valiantly and suffered great hardships during the war is reduced to working as a New York doorman. It is as though he is paying the price for his experiences if not for his actions. "The Rival Dummy," another of the longer stories making up the first half of the collection, is about a ventriloquist who was once at the top of his profession. The performer then sinks into a psychotic state and "kills" his dummy with an axe in a fit of jealousy. Forever after he lives under an assumed identity, fearful of prosecution. The new identity fools no one, and the man becomes the object of jocular pity.

The stories in the second half are shorter and less well developed. Some are anecdotes. Others, understandably in view of the Hollywood pressures under which Hecht wrote, are less stories than scenes from novels never written. They all have a Hitchcockian quality of mystery about them and, as before, they are drawn from personal observation. "The Masquerade," for instance, describes a man about to be hanged in Chicago who, as his last request, petitions for women's clothing and make-up. This eerie story, which Hecht had covered as a reporter years earlier, is pepped-up and lessened by the tacked-on ending — a reprieve from the governor that arrives too late to save the transvestite who only on the gallows comes out of the closet. Several others also concern hanging and murder. One of them, "The Lost Soul," is a brief and chilling description of a man who believes he is in a hospital but who is actually in prison suffering derangement or amnesia or both. He believes he is being led to another part of the hospital but is actually being taken to the gallows room where he is quickly executed.

Many of the stories are hamfisted or, when not awkward, then prosaic, with Hecht's normally peppery style diluted beyond the limits of tolerance. Together, however, they show the Sophisticate at work. Here Hecht is setting himself above the mob as a man of the world rather than an iconoclastic intellectual, and he is looking down on the mob with various sorts of derision. Hollywood life had made him see absurdity everywhere and frequently avarice and pomposity as well, as conspicuous to him by their absence as by their presence. Hecht the Sophisticate took the same view of everyone else that Bodenheim had taken of Hecht in *Duke Herring*. He pretended to see New York as Babylon and to view with distaste the "Broadway sneer" which was frequently his own expression.

It would not be precisely accurate to say that the stories based on Hecht's memories of his newspaper days foretold his last life, as a Memoirist. In one sense, Hecht was forever reminiscing and drawing upon his experience immediately after living through it. Yet it is fair to say that the Sophisticate stories offered the first glimpses of some subjects which later would be of great concern to him, though the concerns at that point were still integrated with other elements. "Snowfall in Childhood," for instance, one of eight long stories in *Actor's Blood*, is a standard display of evocative yet restrained sentimentality. The tone is also obvious in "The Little Candle" in *A Book of Miracles*, in which a rabbi commits suicide because of the Nazi pogroms in Europe. The latter story, however, is an early indication of Hecht's rising anger. The touch of propagandistic fervour shows through the overall mood of gentleness and sentimentality. Perhaps the greatest change in the Sophisticate's fiction is that he now sees society not as a variegated lifesize Chicago or New York but as a microcosm of social extremes often with a Hollywood setting. In fact, show business had come to represent the pomposity and stupidity formerly characterized by sheriffs and politicians. Art, in turn, as distinct from entertainment, had come to be represented by Hecht himself. "An American Kangaroo" in *The Champion From Far Away* represents a wheeler-dealer with an amazing esthetic ignorance. As such, the story is to some extent a comment on Hollywood values. But it is in the title story of *Actor's Blood* and several other pieces actually about movie business characters that Hecht reveals himself most plainly.

The central figures in "Baby Miller and the Pharaoh" and "The Missing Idol," from *Champion* and *Miracles* respectively, are big shot film producers. In personality they resemble Oscar Jaffe of *Twentieth Century*. That is, they take a highly theatrical view of themselves. But it is low theatrics indeed, a sort of mock tragedy that is unintentionally comic. They moan a great deal about being ruined. They grumble about being surrounded by infidels and ingrates. All the while they do turns as moneygrubbers in a continuous vaudeville, every bit as corny as the schlocky movies to which they proudly lend their names. They stand apart from Hecht, who views the world as essentially comic in order to keep from being overcome by the sheer tragedy of it.

Perhaps the best story in these collections is "Crime Without Passion" from *Actor's Blood*, which later became one of the films of Hecht-MacArthur Productions. It is the tale of Lou Hendrix, a sceptical defense lawyer. He resembles Clarence Darrow and Charles Erbstein, both of whom Hecht had admired in Chicago. He is a man of immense cleverness. His cleverness, in fact, consumes the rest of his personality and colours disastrously his view of others. At the back of his self-assurance, however, is a certain fragility of spirit. When he commits murder and allows himself to be done in through a twist of fate and a quirk of his own cockiness, it is a natural ending. Hendrix is Alexander Sterns who is Erik Dorn who is Hechtian man who in turn is Hecht himself considered in light of Hollywood. When the crash comes at last, it is with a sense of inevitability and a feeling of loss at what might have been. It is, in psychological terms, the story of Ben Hecht in movieland.

Hecht had always been the kind of cynic who was actually a disappointed sentimentalist. In Hollywood he became the kind of sophisticate who was actually a disappointed cynic. That fact put him in some demand in the 1930s, when the same generation that had thrown caution to the wind after World War One became frightened, guarded and sometimes bitter. Hecht's ideals fitted in perfectly with the mood of the day, at least among the artistic aristocracy. But, always something of a rebel, he rose up against that unintentional timeliness. He viewed others who appeared to believe as he did, as late-comers and dilettantes who had not earned their outlook, as he had. In the many films he wrote during this period for various bosses (as well as some he wrote for himself alone) he made fun of the new attitudes those around him held dear. The first of those films was *Design for Living*. It was directed by the great emigré ironist Ernst Lubitsch, with whom Hecht would work only one other time, in 1940 doing an anonymous rewrite on *The Shop Around the Corner*.

Design for Living was ostensibly to be a straightforward adaptation of Noel Coward's play of the same title. It came at a time when Hollywood, having already staked out Broadway, was laying waste to the West End as well. The story goes that Lubitsch, a man of quick enthusiasms and dislikes, suddenly turned against Coward and ordered the play thrown out, with only the title retained. Hecht, so it is said, then wrote an entirely new script, foiling Lubitsch by working in several of the choicest lines from two other Coward plays, *Hay Fever* and *The Vortex*. It is interesting that Hecht, although he grew to dislike Coward (who later starred in Hecht and MacArthur's film *The Scoundrel*), would tip his hat to the British satirist with whom, superficially and in his Hollywood writing of the 1930s, he had something in common.

The Five Lives of Ben Hecht

The premise is creaky now but a typical one for the period. Two expatriate bohemians (in the film, Americans) are starving in a Paris garret but keeping their spirits alive, competing for the affections of a flippant young woman. One of them is an unpublished writer, the other an unhung painter. The plot is so light as to be non-existent. In the end, the bohémians, Fredric March and Gary Cooper, lose the girl, Miriam Hopkins, to a US underwear tycoon played by Edward Everett Horton. The craft is mainly in the dialogue, which shows a lightheartedness and an implied bawdiness. It is in this film, for the first time, that the Hollywood Hecht, taking a cue from Coward, has fun without bitterness:

COOPER: I haven't got a clean shirt to my name.
MARCH: A clean shirt? What's up? A romance?
COOPER: I'm not talking pyjamas. Just a clean shirt.

The film contains most of the elements obvious in all Hecht's comedic writing, as well as a number of catch phrases found in his serious work. It is basically the old Hollywood Hecht story – the friendship of two men and a female interloper who first threatens the relationship but, in the end, leaves it undamaged and possibly strengthens it. It is like *The Front Page* all over again with Horton, an effete and somewhat effeminate character, portraying, if not the future Mrs. Hildy Johnson, then at least the role later created by Ralph Bellamy in *His Girl Friday*. Such an interpretation is made stronger by Hecht's (and Hollywood's) view of newspapering and newsmen. There is a scene in which one of the principals takes the boat train which connects with the Channel ferries and is met by a crowd of French reporters – who, although music hall Frenchmen, speak and behave exactly like Hollywood's idea of American reporters. Something of Hecht's *recherche du temps perdu* is also shown when Hopkins, trying to settle a quarrel caused by her presence, says: "Let's talk it over without any excitement – like a disarmament conference."

There is no doubt that Hecht, perhaps even more than Coward, was making light of the Paris bohemians. After all, Hecht disliked Hemingway and was ambivalent toward Fitzgerald. Although he would later use Fitzgerald (who once collaborated with MacArthur) as a symbol for Hollywood's treatment of literary men, he would do so only after Fitzgerald's death, when the generation of

114

the 1920s became united by the simple fact of having survived into old age. In 1933, Hecht was disrespectful of the exiles, partly because he thought them unequal to the old Chicago bohemians but also because it was good box office to be disrespectful. It was only in the middle 1930s that the experimental writers of the 1920s were well enough known at home to be laughed at by movie audiences. Witness the line in *Top Hat*, in 1935, in which Ginger Rogers replies to Fred Astaire's nonsense by saying that he sounds like Gertrude Stein, which she pronounces *Schtein*, in the German fashion.

But in another sense, Hecht, locked into Hollywood now, was writing not merely as an opponent of the expatriates but as a fellow member of their generation. There is something of Margaret Anderson in Miriam Hopkins when she states, "I'm going to be a mother of the arts!" There can be little doubt that Horton, the visitor among them, the expatriate who is not an ex-patriot, the square among the bohemians, is every 1920s writer's dream of a comic George F. Babbitt. By the 1930s, Hecht's regional and artistic antagonisms had begun to wane. It was, after all, a time of escapism — escapism was paying his salary. The audience escaped into what it thought was sophistication while Hecht, a different kind of Sophisticate, escaped into the past. That was the pattern for much of his career. The kind of sophisticate he established in *Design for Living*, rooted in the original *Front Page* and *Twentieth Century* but intensified by Hollywood, would remain unchanged. The scripts for many movies, including *Nothing Sacred*, *Comrade X* and much of the material he wrote with MacArthur, were reworkings of such an attitude. Although during the 1930s Hecht wrote, co-scripted or worked on a long procession of films, it was in the comedies that he did his best work. For a time most every other kind of film he wrote was hack work, at least so far as he was concerned. It was in the early 1940s that he changed and began bringing to other genres as a matter of course and pride the intensity and lyrical quality of the 1930s farces. Alfred Hitchcock was one of the people responsible for the change.

John Frankenheimer has remarked that any contemporary American director who says that he has not been influenced by Hitchcock is probably lying. Certainly Hecht's own direction was greatly affected by him once he set up shop as a director. Hecht, however, was also influenced by Hitchcock as a writer, insofar as the two functions are separable in Hitchcock's case. A good book could be written on the relationship between Hitchcock and his screenwriters, and Hecht would make an interesting chapter of it. He wrote at least five jobs for Hitchcock — two full screenplays and three uncredited co-scripting assignments — and it is Hitchcock who more than any other helped change the Sophisticate of the 1930s into somebody quite different. He elevated Hecht into what might be called the Higher Cynicism, a stance maintained all too briefly before the passion aroused by Palestine took control of his public self.

It is not unrealistic to suppose that Hecht found in Hitchcock another man who, like MacArthur, was after his own heart. Hecht and Hitchcock had had much in common over the years without being aware of the similarity or, indeed, of one another. For instance, the gallows humour, the disrespect for small town life, the joy of letting the audience see through the keyhole, the belief that the authorities were morally no better than the criminals — all the traits which have come to be seen as basic Hitchcock were also all the while basic Hecht. What Hitchcock contributed to Hecht in terms of craft was the feeling that films should be tightly scripted, for Hitchcock concocted very little on the set or in the cutting room; and that a certain Chicago-ness was called for, regardless of what the studios or audiences wanted.

The first Hitchcock on which Hecht worked was *Foreign Correspondent*, a 1940 adaptation of a book by Vincent Sheean. Robert Benchley and James Hilton were among the other eight writers who wrote on the script from time to time. The superfluity of writers makes it difficult if not impossible to determine what part of the final version belongs to Hecht. The film is useful, though, in showing how the two men quite naturally worked well together. Hitchcock was a natural cynic whose cynicism was not rooted in fashion or professional necessity, as Hecht's had been at first, but was a response to a world full of (as he saw it) *potential* moral blackguards.

Potential is the key word, since Hitchcock was concerned with ordinary people — what pains he took to make them ordinary! — caught by turns of fate and psychological accidents. One is reminded of Saul Bellow's description of Hecht: " ... not much of a psychologist and even less of a moralist." That could also be a description of Hitchcock. Both men saw themselves as spinners of tales but betrayed their ulterior motives in proving that the world was populated by anonymous, emotionally fragile creatures. Hitchcock taught Hecht to be a cynic without even the conviction of his own cynicism. He showed him how to make his predetermined sorry view of the human race subordinate to the story, thus making the story, free of stylistic whimwham, all the more powerful and convincing. A part of that conviction was Hecht's introduction to the thriller form. The genre would work well for him except when he later applied it retroactively to some of his fiction.

Hecht's two best Hitchcock scripts − though not necessarily Hitchcock's best films − were *Spellbound* in 1945 and *Notorious* in 1946. The first is a thriller about psychology without being a psychological thriller. It is a murder mystery set mostly in a psychiatric clinic. A new chief of staff (Gregory Peck) arrives and with the help of one other staff member (Ingrid Bergman) realizes that he is an imposter. He has put himself in the place of a man he thinks he has murdered. The film includes a dream sequence choreographed by Salvadore Dali. James Agee suggested that the sequence was inspired by James Cruze's old silent film *Hollywood*, but it likely owed more to Hecht's opening, with screaming witches, in his own film *Crime Without Passion*.

Notorious has a tangled plot involving Bergman again. The daughter of a Nazi, she is now working as a spy among former Nazis in Rio de Janiero. She has to marry the man she despises in the line of duty, rather than Cary Grant, another American secret agent. The influence of Hecht on the characters is marked, as they are cynics with soft centres thinking themselves several rungs above the riffraff with whom they do business. They are, all of them, one big Erik Dorn in an explosive situation, so without time for the self-pity and self-distortion which always mucked up life for Dorn and the other Hecht creations like him. Their best qualities and their worst are implied, never stated − certainly not drawn out, dissected and argued over endlessly. The same might also be said of Hecht in his work for Hitchcock. Their association was a brief respite from Hecht's view of the dominant society and the hack work which continued to support his other writing.

The Five Lives of Ben Hecht

A Jew in Love, published in 1931, was to be Hecht's last novel for twenty-five years (except for the mystery *I Hate Actors!*) and the penultimate novel of his career. It is in many ways a reprehensible book and on most accounts a curious one. The title alone, putting aside the racially snide descriptions in the narrative, was enough to brand the author as anti-Semitic. The critic Leslie Fiedler has conjectured that the book sprang from a self-hatred Hecht felt as a Jew and outsider — a self-hatred he projected on Jews in general, of whom his hero, Jo Boshere, is a sad caricature. Another less psychoanalytical explanation presents itself when the book is viewed in terms of Hecht's career up to that time and his situation at that moment. *A Jew in Love* does not concern Hollywood. It was written before Hecht's involvement in film had reached a peak. Yet the book is clearly the product of the change of mind Hecht underwent in a Hollywood so far removed from his, not ethnic, but literary roots. It is a cynical book to no good purpose, redolent of the self-hatred he felt not as a Jew, but as a hostage of show business, as an outsider from Chicago and all that implied.

Boshere (who began as a character in a short story that grew out of control) is described in the opening sentence as "a dark-skinned little Jew with a vulturous and moody face, a reedy body and a sense of posture." The fact that he is a book publisher led to much comment that the novel was patterned after the career of Horace Liveright. Boshere is clearly much more an amalgam than most Hecht characters, however. There are distinct touches of Jed Harris, Hecht himself and even Bodenheim, though the book is not, like *Count Bruga*, a lampoon of any one mammal (even a composite one) but of modern man. Boshere is an insidious, conniving person who manages to juggle a wife, a mistress and a prostitute. The last is the one he believes himself to be in love with, though, as in Hechtian man, there is at the bottom of his involvement no real passion. Boshere's business life is just as tangled as his personal life. The story is a rogue's progress — sideways.

As Boshere is engaged in an imitation of life, as though to convince himself that his life will acquire meaning once it picks up speed, so Hecht is engaged in an imitation of his former style: an imitation that borders on parody at times. The book lacks precision, form and a sense of purpose. Hecht's clever coinage here comes through dint of revision rather than inspiration. His mots do not generally ring juste. The lack of direction in style and plot dovetail the lack of purpose in his character, resulting in a mood of dereliction on the part of both Hecht and Boshere. There is practically none of the compassion which, blended with cynicism, made the earlier fiction and some of the plays so recognizably Hechtian and so noteworthy. What is wrong with the novel, one could say, is that Boshere has no schizoid tendencies and neither does the book; they both run about in ever widening circles in a kind of confusion excruciatingly free of conflict.

A Jew in Love has an unusual publishing history. In his memoirs, Donald Friede, who had been a partner in the Liveright firm and then part owner of Covici-Friede, relates the problems. The book had grown in Hecht's and Pascal Covici's minds to the stature of a bestselling masterwork. The manuscript finally delivered fell far short of being Hecht's best work. The machinery of promotion, however, had already begun to turn, and the publishers dutifully lent their backs to a project that did not have their hearts. The result was an artistic failure and a great commercial success. A Jew in Love far outsold any of Hecht's other fiction. It is not unreasonable to assume that its popularity had a greatly detrimental effect on his literary reputation, which by 1933 was already so badly damaged that two literary historians, Irene and Allen Cleaton, stated that "it is doubtful if he will ever again produce much of literary dignity."

The spirit of the older Hecht was apparent, though, to the extent that he once again ran afoul of the censors. In fact, the first printing of A Jew in Love was recalled (except for the one hundred and fifty specially printed copies of the limited edition). The reason was a line on page three hundred and six in which Boshere says: "As far as I'm concerned God is a pain in the ass." In the replacement printing, the sentence stopped after the word "pain."

There can be little doubt that his Hollywood work brought about a disillusionment which supplanted the artificial disillusionment exhibited in his early work, and so changed the nature of his writing, or at least his fiction. It is perhaps stating too much, however, to say that the nature of the film script as a form had a pronounced effect on his other work. Still, in his fiction of the 1930s and 1940s, Hecht's style changed in a way that suggests a bit of influence from scenario writing. For instance, Hecht's fiction was now made up of much more dialogue than before, with the narrative elements more on the order of Shavian stage directions and production notes. It was as though the characters had to prove their worth visually, as in film. The fact that he was still bound to the printed page, however, meant that the dialogue was more emphatic, more doggedly like natural speech — in any event the speech of the real Ben Hecht. At least that is true of *A Jew in Love*.

In the stories from the 1930s and 1940s one also detects a trend toward, then a backing away from such cinematic devices as the dissolve and jump-cut. But what really marks the shorter fiction of the Sophisticate is Hecht's asphixiation for want of involvement in his work and the conviction and grace that had once been the result of such involvement. Nowhere is that more obvious than in the *Collected Stories*, published in 1943, and in *A Treasury of Ben Hecht*, a slightly padded version of the same book published in 1959. In these books Hecht not only enshrined as "collected" the stories from the 1930s and 1940s, the good with the bad, he also destroyed the texture and verve of the earlier ones from the 1920s and before.

The best example of such butchering is the story "Broken Necks," written in 1915. In the *Little Review* and later in the two versions of the collection bearing that title, the piece began like this:

> I stood on the corner that day adjusting certain important adjectives in my life. I had seen two men hanged and it was Spring. How the wind ran through the little greedy half-dead swarming in the streets. Yes, those endless, bobbing faces almost looked at each other, almost smiled into each other's eyes — insufferable and inhuman breach of democracy. But there was something immoral about the day. The music of dreams tugged at the endless shuffling feet. The music of desires — little starved and fearful things come out for a moment in the sun and wind — piped vainly for dancers. There was something vague and bewildered about the buildings and the people as if there was a great undying shout in the streets. What a panic this monotonous return of Spring breeds among the little half-dead as they shuffle and bob along with a tingle in their heels and a blindness comes suddenly into their eyes. For it is through the mists of greedy complacencies that the little half-dead are able to

pick their steps with certainty and precision. Now comes this wine and this music and this disturbance as of a great undying shout sweeping the bristling shafts of stone, and the mists vanish for a moment. In the blindness which falls upon them is an undertow tugging at their feet.

I stood on the corner that day observing how in the spring the bodies of women were like the bodies of long, lithe animals prowling under orange and lavender, green and turquoise dresses and how the men with their coats dangling across their arms were like hot beetles that had removed their shells. But as I watched the endless faces filled with half-startled and half-placid confusion, and as I noted what the poets call the gayety of spring in the hearts of men, there came to me out of the swarm and roar of the day the mockery which it is the duty of philosophers to hear. For I had seen two men hanged and had most properly come away a philosopher.

It was pure Hecht at his best, with all the characteristic elements and attitudes: the juxtaposition of the hanging and springtime, the emotional involvement with the state of professed emotionlessness, the sense of himself as detached philosopher and critic. But as revised for *A Treasury of Ben Hecht*, the same story omitted such (to him then, youthful) excess and began with a prosaic description of the room where the men had been hanged. The lovely smell of art had become malodourous to aging nostrils.

It was as though the editing was the last expression of Hecht's desire in the 1940s to disavow a past which had deserted him in Hollywood as the source of any but the most mechanical inspiration and manifested itself, psychically at least, in *A Jew in Love* and other smaller travesties. The *Treasury*, however, was the final belated gasp of emotional rootlessness.

Beginning in the late 1930s, slowly at first, Hecht changed again. His concern, unlikely on the face of it, with the plight of European Jewry turned him into a Propagandist. It was a life he was proud of living all the while he was doing other work and one he would, to some extent, continue living from that point on. The Jewish cause alarmed him and, at last, gave him a forum into which he could throw himself totally. It gave him something to believe in besides cynicism. It stirred him to incredible heights of passion which spilled back into his writing both social and general. Hechtian man was killed off and replaced by a different fellow as full of passion, anger, angst and commitment as the early Hecht, alias Dorn, Sterns et al, had been empty.

8
Where is Zion Now?

*I have always held to the line that the wisest thing
a writer can do is be himself and trust to God that
the people he offends are those he doesn't like.*
BH, *in* A Guide for the Bedevilled

Hollywood certainly changed the style and thrust of Hecht's writing, though it is doubtful whether the experience also altered the nature and essence of it. What finally did bring about such a change was World War Two. The battles taking place in Europe, even before America joined in them, aroused his patriotism or possibly created it in the first place. The common-place patriotism grew into a kind of racial allegiance, much stronger than the merely national kind, and eventually embroiled Hecht in politics. It was a remarkable change to come over a man who had insisted he had no politics and who believed that people who did have were fools, charlatans or worse. Also remarkable is the fact that the rise of Hecht the Propagandist, unlike the rise of his earlier incarnations, took place very quickly.

When Ralph Ingersoll was assembling the all-star staff of his New York daily newspaper *PM* (so titled despite the fact it was a morning paper), he approached Hecht for contributions. Ingersoll recalls that Hecht was fed up with film work at the time and "wanted to be an honest man again." The result was a daily column which, taking advantage of Hecht's lingering Chicago reputation, was headed "1001 Afternoons in New York." During the next

123

The Five Lives of Ben Hecht

two years Hecht, whose copy was sacrosanct in terms of the copydesk, often threatened to quit and devote himself to other pursuits. But he dutifully resisted the temptation to leave until after the country (and his friendly publisher) had gone off to war. He had deeply felt reasons for remaining.

The column was a curious blend of Hecht's new interest in human politics and the old concerns from his days on the Chicago *Daily News*. There was only a watered-down version of the inverted lyricism so pronounced in his earlier writing, though at times Hecht tried writing the sort of copy that had made his early reputation. Although he had lived in New York off and on for twenty years, Hecht never came to know its dark corners as he had those of Chicago. When he tried to determine why an apparently penniless bum died leaving $26,000, or whose cadaver it was that now lay unclaimed in the morgue, it was with his old mixture of compassion and cynicism but without his former intensity and style. In fact, the best of the non-political columns were ones harkening back to his young days and the people he had known then, for Hecht was already beginning to feel the pull of nostalgia.

He wrote good columns about friends such as Gene Fowler and Harpo Marx and a pitying one about Bodenheim, whom he encountered on the street after many years, looking like the rummy he now was. Perhaps his best column related a meeting with another old friend-enemy, Sherwood Anderson, whom he also had not seen for years. Anderson would die a few days after the column appeared aboard a ship carrying him to self-imposed exile in South America. These pieces, however, were not what made the column a popular and controversial feature of the scrappy liberal newspaper. The pieces which gave it its reputation were those written by Hecht the Propagandist, an angry, extremist and surprisingly violent figure.

PM commenced publication in 1939, preceding by a couple years the birth of Hecht the Propagandist. It was not until 1941 that representatives of the Irgun Zwei Leumi, the Palestine guerrilla organization, seeing his columns about Jewish problems, approached Hecht for support. In 1939 war had broken out in Europe, with Hitler's troops invading Poland the first day of September. As the conflict spread, many Jews fled to Palestine, which had been under British control and protection since 1917. They were refused entry. That left Hecht and others in a peculiar situation that was less ambivalent than ambidextrous.

With one hand, the one that was Jewish alone, he sided with the Irgun against the British occupiers of Palestine. With the other, the one that was American and only subordinately Jewish, he was defending the British against the Germans. Beneath the tangle, of course, lay but one enemy: the Nazis. Hecht was confronting the unresolved questions which afflict American Jewish writers – the questions of assimilation versus ethnic commitment. The situation was further complicated by the inevitable when, in 1941, the US entered the war as Britain's ally.

Nowhere were Hecht's contradictions and personal confusion more obvious than in *1001 Afternoons in New York*, the collection of *PM* writings. The book was published two months before Pearl Harbor and was illustrated, in an irony apparently lost to Hecht, by his old German friend George Grosz. It is full of the sort of skillful polemic Hecht was coming to master but which would only achieve full flowering much later, in *A Guide for the Bedevilled*. It was also full of fiery opinions on the world political scene and marked by conflicting attitudes. Those attitudes bespeak the mixture of puzzlement and anger which had now replaced the Broadway sneer as the usual expression on Hecht's public face.

Hecht's new sense of his own Jewishness, his sense of belonging to a world brotherhood suddenly threatened with devastation, manifested itself, not in the study of Jewish history and thought, but in the purblind zeal of the convert. One column was a laudatory and maudlin appreciation of Sholem Aleichem, the writer of Yiddish folk stories. Such a piece would have been unthinkable for the editor of the *Chicago Literary Times*, on esthetic as well as ethnic grounds. Another, more typical column bemoaned the "racial amnesia" of "my Semite brothers" – a disease of which he himself had for so long been the principal carrier, until cured by the holocaust. A third column attacked Joseph Kennedy, until recently the US Ambassador to the Court of St. James, for suggesting that Jews in Hollywood lie low and not use movies as a weapon against anti-Semitism. The language grew stronger as the columns went on. It also became more compassionate as Britain underwent German bombardment and American involvement in the war loomed nearer.

The Five Lives of Ben Hecht

He pulled out every literary trick he knew in defense of world Jewry and against the psychological origins of the Nazis – the two subjects were interchangeable to him at that point and the European war just as simple. When it was necessary to make his point a different way, he would use his allotted space for a parable or a mood essay as easily as for a straight argument or a panegyric. At one point he resorted to verse (never a Hecht strong point) to attack the isolationist opinions of Charles Lindbergh. Recalling that he had seen Lindbergh depart in 1927 on the first solo flight across the Atlantic, Hecht contrasted the one-time Lone Eagle with the present day "crackpot" crypto-Nazi he now considered "nutty as a fruitcake."

The basic literary and political philosophy of Hecht the Propagandist was to meet indifference with outrage, to retaliate with full force when attacked and, when in doubt, to attack anyway for good measure. The technique served him well at first, until Jewish problems became more complex. In the last analysis Hecht did much to split the Jewish people at a time when they most needed to be unified, though that fact must be weighed against the good he did in bringing some issues to public attention. While during these years he remained scrupulously quiet about Mencken – Mencken who believed patriotism a destructive force except in wartime and who sided with the Germans in World War One – he was still a disciple of Mencken's method. Hecht still believed that the first duty of a writer in matters of public concern lay in "stirring up the animals." He did his best, for there was more at stake than merely the continued acceptance of Babbittism and the booboisie.

Hecht's war effort – if it is possible to distinguish it from his work on behalf of Jews, which the war aroused – was in full swing before the United States was mobilized. It included several pro-war plays he termed pageants. One of them, written with MacArthur, carried the unfortunate title *Fun to Be Free*. It and one other were staged by the showman Billy Rose at Madison Square Garden. Once the country did go to war, Hecht began working on something more official. He became involved in Red Cross and war bond work in Washington, all the while writing for Hollywood and doing his own work besides. The latter, while not overty propagandistic, included the little book *A Miracle in the Rain*, which was certainly designed to boost national morale. After the war he wrote a film about the United Nations for the state department. In the public mind, however, such activity was secondary to his wartime proselytizing on behalf of Jews. The most notable result was *A Guide for the Bedevilled*, his flamboyant indictment of anti-Semitism, published in 1944. The title was derived from *A Guide for the Perplexed* by Maimonides, the twelfth-century Jewish scholar.

The work is memorable for its extreme zest rather than its reasoned approach. Hecht seemed to announce as much early on when he wrote: "I have a mission to write about Jews. I have a mission, also, to write about anti-Semitism. And this, too, elates me more than any task to which I ever have set myself." The book is nothing less than Hecht's own story of being a Jew in America. It is remarkable in light of his previous writing, and revealing in light of what came afterward, in being the first sustained effort at autobiography, albeit the autobiography of a circumstance and his reaction to it, rather than a life's story. The main topic, however, is anti-Semitism. The way Hecht viewed it, historically as well as emotionally and logically, was what caused a fuss and foretold his later attacks and counterattacks in the late 1940s and up until the time of his death.

Simply stated, Hecht's premise was that too many people considered anti-Semitism (and wrote books on the subject) as though it were something for which the Jews themselves were somehow responsible. They treated the subject as though it were a social attitude or a point of view. Hecht, in his nimblest, most adjectival style, replied that this was nonsense. Anti-Semitism, he stated, was in its present form murder pure and simple, as witnessed by the three million dead in Europe. (That figure was the accepted number of pogrom victims during the first years of the war; only on later evidence was it doubled.)

Anti-Semitism was not a matter fit for mulling over but only for the most severe retaliation. He considered those who insisted upon looking, however sympathetically, to the victims as the instigators of the crime rather than to the perpetrators as, at best, subconscious anti-Semites. That group, he felt, included about half of the commentators in the us who were purporting to be anti-Nazi. Foreseeing the dismissals that would meet such a charge, he

The Five Lives of Ben Hecht

thought several moves ahead and stated: "The villain who halts our pens is also called by the name Good Taste. Virtue is to an ugly woman what good taste is to a stupid man – a false riches. Writers who are too timorous, too vacuous, too thin-hearted, to set to paper anything but the dullest of matters ... are obviously not people to tackle the Germans."

Tackle the Germans was what he did, for despite the attacks on him from some sectors of his own country, it was only later, in response to the Palestine crisis, that Hecht fought mainly an intramural war. He saw the Nazis as people who, in their bestiality and ruthlessness, were but the inheritors of a less violent anti-Semitism which stretched back in a clear trail to ancient Phoenicia. He traced that trail for some distance but did not take what could be called an historical perspective. While he sought at times to explain the Germans as natural anti-Semites, he spoke little of the Nazis as an ideological group, or of Hitler specifically, except at one point to call him a homosexual. He could not have felt more strongly that, in the face of such staggering annihilation, the best defense was not argument or debate but a vigorous offense. To that end he used every stylistic weapon in the arsenal he had built up during his thirty-five years as a writer.

Hecht's position was similar to that of many other Jewish writers who till then had either no politics or only enough to disdain the whole process. Bodenheim, for instance, had always shared Hecht's disinterest in such matters. He believed that poetry had no politics just as strongly as Hecht believed that journalism had none. Indeed, Bodenheim had gone through much the same racial amnesia as Hecht, and both had ridiculed Jewishness in others while seeking to disguise their own. *Duke Herring* was as anti-Semitic in its caricature of Hecht as *Count Bruga* had been in its depiction of Bodenheim. Now, with the war on, Bodenheim became patriotic, conservative and Zionistic. He frequently made his views known as loudly as possible in the pages of the New York *Daily News.*

The same sort of political inexperience was painfully obvious in Hecht. He had taken little or no part in Hollywood politics in the 1930s, when radicalism worked up to a crescendo during the Spanish Civil War. Instead he had prided himself on his view of politics as a trap for innocents and con men who, once caught, became objects of his satire. Now the tables had turned – just as in the 1950s they would for those in Hollywood whose old leftwing connections would cause many to be blacklisted and even jailed. Hecht who had shunned all politics had to make do without the knowledge and keen-sightedness such experience would have given him. While Hecht's political philosophy (or anti-philosophy) was being turned upside down, some of his basic artistic ideas were undergoing the same disruption.

A Guide for the Bedevilled sees the Nazis as murderers because they believed in their own superiority as a people; because they took to heart the spirit of Nietzsche, which extolls the power of the will and the individual, rather than the letter of Nietzsche, which ridicules the Germans as venal lugs. This is revealing and important. Hecht was now setting himself up, as Erik Dorn and his other creations had done, as an intellect against the unintellectual mob. In this case the mob was composed of Nazis rather than faceless Chicagoans, "the greedy little half-dead" of the early stories and novels. Hecht apparently saw no contradiction in any of this. Nor did he seem aware that he was fighting fire with the exact same kind of fire. All the while he was (in the critic Harold Rosenberg's phrase) getting "satisfaction out of beating the German *Golem* with a Nietzschean bladder and kicking man in the shins for being what he is," he was also labelling Nietzsche as another of the sub rosa anti-Semites:

> He stood in their [the Germans'] midst and cursed brilliantly, lyrically....He found a certain cheer in this for he fancied that some day the Germans would read him, blush with shame, and mend their ways. It is the weakness of all philosophers that they dream of making the world more honest. They succeed usually in providing the Devil with more Scripture to quote.

> I write of Nietzsche because he is more than a philosopher. He is a German phenomenon. A nation is revealed to him. He is German in the same way that Shelley and Swinburne are English. Like these and other English poets who gave expression to something that did not exist in the English – to wit, poetry – Nietzsche was the voice of a nonexistent thing among the Germans – egoism and awareness.

The Five Lives of Ben Hecht

There were lesser contradictions in the book but also less solid reasoning. Hecht lashed out at Voltaire and Hilaire Belloc as great literary anti-Semites. However, in presenting a mock film treatment and outline as part of his attack on the process of stupidity, he dedicated it to Céline, apparently unaware that Céline had become a more vicious anti-Semite than Voltaire and Belloc combined had ever been. All the while he decried centuries of incipient anti-Semitism that made way for the German bullets and lime pits, he also lamented the passing of the Jewish caricature in the media, especially radio and film. The arts, he thought, humanized their subjects (at least when they showed them as kindly, innocent and folksy) ; he did not believe that the arts can also dehumanize and, by their condescension, make violence all the more justified in the minds of murderers-to-come.

Logic, however, accounted for only a small portion of *A Guide for the Bedevilled*. Mainly a book for coming out as hostilely as possible against the Nazi killers, it was, in a sense, part of Hecht's war service. Hecht, being a writer and not a soldier, waxed his most damning. The book rivalled even the preface of *Fantazius Mallare* in its ruthlessness toward those who were, this time, undeniably real and despicable enemies. The book practically sizzles with anti-German epigrams, tirades and turns of phrase, as well as with some that are merely misanthropic. The book was so strong in its time that it was often misinterpreted. Hecht's motives were called into question by some of the moderates he damned as well as by the more recognizable anti-Semites. Maxwell Perkins, who edited the book and had a large reputation as the editor of Hemingway, Fitzgerald and Thomas Wolfe, felt it necessary to defend its publication. He explained that the firm of Scribner's felt a moral duty to publish it "to help the American principle of equality by which true Americans detest prejudice against minorities" and also "because it was a magnificent piece of fiery writing — which is also a consideration for publishers."

Britain was committed to the establishment of a free Jewish state in Palestine by reason of a declaration made in 1917. Hecht and his fellow Irgun supporters in the US (the group had several names but ended up as the American League for a Free Palestine) saw that commitment as hollow. Much of Hecht's work during the war was concerned with trying to get the British to allow an army of Jews from Palestine to fight with them against the Axis powers in North Africa. The goal was shared by the Jewish Agency, the umbrella group of Palestinean organizations. It was mainly through Jewish Agency effort that the proposal was accepted, and the Jewish Brigade fought not only in the desert campaign but later in Italy as well. Still, the British acceptance of the scheme came only after many delays which the Irgunists believed were caused by the British fear that such an army would turn against them once the war was over and foil a British plan to divide up Palestine amongst the various Arab and Jewish factions.

At that stage Hecht was interested mainly in helping win the war and making known the basic inequities of British rule – the fact, for instance, that the penalty for Palestinian Jews carrying arms in peacetime was death or life imprisonment while the penalty for the same act by an Arab was said to be a five shilling fine. Hecht was still ambivalent about the concept of an independent state. While he "would be glad to see a nation of Jews under a Jewish flag," he "could no more feel myself part of it than of any other country beyond the USA." He was, in that instance, treating himself as an American first and a Jew second – the same order of priorities for which he attacked other American Jews. Before the war was over, he would change his mind and also change the thrust of his propaganda work.

Just as first reports of the Jewish exterminations had made a Jew of him ("I had before then been only related to Jews"), so the failure to aid the Jews who remained alive turned Hecht into a militant who angered all factions. Early in the war he learned through Irgun sources that Roumania, facing imminent German invasion, had offered to transport fifty thousand Jewish citizens to safety in Palestine if some nation would pay $50-per-person travel costs. Hecht did much to publicize the offer but was hooted down by those who claimed the offer was fictitious, which it turned out not to have been.

Hecht became convinced that President Roosevelt was in league with British Prime Minister Churchill to keep those and other Jews out of Palestine lest such immigration undermine British authority there. He never forgave the British, nor did he forgive Roosevelt.

His outbursts against the latter only further angered the majority of American Zionists, who looked upon Roosevelt as a man with their problems at heart. Hecht was in the process of composing an anti-Roosevelt play when in 1945, shortly before the war's end, news arrived of the president's death. He put the project aside.

With the war won, the Jewish question focused on the establishment of a free state, an idea Hecht now had more sympathy with than previously. As the British mandate was set to expire in May 1948, Jews feared that at that moment the Arabs would take over the land by force of arms before a Jewish government could be established. Such a government would likely be made up of those involved in the Jewish Agency.

But the situation was more complex. The Zionists maintained an "official guerrilla army called the Haganah whose policy was to bring more Jewish immigrants into Palestine, illegally if necessary, and to prepare for the day of Britain's withdrawal. These people stood in opposition to Hecht's group, the Irgun which, while it also was involved in immigration, favoured driving the British out and establishing the new country before their enemies could get a foothold. To that end, they engaged in terrorist tactics against civilians as well as the British military. The Zionists looked upon the Irgun as troublemakers (just as the US Zionists looked upon Hecht) and repeatedly betrayed Irgunists to the British. Some of those thus captured were hanged.

Hecht's support for the Irgun was based in the belief that they were the sole organization whose first obligation was to Jews as a group, rather than to the notion of a state for state's sake. He saw them as the only ones who at least would have tried to save European Jews in the war if it had been possible to do so; he ignored the rescue of Jewish children from Nazi-occupied territory which had been carried out by the Jewish Agency and the Allies. He thought the Irgun the only ones who stood foursquare against the British, who were the enemy by reason of blocking immigration now and during the war, but also because they were secret confederates of the Arabs, some of whom had been pro-German. The Irgun cause needed both supporters and money. Hecht, as their principal US spokesman, sought to get it for them. He did so by soliciting from the Jews of Hollywood and from gangsters such as Mickey Cohen. He also sought to make money for the cause by his pen.

Where is Zion Now?

In 1946, Hecht wrote a play entitled *A Flag Is Born*. It was a long one-acter opening on a cemetery of European Jews massacred in the war and creating, through a range of symbolic characters, a panorama of Jewish history. It was held together with long speeches by a narrator. Hecht had used the same technique in some of his wartime pageants and he was fond of it as a theatrical device. The play ended with a young Jew making a flag from a prayer shawl and joining the anti-British underground. Hecht knew his audience and was putting aside for the moment all the accumulated cynicism of the ages and much of the hyperbole. He struck at people's emotions rather than their wits as he had often seen others do in Hollywood to much less important ends.

Although the American League for a Free Palestine was listed as producers of the play, it was clearly a Hecht enterprise from first to last. He assembled a remarkable array of theatrical talent including Luther Adler to direct and Kurt Weill, Brecht's old collaborator, to compose the music. Rehearsals took place over a restaurant. It was agreed that none of the cast would work for more than union scale. The principals were Paul Muni and Celia Adler, with Quentin Reynolds as the narrator. The role of David, the young man who turns guerrilla, was played by Marlon Brando, then twenty-two, for $48 per week. It was one of his earliest acting jobs and was in some measure responsible for his continued rise to stardom — a fact Brando would remember years later when Hecht did a rewrite for his film *Mutiny on the Bounty*.

The play was careful not to frighten away patrons from its basic message with a too strident tone. The mood was one of nostalgia and hope rather than hatred. It ended with an address to the diplomats of the world. It shows that Hecht was most effective when he was most general and used his dramatic and literary skills to the lessening of angry polemic. It was important also in that it is said to have raised a million dollars for the league, more than a quarter of which went to purchase a small second-hand cruise ship which was rechristened the SS *Ben Hecht*. It was the only Irgunist ship to reach Palestine full of immigrants (compared with about thirty Zionist vessels) but was captured by the British, who transferred the passengers to a detention camp in Cyprus.

A Flag Is Born was a common rallying point for many of the factions in the Jewish struggle. It was not, however, an end to the sectarian name-calling. For Hecht, in fact, the calumny was just beginning. In May 1947, a full-page advertisement, written and signed by Hecht and addressed to the Irgun, appeared in the New York *Herald Tribune* and fifteen other major newspapers. It was later widely reprinted abroad. The ad congratulated the terrorists on blowing up British trains, killing British tommies and robbing British banks. It also abused the Zionists, American and otherwise, for being weak-kneed in their support. While the advertisement did bring in money for the league from many quarters, it led, for Hecht personally, to a disaster that would nearly ruin his career. Ironically, that advertisement, one of many he turned out in his nine years' work for the Irgun and, to him, just another piece of copy in a writer's life, had more effect on his career than anything else he would ever write.

The British papers, which until then seemed scarcely to have heard of Ben Hecht, launched an all-out counterattack. Lord Beaverbrook's press referred to him as, among other things, "a Nazi at heart." Many papers, in addition to filling their correspondence columns with anti-Hecht blasts, assigned reporters to special feature-length attacks on him. In the United States, the press was equally hostile, with *Time* magazine, run by Hecht's old Chicago legman Henry Luce, leading the way, especially after the Irgun mailed unsuccessful letter-bombs to Anthony Eden and other prominent Britons.

There was nearly unanimous agreement that this time Hecht had gone too far. The Zionists only grew angrier, and many of Hecht's friends dropped away. Not only Jews but leading liberal gentiles such as Dorothy Thompson washed their hands of him. Even Edward G. Robinson, who had worked with Hecht on many committees, and had given of his acting ability in the Palestinian cause, "never acknowledged him again" after the advertisements appeared. The tension was not lessened when Hecht, in a back-handed apology, took out additional space to call the British "the nicest enemies the Jews ever had."

The Irgun were among the fathers of modern guerrilla warfare, and they had their effect on the British. Unlike the French, who would later fight full-scale wars before giving up Viet Nam and Algeria, the British were frustrated by terror tactics. They had been so historically and would be so later in Kenya. It was with some

Where is Zion Now?

relief that on May 15, 1948 they relinquished their mandate in Palestine. Hours earlier the new State of Israel had been formed with Chaim Weizmann as the first president. At once the combined armies of Egypt, Jordan, Syria, Iraq and Lebanon, with some support from Saudi Arabia, invaded the new nation but were repulsed. Thus began not only the new state but also the Israeli-Arab strife which continues to the present time. Hecht saw the dream of the Jewish state materialize, but it was not the one he would have wished, governed by the persons he would have liked.

Although the British were out of Palestine, Hecht was not far from their minds. The Cinematograph Exhibitor's Association, representing some five thousand theatre owners in the UK, passed a resolution refusing to circulate any film with which Hecht had been involved. The repercussions were felt in Hollywood, and Hecht's screenwriting income dried up, except for the smaller fees he earned writing four or five films without credit.

For a time it appeared the controversy would die down and the blacklisting simply forgotten. Some months later, however, in September 1948, the Stern Gang, another Jewish guerrilla group, admitted murdering a Swedish peacemaker, Count Bernadotte. Hecht denied they were responsible, saying: "The assassination ... was that of an ass who wasn't worthy of so fine a death. He wasn't sharp enough to be a villain. He was a professional cat's paw, hired to pull chestnuts out of the fire for the British. Jewish terrorists didn't kill this tool of the British."

In November 1950 the cinema owners met to reconsider the ban on Hecht. They voted overwhelmingly to restrict three new films he had written or contributed to, though in the end the stricture served only to delay the movies' release, not preclude it. Still, the vote meant continued unemployment for Hecht, who contented himself with writing mostly for American magazines and working on books. In 1952 the ban was lifted, but as late as 1956, Hollywood withheld credit from Hecht on the script of *The Iron Petticoat* rather than jeopardize the British market. Slowly the excitement died away, however, and Hecht the Propagandist gave the deceptive appearance of lying low.

Hecht the Propagandist thought of himself as a patriot – to the

135

The Five Lives of Ben Hecht

United States, to Jews in general and to the struggle for a Jewish nation. But he also believed that patriots must be judged by how widely and virulently they are hated rather than by how well they are loved. That Hecht, the public backbone of the Irgun in America, did help to transform a divided and occupied Palestine into a unified and free Israel is seldom doubted. Whether that good is outweighed by the harm he did in stirring up anti-Semitism and generally pitting Jew against Jew remains a controversial question. The only certainty is that the most remarkable revolution was the one which took place inside Hecht himself.

Memoirs describing Hecht in his fifties and sixties paint a very different likeness from those autobiographies and recollections published earlier. They reveal a man now acutely conscious of his own Jewishness and very proud of it, even in conversation with non-Jews on totally non-Jewish matters. In the last decade of his life such feelings were particularly intense. If he seemed to be more at peace with his roots than previously, however, he was not necessarily at peace with the world. He continued to act as a propagandist for causes and ideas in which he believed. A Mencken man to the last, he maintained his belief that the best way to propagate one's views was to stir up all the abuse possible. He held to the view that a battle of personalities was more interesting to the public (and so more useful as publicity) than a battle confined to abstract ideas.

In the mid-1950s, for instance, Hecht became interested in the cause of the Greeks on Cyprus, at that time still a British crown colony. The Greek population, representing about seventy per cent of the island, was agitating anew for union with Greece, a move opposed by the Turkish residents. The violence that erupted was largely the doing of a Greek underground organization, the EOKA. The British tried to quell the disturbances by, among other things, exiling Archbishop Makarios III, the political leader of the pro-union faction and head of the island's Greek Orthodox Church. Hecht was a supporter of both the EOKA and the church, siding not so much against the Turks as, once again, against the British.

He resorted to his old tactic by writing that for every British soldier killed on the island he built a little shrine in his heart. When roundly abused for this, he merely repeated the metaphor. But the Cypriot issue was of small import to Hecht compared with his feelings about the leaders who had run Israel since its founding. He excoriated those people in his last propagandistic work, *Perfidy*, published in 1961.

Perfidy was an attack on "the ruling clique" of Israel — the Zionists generally involved in the Jewish Agency who were natural ascenders to the throne once the throne came into being. These included the late Chaim Weizmann, the first president; David Ben-Gurion, the prime minister at the time; and Moshe Sharett, head of the Jewish Agency toward the end of World War Two and acting prime minister in Ben-Gurion's absence. The foundation on which Hecht built his attack was the Greenwald-Kastner case of 1953-1954. Until the trial of the Nazi war criminal Adolf Eichmann in 1961, that case was the main internal political incident of the new nation.

Malchiel Greenwald was a journalist who accused a government official, Rudolph Kastner, of having collaborated with the Nazis. Kastner sued for libel and, in a trial of public opinion, lost the case on the grounds that the allegation was substantially true. He was later assassinated. Hecht used the precedent to assail in particular Moshe Sharett, dragging up an earlier matter involving Eichmann. During the war, Eichmann had suggested trading the lives of some of the Jews under his control for Allied trucks and coffee. The offer had been relayed to Sharett by a Jewish idealist named Joel Brand, who was convinced the proposal was legitimate and Eichmann would fulfil his end of the bargain. Sharett was less certain and the trade was never carried out. Hecht denounced Sharett as the indirect murderer of the Jews in question. He saw that episode as but one indication of what he considered the moral corruption of Israeli leaders. In fact, he accused not only them and the Jewish Agency but the Jewish community in Palestine and non-European Jews in general of complicity by reason of inactivity.

As might be expected, Hecht depicted the Germans as resting for a couple of generations before their next relapse into genocide and the British as polite but basically insidious. Those accusations alone, however, would not have aroused any wrath except in Britain. It was his attacks on the Israelis which rankled. He described Weizmann as one who "had migrated to London and become, magically, an Englishman" and Ben-Gurion as a man with a "flair for obedience to anyone resembling an Anglo-Saxon." He ripped into them and others for having done little or nothing to prevent the wartime massacres.

It was characteristic of Hecht the Propagandist that he used whatever forum was available. For instance, in his original anti-German crusades he wrote propaganda pieces for any audience that would have them. He wrote not only for the *American Mercury* long after Mencken's departure, when it was relegated to an unimportant place among magazines, but for the *Reader's Digest* as well. Also, it was only as a propagandist that Hecht worked in all the media he knew: radio, film, magazines, newspapers, the stage and books. *Perfidy* was his final expression as a propagandist in the last field. Considered purely as polemical writing, without regard for the correctness or incorrectness of its message, it suffers from being a compound of too many contradictory approaches.

The newspaper ads announcing *Perfidy* (one of them written by Harry Golden) emphasized the "documentation" of the charges. The documentation ran to seventeen pages of source notes at the back, but the argument was not much supported by them. Besides, their presence only muddled the polemic, for Hecht was not a source-note kind of writer. He was rather, here as in *A Guide for the Bedevilled*, one whose power lay almost entirely in his bombastic style.

Perfidy was much the same type of book as *Bedevilled*. In the earlier book Hecht wrote of his life as Jew; here he gave his autobiography as a vicarious bomb-thrower. When his targets were well known public figures, beloved from television and the media if not from personal contact, he lost, by his typical flamboyant stance, what before he had gained. These people were not nameless German fanatics taken from editorial cartoons. Hecht's descriptions tended to distort more than to personify. At least that was the consistent complaint of the book's many critics.

Most Zionists and Israelis hated the book. A typical review from that quarter, published in the US Zionist journal *Midstream*, called *Perfidy* "an evil book, in every sense of the word" and "a McCarthyite book." The author himself was referred to as a "huckster." Hecht, it was charged, "waves at the reader half-truths, outright falsehoods, misrepresentations, quotations out of context, surmises and innuendos, name calling, flights of fancy dressed up to sound like fact and huge glaring omissions of crucial facts and events which can only be ascribed to abysmal ignorance or to equally abysmal disregard of truth." In short, *Perfidy* was "a crime against truth and human intelligence," committed by a man with "undoubted talent for writing scenarios for grade D movies."

Even the more beneficent critics took him to task. James S. MacDonald, whose opinions bore less bias and so carried more authority for the public at large, wrote in the *Herald Tribune*: "As League of Nations High Commissioner, member of the Anglo-American Committee of Inquiry on Palestine and the first United States Ambassador to Israel, I had close personal association with these men, and I cannot recognize the picture Mr. Hecht has painted of them."

Such notoriety ended Hecht the Propagandist's life on a high note that would echo long after the death of Hecht the man three years later. He stirred up a great deal of animosity against himself as well as arousing public debate, and the former would linger when the latter had faded away. In present day Britain there are still those who recoil at his name. Among Jews both inside and without Israel, this part of his career remains an issue – if no longer a hotly debated one, then one attached to his broader reputation as a famous Jewish-American writer.

When the factional squabbling died down, when it was supplanted by more important issues and events affecting the Jewish people – when, in short, one takes the long view – there is no question at least on what side Hecht stood. Time has tended to have a coalescent effect on the good guys as well as the bad. In 1975, when Jordan for the first time made public the titles of books and films it bans for political reasons, the complete works of Ben Hecht were near the head of the list.

9
Shelley in Chains

But among all my fantasies is none of writing and directing a movie that becomes the most famous movie of the week – or even the month. I know why this fantasy is missing. It is because my mind balks at the partner in this day dream – the Audience. I have never fancied the pleasures that come from its applause and approval.
BH, *in* A Guide for the Bedevilled

In a quotation widely circulated in the 1950s, Hecht said of his career as a film-writer, "I have to know my stuff, not admire it." As it refers to his movie hack-work – and Hecht probably undertook more of it than any of his contemporaries – the statement was accurate enough. In another sense, however, it was merely a pose. Hecht was one of the few screenwriters of his time to gain some control over his material and one of an even smaller handful eventually to direct his own films. His attitude toward the movies was at all times subject to complete reversal. Even within his long anti-Hollywood periods he was not consistently damning.

With those projects he treated primarily as literary undertakings (generally, the comedies and expressionist-style dramas done in collaboration with some like-minded friend) Hecht was dedicated to the script as an end in itself. The joy of writing is reflected in such works. He became bitter only when the pages had left his hands and entered the sausage mill. Similarly, in those films he also directed (again, in collaboration) or adapted from his own fiction, he took considerable pride, sometimes even admiring them as para-literary works in cinematic form. Sometimes, indeed, the ratio of admiration to worth was entirely wrongheaded. It was only when he was acting as a craftsman that he assumed the cynical stance toward films for which he was so well known. It is as a screenwriter that all his contradictions came out and his various lives were most intertwined. He was by turns the Bohemian, the Iconoclast and the Sophisticate, as of old, and often the three together. Commentators have tended to make his screenwriting all of a piece, which it was not; yet even the breaking down and labelling of lives and parts does not set the record straight. Hecht served many functions in Hollywood, ranging from the noble to the menial. Even the menial ones contributed to the whole.

While Hecht's was one of the strongest voices in condemning Hollywood as venal, phony and slave-driving, he was careful to avoid the trap those truths generally spelt for other writers. He was a whiner but no shirker, and he early on acquired a justifiable and enviable reputation as a quick and workmanlike writer. It stood him in good stead with the system he derided but profited by. To some producers and directors he was regarded for more than thirty years as a deft hand with dialogue. With others he was mainly a plot-saver. One of his publicly less heralded renowns was a writer of opening narrative titles — the rolling paragraphs which at the beginning of films, historical pictures particularly, set the scene. An example is his opening for *Trilby*, a script he wrote with MacArthur for Jesse Lasky Jr:

> On an evening in 1934 – when an Era was ending – when the world still wore the smile of yesterday – on an evening before the First World War began, two pleasant old fuddy-duddies stepped out of the only atrocity known in that day – a Paris taxi-cab.

Collectively, such flourishes were known as the Hecht touch. The Hecht touch was a readily marketable commodity, especially when combined with the assurance Hecht's name brought that such a project would indeed be finished on deadline, without argument, anguish or nervous breakdown on either side.

Hecht's private practice as a screenwriter (he seldom signed himself to one studio) included everything from original stories and original scripts to such respected-in-their-day adaptations as *Wuthering Heights*, done with MacArthur. He also did a great deal of doctoring and saving of other people's scripts. David Selznick used him extensively in such capacity. The work he did on Selznick's *Gone With the Wind* is the most storied example. Hecht heavily rewrote, in three days, the accumulated material produced by a phalanx of earlier writers; and he did so without ever having read the novel.

The reputation that made it necessary to call him in on such jobs was distinct from, but sometimes supported by, the one he had among the film public, even though for the first kind of work he seldom received formal credit. At length his benchmark became so much in demand that he created a factory of anonymous younger writers to block out and draft scripts which he then revised and signed. The members of this assembly line, who were called into action only when needed for a specific job, did not necessarily know one another's identity, a fact that distinguished them from the gallery of disciples and apprentices employed by artists as far back as Michelangelo's time and revived for iconoclastic effect by Andy Warhol in the 1960s. Toward the end of his career, long after his important screenwriting was done, Hecht's credit still retained, to lesser producers at least, a patina of success that appeared to them as golden. The promise of his name even became an advantage in helping finance an independent production. At least once, in a 1958 schlocker entitled *Queen of Outer Space*, he was given a credit by contract when he had in fact contributed nothing to the film.

Perhaps all this shows is that he was, despite his protestations to the contrary, a good businessman, but then that was something he had learned to be even in the beginning of his association with film. As clever as he was, though, he was not always sumptuary, at least in public. In *A Guide for the Bedevilled* he summarized his view of screenwriting thus: "Money seemed more like applause than part of an Economic System." Indeed, that view does appear to jibe with his work methods. What is more important is that he became a good recycler of his own literary work, like many other novelists of the time. Possibly it was the fact that he was cramming his fiction writing between tenures in Hollywood that made him so much a literary environmentalist; or perhaps it was that the great success of the Milestone *Front Page* made him aware of windfalls.

It is difficult at times to tell when Hecht was writing a non-cinematic work with ultimate film sale in mind and when he was using the possibility of a film version to turn a failed project to good account. It would seem at first he gave no thought to capital gains from his fiction and plays. Even before turning against his early work, he apparently made no attempt at marketing *Erik Dorn*, which he clearly recognized as his best book, momentary enthusiasms and fickle parental pride notwithstanding. It is equally true, however, that he did not stand in the way of such sales, as when in 1935 his 1923 mystery novel *The Florentine Dagger* was bought and produced for the screen. He must have realized early that he could make money and save face by converting, or allowing to be converted, works which had failed in some other form.

When they were both pleading poverty in 1933, Hecht and Gene Fowler collaborated on a play entitled *The Great Magoo* ("magoo," according to Hecht, being a slang word for "female sexpot"). It was a ribald but overblown farce written in a deliberately high-low style and in more fun than seriousness. It was considered quite risqué for Broadway, and it closed in a week, though not necessarily for that reason. It had been mounted in part with underworld money. Hecht claimed that after the opening, Billy Rose, the producer, had to dissuade several hoodlums from assassinating the three prominent critics who had panned it most severely. The next year the play was sold to Hollywood and became *Shoot the Works*, directed by Wesley Ruggles. Later still, in 1939, it was revived again as George Archainbaud's *Some Like It Hot* (not to be confused with the Billy Wilder film of the same title).

The idea of important authors writing with eyes cocked toward Hollywood became common in the 1930s. Steinbeck was but one who worked that way on occasion. A later example was Graham Greene, who wrote his story *The Third Man* as the basis for Carol Reed's film. Hecht shied away from the whole concept, except perhaps with his wartime novella, *A Miracle in the Rain*, which was filmed in 1956. He was so prolific a creator of original stories for films, as well as screenplays and adaptations, that he did not have to bother. As for short stories, such ones as did become films were those he directed himself. In his productivity were the seeds of literary integrity rather than avarice. He did feel justified, however, in selling his plays; plays he never ceased writing, alone and in collaboration, despite the remarkable lack of success he had on stage after the early euphoria of *The Front Page* and *Twentieth Century*.

In 1935, for instance, two of his plays formed the basis for films. *The Scoundrel*, the best of the films Hecht produced and directed with MacArthur, and in fact the best with which Hecht was ever involved in more than a writing capacity, was taken from *All He Ever Loved*, a comedy he had written with Rose Caylor Hecht. Another Hecht-Caylor collaboration, *Man-eating Tiger*, was later made into an undistinguished film. The following year, 1936, another Hecht-MacArthur production, *Soak the Rich*, was based on a Hecht-MacArthur stage play of the same title.

What makes Hecht unusual is that he gave new life not just to his own plays, but even to his old screenplays, written for production by others. These reappeared as elements in new works rather than remakes. For instance, a 1958 film called *The Fiend Who Walked the West*, well regarded in the horror genre, was based, rather gratuitously to be sure, on the *Kiss of Death* script he and Charles Lederer wrote for Henry Hathaway in 1947. This famous gangster film, in which Richard Widmark pushes an old woman down a flight of stairs in her wheelchair (a bit Hecht contributed) was perhaps his last great show of originality and verve as a screenwriter. There are still more remarkable examples of the way he used old screenplays. In 1954, he wrote *Living It Up* from two of his old properties, a musical play *Hazel Flagg* and the screenplay for *Nothing Sacred*. The latter had formed the basis for the book of the former. It was a rare instance of third generation use of a literary property. It shows how thoroughly Hecht and his sensibility were ingrained into the whole fabric of Hollywood, and vice versa – far beyond the degree apparent from a recital of his credits.

The fact that Hecht did his best writing for the stage and film in collaboration is a statement on his greater commitment to the literary than the performing arts. It also speaks of the differences between the two. He once wrote that it is in the nature of old reporters to spend their maturity walking backward toward the days when they were twenty-one, and here again Hecht was very much the old reporter. That is not to say that his scripts were overtly nostalgic in their situations, settings or characters (except when those characters were based on Hecht himself). Rather, the best ones were products of an attitude, the view of himself and society that he had held as a young man in Chicago. It was an attitude that he was usually able to recapture only when working with kindred spirits, whose roles in the collaborations are sometimes difficult to determine. As Richard Corliss has commented: "[Whereas] Hecht is too often ignored in discussions of Hawks or Hitchcock, so are Charles MacArthur, Charles Lederer and Gene Fowler forgotten on those rare occasions when Hecht's work is seriously appraised." To that list can probably be added the names of a few other lesser writers as well as that of Lee Garmes, the cinematographer whose work with Hecht was truly a panmedia collaboration.

Part of the reason for the lack of acknowledgement is that, in the tangle of lost credits, wrong credits and nominal credits that make up Hollywood filmographies, it is difficult to determine which lesser writers worked with what major ones. Fowler and Hecht, for instance, worked together often in the 1930s without sharing any screen credits. They had met briefly in Chicago, but had come to know each other well in the 1920s in New York, where Fowler was then editing a Hearst newspaper. Fowler followed Hecht to the West Coast early the following decade and wrote relatively few but nevertheless solid screenplays until the 1940s. Then his contributions dwindled in direct proportion to his rise as a popular biographer of such figures as Mayor James J. Walker and John Barrymore. During the period of his screen activity, Fowler was in frequent demand as a writer of additional dialogue and as a fixer – so frequent in fact that he seems to have rivalled Hecht for the title of highest-paid screenwriter, and in one year may have surpassed him.

Their similarity of temperment made it natural that they should work together. Fowler too was an old reporter, though in Denver and New York rather than Chicago, and they were much alike in their style and sense of humour, despite the fact that Hecht was Fowler's mentor. They were both literary scamps, or could frequently pretend to be; they both were fond of skewering the establishment on screen while, behind the scenes, skewering the smaller establishment that was the film industry. They both delighted in the picaresque, pixilated quality of the underworld and underground characters with whom they had always surrounded themselves. Also, they both made targets of other people's attachments to sex and money.

Those were also the qualities Hecht had in common with Lederer and which came out, not only in their writing together, but in Lederer's adaptations from Hecht – the Milestone *Front Page* and Hawks' *Twentieth Century*. Lederer, younger than Hecht by a decade, was a product of the Hollywood environment (his aunt was Marion Davies) rather than an immigrant to it. He was a more independent stylist than Fowler, but like Fowler, he was a student of Hecht who stood in awe of Hecht's literary achievement.

The first Hecht-Lederer collaboration was the screenplay for King Vidor's film *Comrade X*, made in 1940 with Clark Gable and Hedy Lamarr. It is a farce in a number of respects. It involves Gable as an American newspaperman abroad, and it treats politics as sort of prizefighting in coat-tails, a view Hecht held consistently even during his support of the Irgun. The very style of the writing, the epigrammatic Broadway quality of the dialogue, and the final scene involving a ludicrous chase with an armoured tank are all pure Hecht. They illustrate the obvious point (which explains away some of Corliss' objection) that whenever he collaborated on original material, or on an adaptation of something other than a recognized classic, Hecht was virtually always the dominant partner. In a working arrangement it would be his humour, his oblique ribaldry, his world view that infected the other person's and, in the end, structured as well as flavoured the finished script.

In 1947 the infrequent collaboration of the two men reached its peak, probably out of mutual restlessness rather than from design. The peak coincided with Lederer's busiest period and also the final disintegration of Hecht's collaboration with MacArthur, whose productivity slowed down once he returned from the war. As well as working at different times on the script of Hitchcock's *The Paradine Case*, Hecht and Lederer worked, mostly in tandem, on three other films: Hathaway's *Kiss of Death*, Robert Montgomery's *Ride the Pink Horse*, a vehicle for Montgomery's acting, and *Her Husband's Affairs*, a forgettable comedy with one of the double entendre titles then in minor vogue. They also worked together on

Shelley in Chains

Hawks' 1952 film *Monkey Business*, which also involved I.A.L. Diamond, Billy Wilder's writing partner.

Perhaps because of the number of cooks tending the stew, or because of Lederer's prominence as a screenwriter now against Hecht's waning reputation, *Monkey Business* is a more balanced collaboration than any of the others, although Hecht's hand is still obvious throughout the structure and dialogue. The film is a comedy of the 1930s type and recalls such Hecht works as *Twentieth Century* and *Nothing Sacred*. In a direct link with the latter, Cary Grant finds a serum that will ensure perpetual youth. The story concerns the effects of Grant's rejuvenation upon his wife (Ginger Rogers) and employer (Charles Coburn). The dialogue, at its best, also bears Hecht's stamp. In one famous bit, Coburn addresses his secretary played by Marilyn Monroe (already typecast as a voluptuous but oh-so-dumb blonde from *All About Eve* two years earlier). He has the draft of a letter in his hand and, looking down at Monroe, says, "Get someone to type this."

For all that, however, Hecht's usefulness as a collaborator was beginning to slip. *Monkey Business* is far from the undeniably Hecht script that *Comrade X* was. In the latter Hecht and Hollywood seemed to go hand in hand, with his co-writers tagging behind. The script brought to life a ridiculous view of politics, specifically European politics. If Hecht could create a ludicrous Russian streetcar conductor, Hollywood could descend to the occasion by casting in the part Hedy Lamarr, an Austrian. If the film was in many ways riding on the tail of Lubitsch's *Ninotchka*, a much better satire on communist-capitalist interaction, it was also gliding on Hecht and MacArthur's *Soak the Rich*. It illustrates the point that the best films Hecht wrote in collaboration with Lederer, Fowler or whomever else were, at their finest, only equal to those he did routinely with MacArthur, his most frequent partner and the one of whom Fowler, et al were pale imitations.

In Budd Schulberg's novel of Hollywood, *What Makes Sammy Run?*, there is a scene in which Sammy Glick, a hustler masquerading as a screenwriter, sets up his more talented partner for the kill by assuring him that together they will be "the biggest thing since Hecht and MacArthur." That line is but a small indication that the two names are linked together inextricably in the lore of American motion pictures. Despite the relatively short duration of their collaboration as film writers, the two go together in memory as naturally as Burke and Hare or Bonnie and Clyde and, to hear some film producers tell it, just as logically. Ever since *The Front Page* opened on Broadway, they were thought of as a pair whose frantic style of writing was a pale crystallization of their off-stage revelries. That reputation was bolstered by Hollywood, where they represented a lifestyle as well as a style of writing, though the latter was unmistakably theirs. The two styles were so inseperable that in 1938 Warner Brothers released a comedy entitled *Boy Meets Girl* about two screenwriters whose eccentric ways carry over into their writing, or vice versa. The thinly disguised Hecht and MacArthur team was played by James Cagney and Pat O'Brien respectively.

Although they worked together as playwrights more than as film-writers, many of their dramatic projects were never completed or else were produced and quickly forgotten, at least in the years following *Twentieth Century*. As a film team, they were notable in three ways. First, they worked behind the scenes as doctors and dialogue specialists for various producers, once even going under contract to Metro-Goldwyn-Mayer, where they found the regimen unbearable. Second, they worked together in the 1930s on adaptations such as *Wuthering Heights*, doing creditable jobs of infusing into the films the spirit of the originals without adhering too closely to the texts. Third, they collaborated as a writer-director-producer team, and it was in this capacity that they were most ambitious. In their curious experiment in independence, so uncharacteristic of the old Hollywood, they rose to their greatest success as a team and sank to their lowest failure. It was not that they were unusual in working as a team, nor that they were unusual in the kind of team they were. Rather, they were, throughout the 1930s, the quintessential team, a fact they used to bargain for a license virtually without parallel for American film writers until very recent times.

The genesis of their career as filmmakers, a career that has been called everything from a noble experiment to an expensive practical joke, rested in Leyland Hayward, the agent. It was he who negotiated with Paramount Pictures a deal whereby Hecht and

Shelley in Chains

MacArthur would virtually take over the company's studios at Astoria, Long Island, though they would remain nominally under the supervision of Walter Wanger, who had been exiled there following a corporate scuffle. The contract stipulated that Hecht and MacArthur would make four features, which they proceeded to do in an eighteen-month period between 1934 and 1936. For the studio, it was a small expenditure well worthwhile in retaining the writers' good will and getting them off its back. For Hecht and MacArthur, it was an opportunity to make what they hoped would be good films for the small minority who shared their tastes.

From the start the Astoria studios took on a circus-like atmosphere. The writers, who had so hated being tied down to the crass marketplace of MGM, erected a huge banner with their motto: "Better Than Metro Isn't Good Enough." They also hired prostitutes from a local bordello to act as secretaries or at least give the appearance of secretaries. When shooting on the set, they would retain waiters from the plush "21" restaurant in Manhattan to cater by taxi. The atmosphere in which the films were made, however, was only marginally more bizarre than the films themselves.

Their first picture, an adaptation from Hecht's story of the same title (which later appeared in *Actor's Blood*), was *Crime Without Passion*. It is a good indication of Hecht's directorial as opposed to literary style; it gives full measure to the expressionist tendencies, satire and social attitude found, in weaker dosages, in other films. It shows beyond doubt that, left to his own devices, Hecht was a literary director and an atmosphere director, in that order.

Crime Without Passion is a work involving Hechtian man, the self-consciously and deliberately brilliant fellow who suffers from thinking he has no peers. He blames himself and God for that circumstance while relegating the burden to those around him. Here Dorn, Sterns and all the others have become Lee Gentry (Claude Rains in his second film). He is a thoroughly urban man, with the same torturously symbiotic (or mutually parasitic) relationship with the city as earlier characters of that type. Also, he lives in an expressionistic world. The film opens with a montage, designed by Slavko Vorkapick, of three furies screaming above the cityscape and then crashing into windows of a skyscraper. The skyscraper contains the law office where Gentry earns a living with some of his innate cleverness, only to be poisoned by the part that remains.

As Hecht had once tried, and generally failed, to outwit the literary censors, here he succeeds in foiling the Hays Office. Gentry nearly gets away with commiting murder but in the end is unable to escape being arrested after his cleverness leads to carelessness, with a little assistance from fate. The censors saw the message clearly enough: that intellectual sharpers in the end lack the common sense and divine good will to succeed. To Hecht and his small minority, however, another thought presented itself: that the establishment of dullards always gives exceptional people more than enough rope to hang themselves.

Crime Without Passion, a critical success, showed clearly the origins of Hecht's way of thinking and also the various styles he was then juggling. When the film was made, he had published *A Jew in Love* and was working on the stories which gave off such a smell of sophisticated bitterness. While the picture contains at least a whiff of the same odour, there is here, much more than in the novel and the story collections of the 1930s, the mark of an earlier Chicago period. Indeed, it is as though all the old impulses toward smokestack imagery and exaggerated metaphor had been welling up in him, only now to be released. There are also many traces of the expressionism he came to second hand from Huysmans and others, and first hand in Berlin. The film is full of jagged geometrical puzzles and odd lighting, particularly in very expressionistic scenes involving a bar and a courtroom.

The second Hecht-MacArthur film was far less successful. *Once in a Blue Moon*, based on a story by Rose Hecht, concerns a clown who leads a group of Russian aristocrats to safety during the Revolution by disguising them as a circus troupe. Here similar stylistic tendencies are employed, though they are watered down. Nowhere is there that character at whom Hecht excelled, the emotional cripple whose weakness precludes his being a spiritual athlete. Nowhere is that failing more obvious than in the inclusion of a dreadful dream sequence. It lacks every bit of the correctness that the furies had in the first film. The film also features Hecht's daughter Edwina in a small part, playing under the name Armstrong.

Shelley in Chains

For all its shortcomings (which extended to the critical and fiscal) the film does show the war between Hecht's old influences and his current fiction — namely, the sort of uninformed mysticism implied by the title of *A Book of Miracles*. A miracle was not only often a good way out of a plot squeeze, it was also basic to what Hecht was then working his way through; it had to do with his imminent political awakening and the return of the passion so noticeably absent from Hechtian man.

The pseudo-metaphysical quality is more striking in *The Scoundrel*, the third film he made as an independent. It is the only film in which the mysticism was in harmony with the Chicago literary style and the later version of his expressionism. These elements, combined with some of the best and tightest dialogue he ever wrote, create what is Hecht's best achievement as director. Noel Coward, who had admired *Crime Without Passion*, agreed to play the part of Anthony Mallare, a publisher who is once again based, at least in his choice of occupation, on Horace Liveright, but whose personality is Hecht's own alter ego. As *Gargoyles* was *Erik Dorn* rewritten and diluted, so *The Scoundrel* is *A Jew in Love* minus the venom and overkill and imbued with *Count Bruga's* comedic spirit.

Anthony Mallare is on the surface a thoroughly dastardly and heartless character. At one point he accuses a poet who has just committed suicide of having taken his life to call attention to his substandard verse. The Broadway mysticism comes into play when Mallare is killed in an airplane crash. His spirit is doomed to walk the earth until someone comes forward who honestly liked him in life. Hecht, fuelled and kept from excesses by MacArthur, was in his stride, with a swift plot and the kind of crisp dialogue not heard again in American movies until Joseph Mankiewicz's *All About Eve* fifteen years later.

MALLARE (to his mistress): The earrings are something new.
CARLOTTA: My psychoanalyst advised them to give me confidence.
MALLARE: You never needed confidence.
CARLOTTA: That was before Mallare —
MALLARE: — wrecked your life?
CARLOTTA: No. Decorated it.

The Five Lives of Ben Hecht

The whole production is a Hecht carnival. His stock company of characters are in their top form with their neuroses and bitchiness burnished and shining. There is even an inside joke in the form of a number of x's recalling those in *Scarface*. It was such a combination of standard elements as to appear as something fresh. Not coincidentally, it was the one film for which the majority outnumbered the small minority in its appreciation. It should have won several Oscars but fell within a quite competitive year, so that Hecht and MacArthur took only one prize, for best original story.

Perhaps it was because they were buoyed by this popular success, of a kind that had not greeted their work in five years, that Hecht and MacArthur next chose a vehicle that from the start bore a popular stamp. *Soak the Rich* was to be their final picture together under the Paramount contract. More disorganized and disjointed a film than any of the others, its small esteem was due to its genre, for it was something on the order of a typical 1930s screwball comedy. Here artifice, phony mysticism and moralizing are foresaken for Hecht's long-established love of political bearbaiting. Here he makes fun of the radicals and the reactionaries with equal ease.

The plot has to do with the demands of students at a mythical university for the reinstatement of a professor who has been dismissed for advocating a soak-the-rich tax. It is a tangled and somewhat theatrical comedic plot, with characters entering and exiting neatly, throwing their fellow players into one confusion after another. The difficulty with the film is, first, that the style of the writing and filming are not plush enough to match the crowded action. Both script and film are almost as sparse as *Crime Without Passion* but without good reason. Second, the gag premises and throw-away lines, which should have the effect of wet towels snapped at the audience, are much too slack. The film limps along mainly by force of genre, one that the two authors actually seem to be spoofing. They introduce an heiress who is identified as "the world's dopiest heiress." *Soak the Rich* is too much 1936 and not enough Hecht and MacArthur.

Around the time the last Hecht-MacArthur film was being made at Astoria, Walter Wanger took a liking to their adaptation of *Wuthering Heights*. The two writers returned, perhaps enriched if not exactly satisfied, to their work as screenwriters. Hecht, how-

ever, directed three more films before the end of his career. First
was *Angels Over Broadway* in 1940, another convoluted script like
Once in a Blue Moon that failed to zero in on the point. This was
followed in 1946 by *Spectre of the Rose*, a film about which Saul
Bellow once stated that he would rather be forced to eat ground
glass than have to sit through a second time. It concerned the love
life of an insane ballet dancer who becomes a murderer, without, it
should be said, its having much effect on his emotional or personal
life, despite a lot of balderdash to the contrary. It is the sort of story
Hecht would have thrown away in his early years in the Chicago
attic.

The final film, in 1952, was *Actors and Sin*, based on two of his
published stories, "Actor's Blood" and "Concerning a Woman of
Sin." Both stories involve Hollywood. They are tied together by a
voice-over of Hecht good-naturedly deriding the manners and morals of the film capital in the way for which he had become re-
nowned (though on the prints for the British market his voice is not
identified). The film features a musical score by George Anthiel
(he also scored *Once in a Blue Moon*), the avant-garde terror of the
1920s who, like Hecht, had watched his advances become com-
monplaces and himself grow old and cautious.

In the first story, an aging ham actor (Edward G. Robinson)
stabs himself to give the impression that his actress daughter
(Marsha Hunt) has been murdered. She is an overnight star who
has brought renewed glory to the family. The truth of the situation
is that the father has himself killed her, shooting her twice in the
heart in an act of critical euthanasia. He doesn't want her to wake
up one morning a nobody like himself. That terrible bit of melodrama is *The Scoundrel* turned inside-out. The material is domi-
nated by Hecht's literary style of the moment instead of being
textured by the past and present styles available to him.

There follows the second story, in which the character from *I
Hate Actors!*, an amusingly clever hotshot Hollywood agent
named Orlando Higgins, sells an epic script ("Bigger than *Gone
With the Wind*") to Empire Studios. The character was based on
Leyland Hayward and played by Eddie Albert. The script has come
in over the transom, and it is only later that Higgins learns the
author is a nine-year-old brat. The part of the brat is the debut of
Jenny Hecht. Higgins, being by nature a confidence man in a busi-

ness where con men prosper without prosecution, promotes its author as a young genius. That touch is rooted in the Hollywood lore concerning Anita Loos, who was selling stories to D.W.Griffith while still a schoolgirl. Like many of Hecht's later stories, the two that were the basis for this film were merely anecdotes, without the style and polish which made the *Broken Necks* pieces so worthwhile as literary exercises.

For his knowledge of filmmaking Hecht was obliged to endless rewrites and story conferences going back to silent days. That experience gave him only a journeyman's familiarity with scripts, as well as Sunday quarterback's hindsight. At his best he brought to films the literary ideas and wit he had been honing elsewhere. Only occasionally, as in *The Scoundrel*, could he bring them together on the screen, released but harnessed. He knew relatively little film production and so had to rely on Lee Garmes, a cinematographer with a long list of credits. Garmes worked with Hecht and MacArthur at Astoria and, on *Angels Over Broadway*, was credited as co-director. He probably deserved the title earlier but was deprived of it by contract and other people's egos. The result was that the films in which Garmes had a hand were photographed at least competently and sometimes strikingly. In some scenes, Hecht either fell down or resorted to the only experience he had – theatrical experience. The result was that many scenes had a stagey look.

Hecht occasionally treated film as a new and strange toy, and enjoyed the freedom of editing not found in the theatre. While many of his sets were much too theatrical, often detracting from the scenes, his editing tended to be brusque and uneven. Too often his attempts at saying something were marred by poorly judged camera set-ups and inferior lighting. Another problem was that Hecht really did not know much about directing actors. He treated them as his own preposterous fictional characters and made them move about like mannequins. His best non-literary creations tended to centre around roles which demanded over-acting. Their successful realization depended too much upon the luck of the draw. Jenny Hecht, for instance, looked at the camera and recited lines as though she had just memorized them without having said them aloud. Some of the old pros, such as Barrymore and Edward

G.Robinson, knew where to stop, while others with similarly long experience lacked their grace.

Filmmaking was a new medium for Hecht despite all his years of screenwriting. He worked in it best when he was adapting it to his literary skills rather than the other way around. That is not to say that he viewed his own films merely as vehicles for recycling old phrases and ideas (though he did so from film to film and, by the time of *Once in a Blue Moon*, they all seemed somewhat tired). It is rather that he functioned best when bringing to film in cinematic terms, something that was new to the screen but that for him was the end result of a long process of perfecting and reshaping in other media. He did this most successfully in several films with MacArthur, films which incidentally lost money and discouraged other studios from ever giving writers such freedom again. It was a noble experiment while it lasted, but for Hecht it was more than a gamble. It was a way of bringing together (as in *The Scoundrel*) many of the elements formerly so troublesome to him by their very disparateness.

Toward the end, however, it became too much a game. In the second half of *Actors and Sin* there are many inside jokes at the expense of a Hollywood he had warred with too often. As in some of the stories in *A Book of Miracles* and *Champion From Far Away*, he makes fun of the imbecility of producers and the system, but with more of a heavy hand than a quick wrist. There is an archetypal studio boss who, looking over the proofs of an advertising campaign, tells a minion to scrap the "I love you" tag line. "That line's twenty-five-years-old." There is also a put-down of William Saroyan as well as kindly inside reference to Gene Fowler. All are signs that Hecht was placing the Hollywood experience behind him, as a challenge almost, and coming increasingly to look upon film as a simple livelihood. Shortly afterward, when he began publishing the first of his memoirs, he would view Chicago and even New York as places, as good environments in which to have written. Hollywood, however, would be remembered mainly in terms of a few select cronies with whom he endured the surroundings, and a larger number of adversaries who had made his life there that of a "Shelley in chains."

10
The Champion of Long Ago

I am at my nimblest as a composer of epitaphs.
BH, *in* A Child of the Century

Mellowness was the stylistic characteristic that most set Hecht the Memoirist apart from Hecht in the other phases of his career. When it came time to write his memoirs, he seemed to find quite naturally a middle ground between the raucous excesses of his youth and the sloppy brio of much of the fiction and movie writing he did in the 1930s and 1940s. The spirit of the rebel was there, but it was made all the stronger by the general consistency and directness of style – consistency, at least, being something Hecht had not hitherto been known for. That style, in turn, fitted in perfectly with what seemed to be a new attitude toward himself and his work.

Perhaps the war and the problems of Palestine, as well as the sausage factory atmosphere of Hollywood, had much to do with the metamorphosis. Hecht was no longer at odds with everyone and everything above or below his level of social and esthetic tolerance. Instead he was secure in his position as a flamboyant player of the second rank who had spent his time among colourful personalities rather than important events and ideologies. It was those personalities – including the one of himself when young – that he set out to chronicle.

Hecht wrote not just one memoir but a long uneven series of

156

them. They were distinct from the stories and scripts in which he had simply turned his experiences to account by disguising them slightly. In a sense, the memoirs began with *A Guide for the Bedevilled*, in which he related flat-out some of his upbringing and Hollywood experience, even some not particularly relevant to the points he was making about Jewishness. It is not entirely coincidental that at the time that book was being written, his autobiography *A Child of the Century* was germinating.

This massive work, begun in the 1940s and written on intermittently until 1953, was in many ways the putting to rest of all Hecht had been. Even though he lived another ten years after its publication in 1954, and even though he flared up later as other selves, this was his final assessment of what he was and had been. It was his last major work. He was still to live again (on his television show) as the Iconoclast and (in *Perfidy*) as the Propagandist, but from 1954 such lives were selected carefully from a wardrobe of last season's personalities.

A Child of the Century, written in his fifties and published when he was sixty, was his assessment of the Bohemian, the Iconoclast, the Sophisticate and the Propagandist. By its very existence it was also therefore an assessment of the author in his final phase as Memoirist. It is, then, a living document of the writer at the moment rather than a postmortem. Hecht was truly, as he said, a child of the century: a member of that generation born close to 1900 and the first to come of age with the big-time gangster, the automobile, the world war, the skyscraper and the interior monologue. His sensibility was peculiar to his age, but was tempered by individual experience. While the book is a statement on America at mid-century, it is also the record of someone unique by reason of the course his individualism took. In its depiction of one person's progress across the landscape of his time, it falls within the tradition of the best American autobiography that stretches from Benjamin Franklin through Henry Adams to Emma Goldman.

Many aspects of the book are striking. One of them is the verve with which Hecht invokes the environments of his past, as though he had never left them, while at the same time analysing and appraising them. The two actions are not distinct but take place simultaneously, giving the whole work an unusual quality of detached exuberance. In the course of the book, with all its energy, he will change his mind about himself completely, alter his ideas and contradict himself. He writes damningly of Hollywood, for example, in such a way as to indicate that he actually loved every minute of it, not nostalgically, as most people would do in their memoirs, but at the time, even as he was cursing. More interesting, however, is the fact that the book is an intellectual autobiography as well as a memoir, with all the honesty that the former implies. For example, Hecht deals frankly, and without cosmetics, with his various money-raising schemes, such as his involvement in Florida land swindles of the 1920s. He sees himself at times as little better than a con man and with the same love of con men he tried conveying in *Count Bruga* with regard to Bodenheim. For all that, however, it is not a literary autobiography. Hecht discusses his work surprisingly little in this huge hulk of a book. It is written as another work, not as a distillation or apologia for all the previous ones. It is its own justification.

Graciously, Hecht takes few swipes at his enemies, except generically; but there are several reasons for this. In some cases, events ending in animosity had not yet progressed to the stage of serious bad-mouthing, especially in the glow that must have illuminated him during the task of writing. For example, although he worked out his ideas about Zionism more clearly here than elsewhere, he has far kinder words about the Haganah and the Israeli leaders generally than he would have later in *Perfidy*. Another reason is that, writing as he was in middle rather than old age, Hecht was dealing in the main with people who were still alive. That is particularly important insofar as *A Child of the Century* is a memoir of other people, which it is to a very considerable extent.

The cast is enormous, especially when he discusses life in the three centres of his life: Chicago, New York and Hollywood. While the sketches of his family are as memorable and evocative as anything he would write, those of his actual professional contemporaries tend toward the anecdotal. Indeed, the book depends for its impact upon hundreds of "wild hearts and fabulous gullets."

With the dead, Hecht was understandably less jocular as well as more careful. Sherman Duffy, for instance, one of his old *Journal* editors, had died while the book was being written. Hecht eulogizes him at some length. Herman Mankiewicz and Horace

The Champion of Long Ago

Liveright, also recently dead, are given shorter but equally appropriate treatment. John Barrymore, whose life like the book depended upon the accumulation of wild anecdotes, is given more space but probably less than he would have received had it not been for the appearance of Gene Fowler's Barrymore biography, *Good Night, Sweet Prince*, in 1944. On one level, *A Child of the Century* is a catalogue of Hecht's friends. Whereas this might be a fault in another book, it is here a vision of his life not unlike the vision of the cityscape held so long by the Hechtian man he was now putting to rest. It fashions a view of society he changed by passing through; one he was part of without being directly responsible to or derived from. It creates a sense of the giant among smaller people in the communal enterprise of the large world they all inhabit together. It thus resolves all the conflicts which had produced *Erik Dorn* and other early works. It elevates therapy to the level of literature without ever quite being aware of doing so.

Hecht's style was never better or better suited to its purpose than in *A Child of the Century*. He used simple straightforward electricity to marshall his arguments and impressions as he never quite managed to do as a Propagandist, without reducing the level of his discussion. At times he rose to his own brand of the High Style. There had been nothing quite like it since *Erik Dorn* and the better stories in *Broken Necks*, which he now felt were excessively arty by comparison. An example of the style is this part of a long description of Chicago as he had known it amid the folly of youth.

> I have lived in other cities but been inside only one. I knew Chicago's thirty-two feet of intestines. Only newspapermen ever achieve this bug-in-a-rug citizenship.
>
> I once wore all the windows of Chicago and all its doorways on a key ring. Saloons, mansions, alleys, courtrooms, depots, factories, hotels, police cells, the lake front, the roof tops and the sidewalks were my haberdashery.
>
> Frown on me now or give me a stranger's eye, good town; or cackle meaninglessly over my head and hide like a runaway bride in a forest of stone walls — I know you still. Listen!
>
> A man lay on his back in Barney Grogan's saloon with a knife sticking out of his belly, and I made notes.

The Five Lives of Ben Hecht

A naked woman with a smoking gun in her hand knelt and moaned beside a dead dentist, "Why did I do it? I loved him so!"

And there was a dentist arrested for raping a patient during office hours whose crime was immortalized (for one edition) by the headline, "Dentist Fills Wrong Cavity."

Clarence Darrow in his poor-man's suit, baggy pants, floppy jacket, stringy tie, sang his song of humanity to the jurors trying an ex-chief of police for shaking down whores, pimps and madams. He said: "My client, after twenty-five years on the police force, is a poor man." His client, Chief Healy, went free.

Teddy Webb's sweetheart called the police and told them that the fearsome bandit was lying in a bed in Cottage Grove Avenue with another woman. Four policemen darted forth to capture the wanted killer. They nabbed him as he was trying to pull his pants on, but one of the cops dropped dead of heart failure in the excitement. Chief of Police Scheuttler came on the scene and fired a bullet into the armpit of the dead policeman and saved his honor.

A fire gutted the Stockyards and seven fireman died trying to shoo the bellowing cattle out of the flames.

A man stood naked in front of the Congress Hotel screaming that the world was coming to an end, and he bore out his contention, in part, by dropping dead when the police laid hands on him.

The school board was arrested for graft. Investigators revealed the new country hospital had pillars stuffed with straw instead of cement and was menacing the lives of all who entered it; and the assistant keeper of the morgue died of poison from eating the leg of one of the corpses in his custody.

A minister of the Gospel and his paramour died in the basement of his church, overcome by escaping gas. The impassioned reverend had kicked open a gas jet while doing homage to Eros. Preoccupied by love, he had smelled no other fumes than those of Paradise and given up the ghost while still glued to his parishioner...

The mayor of the city, William Hale Thompson, was accused of stealing all the money out of the treasury and giving it away to friends.

The yellow cabs fought the checkered cabs, and passengers were tossed into the gutter. The Hearst Chicago *Examiner* fought the Chicago *Tribune*, and each publication sent stern and muscled minions through the rush-hour streetcars to snatch the rival paper out of passengers'hands, and, on resistance, tossed the readers into the gutter...

A linen fetishist tore up all the bed sheets in the storerooms of the Sherman Hotel and was captured as he lay sexually exhausted on the fire escape.

A janitor ravished a child behind a coal pile in a Halstead Street basement, and Theodore Dreiser wrote a play about it called *The Hand of the Potter*.

An automobile salesman killed a reluctant customer by bashing in his skull with a baseball bat, and died gamely on the gallows, so we wrote.

Carl Wanderer was hanged for killing his wife and a Ragged Stranger whom he had hired to hold them up as they were coming home from a movie show; and with the rope around his neck, Carl sang a ballad called "Dear Old Pal of Mine."

Blackie Weed, a white man, died on the gallows for killing a representative of the gas company and a policeman come to collect a bill he had already paid. The receipted bill was his only defense. Blackie, a firm man, spat at the cross the priest held up for him to kiss, a moment before the trap was sprung.

And a Dr. Hugo succumbed on the gallows in the oddest manner of all the seventeen I saw twisting in their white sheets on the end of the shining rope. Sheriff Hoffman, always eager to hear a confession of guilt from the guest he was scheduled to hang, made a deal with the doomed doctor at four A.M. of his final morning. In return for a full confession, he granted the medico a last request — a ladies' make-up kit. I hurried through several brothels, secured a "vanity" case and darted back with it at five A.M. to the death cell. Dr. Hugo had time to rouge his cheeks and lips, mascara his eyes, pluck his brows and heavily powder his neck before the death march started. He stood thus on the gallows, painted and simpering and oddly triumphant. The sheriff, unnerved by this indecency to which he had committed himself, worked fast. The doctor went through the trap in jig time. Out of him, hanging and turning in his death throes, there came a woman's high falsetto screech.

And on Wabansia Avenue two men were burned to death while trying to stab each other in argument over a pinochle game. They were found in the charred rubble, each with a knife in his blackened, un-fleshed hand.

A lover tied his beloved to the bedposts on the fifteenth floor of the

161

The Five Lives of Ben Hecht

Morrison Hotel and whipped her to death for not loving him enough. Then he jumped out of the window into the noon traffic.

A machinist shot and killed his wife and then killed himself, leaving a note: "Nobody else will ever have her." This tale took a strange turn when an alert undertaker, preparing the bodies for burial, announced that the "machinist" was a woman, fully equipped in every respect. And thus I was introduced to the marvels of psychiatry.

Federal Judge Carpenter listened to evidence contending that the "Oceana Roll" was a piece of musical plagiarism. And he handed down the judgement that since the "Oceana Roll," to which he had listened with an open mind, was not music, it could not be a musical plagiarism. Case dismissed.

But not so the "Oceana Roll," or the tide of jazz that came rolling to town with it. A colored band up from New Orleans appeared for the first time in a white café, operated by Ray Jones on the South Side. Turkey Trots, Bunny Hugs, Stomps, Blues, Grizzly Bear Hugs, the music that was not music filled the joints and cat houses of Chicago. Only New Orleans and Memphis had heard these brassy, snorting, wailing incantations before. Now South State Street heard them, and North Clark and Archer Avenue; West Harrison and the lava bed precincts beyond. And a new tribe of hopped-up horn tooters was born, to provide a faster, wilder obbligato for love, crime and liquor...

There were swindlers, funerals and weddings; a rash of bichloride of mercury suicides; and the arrest of Mrs. Ginnis, who ran a nursery for orphans in which she murdered an average of ten children a year.

Counterfeiters sold ten-dollar bills for eight dollars to the America-infatuated inmigrants in Maxwell Street...

A colored man named Henry knelt in his Desplaines Street basement flat and prayed to God to save Chicago from its sinful ways. God heard the prayer and sent His Wrath to punish the wicked city. His Wrath was Henry, who came out of his flat with three loaded guns and shot dead eight Polish workingmen starting out on their day's toil. The workingmen fell in front of their doorways, their lunch boxes in their hands. The police came to get Henry, but Henry the Wrath of God smote them for five hours. He barricaded himself behind a bureau. His wife, singing hymns, loaded and reloaded his rifles. One policeman was killed, and three wounded. Henry, untouched behind his bureau, cried out, "Hallelujah! Thy Will be done!" each time he fired. At one o'clock the police dropped dynamite through a hole in the roof and blew up several buildings. In the debris were the remains of Henry the Wrath of God and his loyal hymn-singing wife.

Orators spoke at luncheons, thousands of them. Presidents, vice-presidents, senators, royalty, geniuses, billionaires, lecturers, beauties and dowagers, priests, educators – made an unending parade before my reporter's pencil, ninnies all, talking through their hats, which is the only way "greatness" dare speak for publication

Revivalists bellowed, organs played. Evangelist Rodeheaver blew his hot trumpet and men and women were saved and cured of paralysis and blindness. And the Stockyards' owners imported Billy Sunday to di - vert their underpaid hunkies from going on strike by shouting them dizzy with God.

A psychoanalyst (like a first robin) appeared with a beard and a Viennese accent. His name was Dr. Stekel and he brought the good news to town that chastity was a disease responsible for most of the lunacy in the world, especially among ladies.

Jim Colisimo, genial owner of half the whore houses in town and possessor of one of the greatest collections of rare cheeses in the world, was shot and killed in a phone booth. The great cortege of jurists, politicos, financial and industrial nabobs was halted outside the gates of the Catholic cemetery. Burial in Catholic ground had been denied the corpse by the local priesthood. For five hours officials of the city pleaded with Pope Pius over the transatlantic telephone. The connection was bad and the Pope irritable. A great jurist finally informed the press, "He hung up. Let's take Jim some other place." And Jim's bullet-riddled remains were wheeled off to a heathen grave.

Tommy O'Connor skipped out of his cell in the county jail while the sheriff was testing the gallows on which he was to hang in the morning. A thousand cops combing the town failed then and ever after to find any trace of Tommy. Straining a number of points in this story, I wrote it as my first movie, *Underworld*.

Jack Johnson, the colored World's Champion, was married to a white girl, Lucille Cameron. They waited in the South Side parlor surrounded by an excited wedding party, and none of the pictures we took could be used, because Lucille had sat soothing her powerful but nervous groom by tenderly stroking his genitals.

Trains were wrecked, hotels burned down, factories blew up. A man killed his wife in their Sedgwick Avenue flat, cut off her head and made a tobacco jar of its skull.

The Five Lives of Ben Hecht

Beautiful women jumped off the top of the Masonic Temple, the High Bridge in Lincoln Park and the Frances Willard building in La Salle Street.

A surgeon named Dr. Pratt was arrested for removing unnecessarily some nine hundred uteri.

A butcher in Division Street killed his wife, ground her up and distributed her to his sausage-loving customers. The presence in one of the sausages of a wedding ring bearing his wife's initials led to his arrest and hanging.

And these things went on every day in these streets, and I was there among them. I could cover a hundred pages with lists of fascinating cadavers. They all clamor for cataloguing. But I stop my pencil and sit sighing among my phantoms, and feel pleased. What better is there to sigh for than happiness, yesterday's or tomorrow's. And that was happiness. Skyscrapers banged at a cymbal sun. The headlines of murder, rape and swindle were ribbons round a May pole. The Elevated squealed hosannas in the sooty air. The city turned like a wheel. The chimney smoke lay in awning stripes against the white clouds. The days leaped away like jack rabbits. Night sprinted across the Illinois sky, and a jack pot of moons tumbled out of the heavens. Swiftness was in all the hours – yet nothing moved. Everything stood still and was changeless, for it was youth. Youth holds time like an arrow in its hand. The hand and arrow stay motionless.

The point is not that this is precisely the way a realist or naturalist would painstakingly describe it all, but rather that, by describing it his way, Hecht makes real a sort of imaginative Chicago. He alone could do it because he was and remained its only inhabitant. The facts are somewhat eccentric in places, though Chicago is not made any better, worse or different than it actually was in spirit.

Hecht the Memoirist was a fine and moving eulogist but a poor biographer. He simply did not bother with those facts which did not hold his interest and was often loose with those he did employ. Rather than record and analyse his subjects, he tried to capture their spirits. Such attempts, however, were couched in a literary style better suited to his own nostalgia than someone else's. There are many short examples of Hecht's reaching for, and missing, the

164

essence of various friends and colleagues, many of whom come away sounding like so many Ben Hechts in tawdry disguise. All together, however, these writings do not match the glaring failure of Hecht's only book-length biography, *Charlie: The Improbable Life and Times of Charles MacArthur*. It appeared in 1957, the year following MacArthur's death, and is curiously mis-subtitled. The life and career of his longtime friend and collaborator were indeed colourful, but Hecht wrote only of their similarity to his own. He missed whatever made MacArthur a character unto himself.

In a way, MacArthur was what Hecht would have been if Hecht had not been a writer. MacArthur was a man haunted by the desire to create an imaginative world for himself and guilt-ridden by the masking of his failure to do so in literary and social shenanigans. The basic outline of Charles MacArthur's story is told best, not in the text of Hecht's book, but in a shortened version of the index.

antipathy to New York, 76-77
awareness of death, 5-6, 20
blooms as man of letters, 87
bombards Berlin with empty Scotch bottles, 211, 231
brothel experience with Keeley, 45-47
drinking, guilt feelings over, 211; reason for, 218-219
drinking bout on Turkey Hill, 178-183; in Europe and Africa, 210
early journalistic days, 40-41
fist fights, 18
Hollywood period, 157-191
knowledge of whores and whorehouses, 38
loyalty to Chicago, 76
as movie writer, 157-61
portrait of Christ by, 31
sense of sin, 39, 128
streetcar-stealing incident, 78-80
unconformity of, 127-128
writing habits, Nyack home, 151-154
years of silence as playwright, 162
"youth" as religion of, 74

That picture of MacArthur can be fleshed out almost indefinitely, but extra facts do not alter its shape. He was the son of a Scottish evangelist who thought the rod a proper means of instilling piety in his sons, two others of whom became millionaire businessmen. The future playwright, naturally, rebelled against such a background and, when a Chicago reporter, led a number of crazy escapades which lingered on in the countless recollections of his contemporaries. Like so many, he strove to be more than just a reporter but, unlike Hecht, failed to create a body of work from the imaginative world they helped create for each other. There was always something to conveniently distract him from the work at hand: two world wars, New York café society, Hollywood, after-hours cynicism and, finally, the bottle.

The work he did alone or with some collaborator other than Hecht was competent and in the vein of the *The Front Page* and *Twentieth Century* much of the time, but it failed the test of endurance because its author failed the test of discipline. For instance, his short story "Rope," about the love life of a Chicago hangman, was a fine piece of irony and has had to stand as his stock anthology piece, mainly because it is virtually his only story of consequence. Hecht's personal confusions − the tribulations of Hechtian man, his angst about his Jewish roots − in time became urgencies that had to be resolved in his writing. In contrast, MacArthur's inner struggles − for and against the Christianity of his youth − became more and more involuted without surfacing as pages of manuscript. These were the problems of MacArthur which Hecht never got a hold on in *Charlie,* even though he admitted early on that he was not writing a biography but what "is obviously a letter about a friend who died." It is a curious letter.

The book contains several notable "flaming factoids," as Norman Mailer would call them when mentioning Hecht years later in his book on Marilyn Monroe. There is, for instance, the case of the gangster Dion O'Banion (whose name Hecht always misspelled O'Bannion). Hecht states that this mutual acquaintance of MacArthur and himself was murdered in retaliation for the St. Valentine's Day Massacre of 1929. In truth, O'Banion's murder, one of the best known in underworld history, took place in 1924. It was one of three murders, by the Capone interests, of successive North Side gang leaders, and was part of a war which the massacre brought to a close by scaring the fourth heir (Bugs Moran) out of the bootlegging business. Such errors, however, are not what Helen

Hayes MacArthur, the subject's widow, was referring to in her preface when she graciously allowed for a considerable discrepancy between the MacArthur she knew and the one to whom Hecht was paying tribute. She meant instead to warn the reader of something newcomers to Hecht might not be aware of − that Hecht's reminiscences were, factually, part-truth and part-untruth but that, imaginatively, they were almost a new form in themselves. Hecht the Memoirist was the kind of writer their detractors accuse the present day New Journalists of being. He shifted the focus away from a careful analysis of the facts toward an impressionistic truth supported by a mesh of tiny detail. Much of the detail was certainly as he remembered it, but some was included because it sounded plausible. None of it was researched.

In the interests of that peculiar brand of accuracy, the Memoirist was often caught up in minor inner struggles resembling tugs of conscience. Now that MacArthur was dead, Hecht made numerous allusions to his friend's alcoholism and even began to consider the reasons for it. Then he faltered and let the subject drop. Such picking up and sudden dropping of threads is only exacerbated by Hecht's style. At times the book reads like a rough draft. There is an apparent lack of organization, melted with Hecht's gift of metaphor at its most uneven, and a marked overuse of literary, biblical and mythological allusions. Such lack of precision, in turn, reinforces, not just the failure to make us certain what kind of fellow MacArthur was, but also what Hecht, in this work, hoped he would become. The problems are most unusual, even given Hecht's sometimes selective memory.

For instance, in *A Child of the Century*, he had glossed over certain periods of his life and, in other periods, simply omitted salient facts − when it was convenient to do so. While eulogizing Mencken, he had even neglected to mention Mencken's strong pro-German bias, even in wartime: a considerable anomaly in light of what Hecht, as a Propagandist, had had to say about the Germans. In *Charlie* there are apparently no omissions of such magnitude, but Hecht does resort to other tactics. Instead of turning a blind eye to some facts, he views them with rose-coloured glasses. He even goes so far as to attribute to MacArthur at least one of his own triumphs. In his discussion of the Carl Wanderer murder case of 1920-1921, Hecht credits MacArthur with solving it in his work with the *Herald-Examiner*. In fact, the evidence (some of it reprinted in Snyder and Morris' *A Treasury of Great Reporting*, the standard anthology) suggests that the discovery of the culprit was made by Hecht in the rival *Daily News*. Everywhere the tone is consistent with such new-found generosity becoming to the Memoirist, who now suddenly saw many of his close friends and fellow survivors crumple around him.

Such awareness of mortality was the last great confusion of Hecht's decidedly confounded life. His friendships were important to him because they had replaced the crimes, sensations, intrigues and scandals through which he had lived for so long. With his life quieter, after the excitement of Chicago and the whirligig of Hollywood, he found such vicarious relationships, in which each friend was, in a sense, a collaborator in the myth of Hecht's own past, disappearing. So he began writing his memoirs relatively early in life and never looked back – or rather, seldom looked forward, except to wince at a friend's grave and resume remembering. What made the Memoirist unique in his time was that the process of remembering was in itself a creative act. So long as the past could be improved upon there was hope for the future or at least comfort in the present.

The Memoirist, like the Propagandist and various other Hechts, worked in more than one medium. In the 1950s, for instance, Hecht did dramatic writing for television, including some for David O. Selznick, who was now reduced to the ignominy of the home screen after having, like his father before him, gone broke as a Hollywood tycoon. One of Hecht's television credits was a play "Hello Charlie," produced in 1959 on the Screen Gems series *Award Theatre*. The script, about one of MacArthur's Chicago adventures, concerns the case of a man presumed to have locked himself in the time vault of a downstate Illinois bank.

In the actual case, according to MacArthur, a safecracker was recruited from the Joliet prison only to find that a thief had left his coat outside the vault while making his getaway and that the safe was empty both of cash and victim. As retold by Hecht, the story is that of a local schoolgirl locked inside. MacArthur, portrayed by Tony Randall, remarks at one point that the safe must be opened by such-and-such an hour because "that's the deadline for the little girl – and also our home edition." The programme was an example of the way Hecht used one of his friends, this time not even disguised, to relive again a bit of his own past attitudes, glossing over those peculiar to the friend in question.

Something of the same technique, but on a more ambitious and, as it happened, more controversial scale, had been used before. Hecht's play *Winkelberg*, based on or at least heavily inspired by Maxwell Bodenheim, was produced off-Broadway in 1958. The story of the production is another example of Hecht's strangely insensitive yet benevolent attitude toward the poet, who had been foully murdered in 1954 after thirty years' degradation and living martyrdom. It was also another instance of how Hecht projected his own personality onto other people's, however unconsciously, with the resulting mixture of eulogy, memoir and fiction.

Hecht's relationship with Bodenheim is perhaps the most complicated and subtle he had with any other writer, including MacArthur. Many of the complications arise from the temperment of the poet, who was unlike Hecht, except in his public quasi-official pose. Even then the similarity was mainly in their younger years. They had first met in Chicago when teenagers. While they went their separate directions after that in their personal and artistic lives, each seemed somehow hurt by the parting and each blamed the division on the other.

The facts of Bodenheim's life are clouded at best. His biography appears to consist largely of adjectives describing him, most of them abusive. He was one of those figures – like Robert Johnson in blues or Richard Savage in English literature – who becomes legend through the ultimate satisfaction of his martyr-hunger by the destruction he brings on himself. He was, in a word, a loser, but on a magnificent and profane scale. He was born in Mississippi and began his writing life in Chicago, apparently after being dishonourably discharged from some branch of the military. As a young man he would stroll about with one arm in a sling he did not require and gratuitously offend those around him. He derived a satisfaction and joy from the way in which he informed people of their faults, real or imagined, and even attributed to them some of his own. For a time in the 1920s he was a popular literary figure, though more of a novelty than an artist in his public's eyes. His notoriety rose with a series of scandals, several of them involving the suicide, accidental death or discomfiture of young female admirers. But the reputation, like the man, declined sharply in the Depression, when such people as Bodenheim, clowns with a clown's essential sadness, ceased being funny. By that time, he was already well on the path to ruin. For decades he was little more than a cadger of drinks in Greenwich Village, a frequenter of flophouses or, when flops were not open to him, streetcorners and deserted subway trains.

Underneath all that, however, was a man Hecht must have known but never wrote of: a serious craftsman who continued to write in his 1915-style Imagist verse long after the fashion had outstripped his talent and his audience; in fact, until the day before his death. He possessed a keen and well-defined sense of artistic integrity and discipline, and was inordinately proud of his ornate and vituperative vocabulary. It was the last vestige of his Chicago youth and his place in the world of letters. It was all that was left to distinguish him from his doss mates, and from the middle class, once the bohemian had fallen away, leaving only the wino and bum. Through the last couple of decades of their lives – they saw one another infrequently and usually by chance – Bodenheim resented Hecht's facility and material success as a writer. Hecht, for his part, envied Bodenheim's singleminded dedication to his personal voice. He admired the way Bodenheim hurdled all the obstacles in his path, both the ones society put there and the ones he himself erected as tests of endurance.

Winkelberg is primarily a testament to Bodenheim's vocabulary and the pathetic soul behind it, rather than a search for the complicated and oddly self-deprecating creature who took refuge in insults and affectations. Its main device is a series of soliloquies and conversations presented by Jonathan Winkelberg, a name that as early as *1001 Afternoons in Chicago* had been Hecht's choice for a fictional character like Bodenheim. Hecht, who had been away from serious theatre for a long time, rewrote the play many times – an unusual procedure for him – in the several years before it was finally performed. Its production was hampered by a snowstorm, a taxi strike and hostile reviews.

It also met with criticism from several of Bodenheim's friends, who had stayed with him through the last terrible years in the

Village. Hecht had given Bodenheim "my own words, which, in our youth, were not too different from his own." He had also, as he went on to explain in a puff piece written for the New York *Times*, "written all Winkelberg's poetry for him, for Bodenheim's poetry was in my eye a bit too fragile for public ken ... there are only two of my friend's phrases in the play." Such liberty, a clear indication that Hecht was as much interested in reliving his own past as in exorcising the ghost of Bodenheim, infuriated some Villagers who picketed the theatre and distributed anti-Hecht broadsheets.

Nowhere did Hecht do for Bodenheim what he had done in *Charlie* for MacArthur by including a dialogue (one of the best he ever wrote) between the two friends which, for once, got near the essence of the subject. In the play, however, Hecht does put in a partial appearance as the character Stanley, a painter at the time of the Chicago Renaissance. This curious bit of transparent modesty enables him to allude to some of the wild occurrences of that time, as when one of the female characters much later inquires of the poet: "Did you and Stanely really have that debate in front of the ritzy Book and Play Club — Resolved: Are People Who Attend Literary Debates Fools?"

It is significant, however, that even as he is ridiculing Bodenheim's poverty and failure, Hecht is admiring Bodenheim's steadfastness under the circumstances; that even while stooping to write Bodenheim's verse, he is allowing the character some of the best lines he can come up with ("You may add that the English stiff upper lip about sex is a matter of misplaced firmness"). There are masked references to many figures of the Chicago days which were doubtless lost on the audience, even in their primary function of showing the environment from which Bodenheim sprang into uneasy bloom. There are also still more oblique references to seminal characters in Bodenheim's past — to his father, a merchant, against whom he first rebelled, and to Fedya Ramsay, an actress who took her life, apparently in despair of her romance with the poet. The latter's death, sometime before 1920, was a shock from which Bodenheim never recovered. He dedicated virtually all his work to her memory for the remaining thirty-five years of his life.

Such allusions indicate that Hecht really knew more of Bodenheim than he was prepared to admit. Instead of probing psychologically, he was content to concentrate on what he knew

The Five Lives of Ben Hecht

by heart, the resemblance between the Chicago Bodenheim and himself when young. Little was ventured and, inevitably, little gained in the exercise. Hecht was dealing with his own past. What had been part of that past he attacked with vigour, but also with the melancholy characteristic of the Memoirist. What was not part of the author's own experience – and that was the better part of Bodenheim – was guessed at. He would have other chances later on and come somewhat closer to the truth. A blind spot caused Hecht to include *Winkelberg* as one of the best things he had written in his omnibus volume *A Treasury of Ben Hecht*.

Hecht's autobiographical writings, and even his biographical extrusions into the lives of other people, were concerned with trying to find the essence of his youth. It was the youthful spirit, and his reaction to the gradual lessening of it, that governed his life once his early tastes changed. His works of remembrance approached the problem from several different angles. Not that Hecht had failed in his initial attempt, for *A Child of the Century*, as well as being a brilliant self-assessment, is an insightful elegy on his roots. Rather, he continued trying to better that book's success by other avenues.

In his search for the spirit of the time he had lived through, he often resorted to key words and phrases of his early work to uncover old attitudes and enthusiasms. One example is the phrase "gaily, gaily" from a poem by Bliss Carman, popular early in the century. Hecht used the words in *1001 Afternoons in Chicago* as a shorthand symbol for the carefree disregard of mortality held by the reporters who lived with so much death and destruction. They turn up thirty years later as a heading in a *A Child of the Century*, and in 1963, became the title of a collection of autobiographical semi-fictions which, if inferior in style and depth to *A Child of the Century*, are Hecht's best single pieces in this peculiar factoidal form.

Gaily, Gaily, is comprised of nine stories, each built around one episode or set of characters from his days on the *Journal*. The years covered are those before the start of his literary career, which (allowing for a few poems and some discarded fiction) blossomed only later, when he had gone over to the *Daily News*. Six of the stories appeared first in *Playboy* which, from about 1960 until his death, gave him an audience of young people not otherwise familiar with his work and mythology.

For a book written as a loose kind of serial, it is surprisingly well integrated. Before putting them between boards, Hecht revised the chapters extensively and, for once, revised upward instead of down, tightening many of the bifurcated passages and polishing the style considerably. The result is an energetic tone characteristic of Hecht as a whole, without the sloppiness of *Charlie*. The effect is rather that of certain passages in *A Child of the Century*, but mellower in its assessment of the callow young journalist to whom the author professes to see little resemblance. What in *A Child of the Century* veered at times toward embarassment at what he had been was in *Gaily, Gaily* a jocular understanding of his former recklessness and naiveté.

Even his digressions contribute to the flavour. He manages to recreate the atmosphere of his early experiences in a series of more or less straight narratives rather than a mosaic of vignettes and musings, as he had in all his other prose memoirs. Nevertheless, he is still able to weave an underpadding of facts, dates and proper names which serve as background information as well as background music. Not that the facts are always any truer than they had been in other memoirs. The book bears no sign of research, except for consultation of a diary he kept in his early *Journal* period. Rather, the facts create an ambience which primes the wells of invention and memory (a throw-back perhaps to his creative way with newspaper assignments). When his memory failed him, he simply grew looser with the facts and carried on.

The best chapters, such as "The Lunatic," are thus a strange combination of the probable, the impressionistic and the atmospheric. They are much more successful as tales than any of the short stories he wrote from the early 1930s onward. There are stylistic excesses, chapters written as bridges and catch-alls and the usual percentage of abortive metaphors. For all that, *Gaily, Gaily* is one of his best shorter works. It reveals the way in which he set about reordering his own myth by incorporating, as semi-fictional characters, some of his previous selves.

Such incorporation was one of the essential traits of the Memoirist, to which his use of hard fact was usually subordinate. His contemporaries, however, did not all see the situation in that light. One example is Carl Sandburg (himself not always a strict factualist). He complained at least twice to Harry Golden, his biographer, of Hecht's casual attitude toward details of Sandburg's Chicago career in *A Child of the Century* – even while writing Hecht warmly upon the book's publication. What Sandburg failed to see, or what he perceived and decided to ignore, was the inevitability of Hecht's misuse of acquaintances' biographical data in the sorting out and reshaping, for literary purposes, of his own. The process is central to *Letters From Bohemia*, the last book Hecht completed.

Gaily, Gaily was largely a collection of pieces written for serial publication, but *Letters From Bohemia* was literally a paste-pot book. It came about when Hecht, rummaging in the house at Nyack, discovered several old letters from friends who had died. The correspondents were Gene Fowler, H.L. Mencken, Sherwood Anderson, Maxwell Bodenheim, George Grosz, George Anthiel and Charles MacArthur. Some of the letters dated back to the teens of the century while others were from the 1950s. Hecht's idea was to reprint the letters without annotation, prefacing each section with a memoir of the writer in question.

There was no question of its being a selected correspondence of those public men. None of the friends (except perhaps Mencken, with his short, witty notes) expected the letters to ever be published. Nor was it even a selective correspondence showing an exchange of ideas. Hecht, being an old reporter, did not keep carbons of his replies. Besides, the incoming letters were fragmentary portraits at best, ranging from only two MacArthur letters to a series from Bodenheim. The latter were from the years when Hecht was helping support the poet by long distance on the condition that he continue with his literary career. The book would be nothing but background information without the accompanying reminiscences, which add up to another summary portrait of Hecht.

A Child of the Century was Hecht the Memoirist revealing himself by remembering his actions, friendships, causes and thoughts, while *Gaily, Gaily* was a smaller assessment of his actions alone. *Letters From Bohemia*, however, depends solely on portraiture through association. Coming after so many similar books, it must have presented certain difficulties. Hecht was at pains not to repeat anecdotes used in earlier works. The result is that some of the stories about these people are too fantastic to be true; at least, too fantastic not to have been used earlier. When he was writing *A Child of the Century*, all the subjects except Anderson were alive. Still, it seems incredible that he could have failed to use then, in what he doubtless thought would be his one final account, some of the stories in *Letters From Bohemia*. How could he have saved for so long the story of Fowler libelling his employer William Randolph Hearst and getting away with it, or Mencken misplacing the ashes of Percival Pollard, one of his critical mentors, and interring instead a box of cigars?

Nonetheless, the anecdotes are in character. The sketches of "seven dead friends who, in a fashion, molded much of my life" are moving and faithful to Hecht's conception of the reality, despite a reversion at times to the stylistic carelessness of *Charlie*. It is a pity that the book was dependent upon the happenstance of the letters, for the selection of subjects is a mixed blessing. Anthiel and Grosz, for instance, were minor compatriots at best compared with Charles Lederer. Lederer, of course, had lived in Hollywood, where Hecht spent much of his time, and so the two men would have had less occasion to correspond.

To the others, however, Hecht lends some insight. Of Anderson, whom he saw hardly at all after the breakup of the Chicago group, and who resented and disliked Hecht the Iconoclast and Bohemian, he says: "There was something remarkable in him for him to love. He had a way of talking and writing that was different than [sic] anyone else's. He was Modernism – the unwanted orphan on the doorstep of complacency." So indeed it must have appeared in 1917.

The book continues Hecht's boosting into legend of Fowler and MacArthur (Mencken needed no such help), and continues also the wrestling with Bodenheim's spirit. Here again, however, Hecht is perpetuating an image Bodenheim alternately welcomed and vigourously denied in life. This section (printed first in *Playboy*) shows Bodenehim as "more disliked, derided, denounced, beaten up, and kicked down more flights of stairs than any other poet of whom I have ever heard or read." Once again, Bodenheim was, underneath, the fellow Hecht had once feared becoming. Behind Bodenheim's affectations there was more than a little real ghetto poverty. Hecht had outdistanced this kind of poverty early on but the fear of it haunted him even as a Memoirist. Such fear, along with a distinct and bothersome sense of his own impending end, were the Memoirist's only concessions to the future. As he went about making a present identity from what had gone before, the fears proved well founded.

Letters From Bohemia was published posthumously.

11
Special
Effects

*Perhaps I am even a trifle overdone, for I have less
anger in me and less love than I had a few years
ago, and my sentences have grown a little longer.*
BH, *in* A Child of the Century

Hecht's last years appear to have been a tangle of transitory works
and uncompleted projects. There was about him, it seems to the
observer now, a long period of diffusion. His various personas were
scattered on the winds of money-making, controversy and melancholy. As of old, he thrived on the activity, but what he accomp-
lished seemed to add to the confusion, not define it. He continued
to turn out a large amount of work, but it reinforced his reputation
as a gadfly without strengthening or changing it. It was as though,
by sorting out his past as a Memoirist, he left nothing ahead of him
but a mad scramble to catch up with the present.

The melancholy or mellowness cannot be over-stressed but
neither can the controversy that was its chaperone. In 1947, in the
midst of the Palestine turmoil and his last serious assault on Hollywood, he paused long enough to compose his only work for children, *The Cat That Jumped Out of the Story*. Such a book would
have been unthinkable to those who knew only Hecht's ferocity
and cynicism. Yet this bit of whimsy was natural to a Hecht living
out a number of roles all at once. It was also natural to a Hecht few
readers cared to recall from *A Child of the Century* — that is, the

aging family man grown fond of what he stopped short of calling the eternal verities. The book was dedicated to, and presumably written for, his daughter Jenny. She would soon begin (in her father's film *Actors and Sin*) a career as an actress that would erupt in the kind of controversy that seemed to be a genetic inheritance.

Early in 1953, Jenny, then nine years old, was selected for the cast of the play *Midsummer*. Her part was that of a precocious daughter of a school-teacher trying desperately to become a Broadway songwriter. The play, which previewed in New Haven and Boston before moving to Broadway, starred Mark Stevens and Geraldine Page as the girl's parents. The controversy arose when other members of the cast laid charges against Jenny through Actor's Equity. Apparently, the accusations involved tardiness, mischief and insubordination, including scene-stealing from the adult players. Pending the investigation she was suspended from the role, which had been paying her $175 per week. Jenny, even offstage as precocious as her father, holed up reading Chekov.

Mr. and Mrs. Hecht leapt to their daughter's defense, and the media, mindful of Hecht's disputatious streak, jumped upon the story with equal vigour. The Hechts charged that their daughter had been the victim of psychological warfare, claiming that her safety was being jeopardized by rivals jealous of the critical attention she had been receiving. In an open letter to the union, Hecht dismissed as "trumpery" the grievances, which were later quietly dropped. At one point the angered parents considered litigation against the union and even went so far as to discuss possible action with no less powerful an attorney than Louis Nizer. It was a spirited conflict for a time, but it passed. Jenny's career, however, persisted. At length she became a member of New York's Living Theatre, the most famous and outrageous experimental group of the 1960s. She died tragically at an early age less than a decade after her father, who had meanwhile been involved in other fracases.

The publication of *A Child of the Century* in 1954 made Hecht publicly what the composition of it had made him privately: a survivor from the glorious days of the 1920s and beyond. In the popular and literary histories of that period, which had begun appearing early in the Depression, Hecht had little place. Sorters through the debris of an era had generally written around him. Now, however, all that was beginning to change. The historians of

Hollywood who would resurrect his memory and renown were still in the future, though chroniclers of the Chicago period were beginning to appear. The publication party for the autobiography had been held in Chicago at the bookshop of Stuart Brent, then a gathering place for a new, smaller and tamer generation of local writers, such as Nelson Algren and Studs Terkel, who nonetheless were making themselves heard. At about the same time there was a long anniversary celebration of the Renaissance veterans. They were welcomed back for visits, already enshrined in the history of that American city most conscious of and plagued by its past. The first book-length retrospective critique of the Renaissance appeared the same year.

In order to enjoy the leisure of his newly-codified past, Hecht spent much of his time travelling to Europe and elsewhere for screenwriting and doctoring jobs. He also maintained at home what would have been, for any other writer, a full schedule of such work. One such job was the screenplay for Howard Hawks' comedy *Monkey Business*, surely one of the most presentable of the many, generally undistinguished films through which he flitted in the final years. It was in 1952, during the writing of that script with I.A.L. Diamond and Charles Lederer, that he renewed his acquaintance with Marilyn Monroe. The meeting would result in another controversy of sorts, though only after both principals had died.

It is asserted that Hecht helped Monroe write an autobiography, "My Story," which two years later appeared serially in a now defunct British tabloid, the *Empire News* of London. There is little evidence to seriously suggest that the manuscript was actually the work of Monroe and not a team of studio hirelings. There is far less to connect it with Hecht. Certainly the book carried no "as-told-to" credit, although that might be explained by Hecht's position in Britain at the time, during the banning of his films there. In any event, through a few stylistic flourishes, which just as easily could be the mark of some other hard-boiled newspaperman, and through a certain amount of legend, the work came to be considered Hecht's. It was presumed to be such in the early 1970s when a spate of books began appearing on the actress's tragic life.

In 1974, on the heels of the other Monroe biographies, the controversy came about when a version of the manuscript was scheduled for publication in New York as a new and original work.

The Five Lives of Ben Hecht

As it was being produced, the detective work of Digby Diehl, the literary editor of the Los Angeles *Times*, showed the impending volume to be only the old serial with a few minor alterations. Hecht's name was again brought up, and attempts were made to prove his connection with the manuscript. Once again, the issue quickly blew over after a few days of big headlines.

Such talent for disposable controversy made Hecht a natural candidate for television, a medium he took to with as much flair and alacrity as he had once taken to the talkies. It made him, first, a sought after guest on some of the pioneer talk shows, such as Mike Wallace's. There and elsewhere he found it easy to lay out an unending stream of indignant and deflating opinions that would have done justice to Mencken. He revealed all his contradictions most blatantly in the new medium. He stated, for instance, that he cared not a hoot for religion, cared no more about being a Jew than if he "was a Kentuckian" and rejoiced in the news that Judaism was on the decline in the United States. Odd opinions to come from the once and future Propagandist, but not odd at all for a bewildered, aging man who sought only to divert himself by entertaining others with outrageous banter.

Talk shows, not yet the staple of television they are today, were nevertheless the rage, often on a local basis. For instance, the musician Oscar Levant, an old friend-antagonist of Hecht and composer of the score for *Crime Without Passion*, hosted a popular programme of that type in Los Angleles. It was in some measure a response to Levant when Hecht was retained by the ABC flagship station in New York to conduct what the corporation called "an intellectual variety show," beginning in September 1958.

Almost from the start it was a controversial show, due in part to bizarre programming. In November, for example, one of the nightly installments was blacked out by management minutes before airtime when it was learned that Hecht planned to bring more than half a dozen Bowery winos into the studio for an unstructured discussion. Earlier he had tried and failed to get Jack Kerouac, then at the peak of his fame, to denigrate other Beat Generation writers. Later, 1959, when the show finally went off the air, Hecht led Dorothy Parker, of all people, in a public slaughter of the old Algonquin Round Table. In that case, his feelings were no doubt whetted by memories of MacArthur, whose irregular attendance at the famous group was a sad symbol of his unproductiveness as a writer.

Perhaps the two most remembered programmes in Hecht's brief flirtation with a more public oraculousness are also the most revealing of his attitude at the time.The first programme was one in which he himself was interviewed about books which had affected his life. The list is interesting both for its consistency with his past public lives and the breadth of his one unbroken private self. He listed and commented on Huysmans, Mencken, some of the long ago erotic masters and other influences of his youth, who still meant a great deal to him. He also enthralled the audience with his familiarity with art history, entomology, archaeology and general science as well as with the classics. All were filtered through Hecht's claim to being a child of his century, enabling him, for instance, to say that "Suetonius was an early Walter Winchell." The show was by far his most popular. More than ten thousand viewers wrote requesting copies of the list, and Hecht reprinted the full transcript the next year in *A Treasury of Ben Hecht*.

The other noteworthy show featured Mickey Cohen, the Los Angeles gangster who had helped Hecht raise funds for the Irgun. Under questioning, Cohen revealed on the air that he had never killed anyone who, in his opinion, had not deserved killing. The resulting furor could have been foreseen. It was the most mileage Hecht was to get from Cohen, who figured in one of the large number of abortive or inconsequential projects that occupied his time.

One does not have to research diligently to discover that Hecht was attempting to juggle a large number of literary, theatrical and film projects, some of which developed but many of which did not. In 1955, for example, Westbrook Pegler, the Hearst columnist, mentioned in a piece that he, Gene Fowler and Hecht were then collaborating on something called "The Life and Death of Al Capone." Pegler's father had been one of the grand figures of Chicago journalism when Hecht was young; Hecht and the son apparently got on despite the latter's notorious rightwing political stance. The

Capone project was probably a film property, though what became of it is uncertain. It simply sank beneath the tangle of work Hecht was undertaking around that time.

In 1958, Hecht returned briefly to Chicago and conducted, for nostalgia's sake, a guest column in the *Daily News* under his old standing head, "1001 Afternoons." What with the way Hecht had treated his tenure there in *A Child of the Century* — as perhaps the most productive and happiest years of his life — all was now forgiven at the newspaper that had once dismissed him so callously. Indeed, Hecht was a large part of the paper's legitimate claim to a distinguished and colourful past. In 1976, when the publication celebrated its centennial, it would note, in proudly reprinting Hecht's final column from 1922: "If ever a ghost ought to walk the corridors of a newspaper building, it should be that of Ben Hecht." The 1958 column was, as to be expected, little like his original one. The almost incalculable changes that had taken place in the city did yield, however, an article for *Playboy* early in 1959, which was one of Hecht's busiest periods.

The subject of the article was prostitution, or rather the total disappearance of prostitution as he had once known it in the era of posh houses, cheap perfumes and piano players addressed as "perfesser." He pretended to take a somewhat naive stance, as though taken aback by the remoteness of his experience from the present situation. Such a position was a device for relating another brief memoir in the guise of an article, though it also has real implications as regards the course of Hecht's writing. His contemporaries, like the Chicago he had known, were dying off, and he found fascination in vicarious associations with olden times in general, if not always his particular olden times. Also, he came to contrast some of his work on contemporary themes with the way such work would have been undertaken in his prime.

He had two books underway in 1958. One was a biography of Mickey Cohen, whom he had come to know better than many of the old time Chicago bootleggers. In the late 1940s and 1950s, Cohen virtually symbolized the American gangster with his life of bloodshed and opulence, his infiltration of legitimate business and his association with politicians and entertainment stars. Cohen was the gang lord of Los Angeles. He was a fitting symbol for Hecht, whose interest in the old Chicago lifestyles and ethos remained even after the reality had changed and he himself lolled amid the palm trees.

Hecht worked intermittently on the biography, taking advantage of the gangster's full co-operation. He wrote in a vein similar to that of *Charlie*, but in a tighter, crisper style. The project had to be abandoned, however, when it was well underway, partly because Cohen, ignorant or treacherous in the ways of journalism, gave a revealing interview to a free lance, thus compromising the exclusivity of Hecht's work. The unfinished manuscript was finally published in 1970 in the premier issue of *Scanlon's*, a short-lived muckraking magazine edited by Warren Hinckle, formerly editor of *Ramparts*, and Sidney Zion. The latter was passionately interested in Hecht, largely because of Hecht's Jewish activities, and was one of a small but vocal group who championed various facets and lives of Hecht following his death.

The other project at the time was *The Sensualists*, his last attempt at serious fiction. It was structured as a murder mystery, although it otherwise bears little resemblance to the genre, and is concerned with the methodology of eroticism. In an open letter announcing the publication, Hecht wrote of how the authors of his youth, such as Anderson and Dreiser, had mixed a frank approach toward sexual expression, daring at the time, with a reticence about the intricacies of sex. Such reticence was the last vestige of the Victorian prudery against which they were rebelling. He contrasted it with the tendency of present day writers to treat the subject with a clinical accuracy unknown in the 1920s, but with little of the psychological searching that had made their predecessors important.

His response was a compromise that sought to be something fresh. It was not didactic except insofar as it preached the virtue of intellectual hedonism and the study of psychological cleverness in which he himself was so well-tutored. It is interesting that one of the book's characters is a sophisitcated but callow New York book publisher. Perhaps Hecht was also criticizing the excesses of his own earlier work, trying to get at the roots of the character he had treated with such artifice in *A Jew in Love* and *The Scoundrel*. But that was a private concern. Publicly, Hecht, with his often unreliable impressionistic, metaphorical pinpointing, saw the novel as "a sort of seminar on modern eroticism, such as Ovid might have set down had he been cross-pollinated by Raymond Chandler."

Except for *Gaily, Gaily*, which was largely stitched together from his still prolific magazine writing, few book projects bore fruit. The results in other media were equally discouraging. In 1960, for instance, he formed a company with the intention of returning to independent film production. The plan was to shoot, mainly in Greenwich Village, a film version of *Winkelberg*, which Robert Parrish would direct from Hecht's own adaptation. Hecht was to be the producer as well. This, too, came to nothing.

For a time, Hecht's name was almost as prominent in controversies and magazine by-lines as in author's credits. One imbroglio was innocent enough as far as its perpetrator was concerned. The charges and counter-charges came about when Hecht contributed a Hollywood memoir to the November 1960 issue of *Playboy*. The article, which is surprisingly good-natured about the Hollywood experience and a useful source for clues to hidden screen credits, contained a reference to the death, in 1932, of Paul Bern, an MGM executive who had recently married Jean Harlow, then the studio's most important female star. In an aside, Hecht wrote that the death, presumed a suicide, had been no such thing. He repeated as common inside knowledge that Bern had been murdered by his mistress, who had then taken her own life as well. He casually stated (charged would be too strong a word) that the studio, fearing for Harlow's reputation, had forged the suicide note found beside Bern's body. People in the business, he asserted, had known this for years. He went on to state that the director Henry Hathaway knew the full story.

All hell, as it had a way of doing for Hecht, broke loose for a short period. The Los Angeles district attorney announced plans to question both Hecht and Hathaway, citing Hecht's literary stature as sufficient reason for reopening the case. Hecht was caught in the middle again. He admitted that he had no evidence for his statements and was repeating gossip common at the time, twenty-eight years earlier. The uproar followed him wherever he went. In Toronto, where he had gone with Billy Rose to attend rehearsals of Robertson Davies' play *Love and Libel*, apparently with the intention of perhaps securing film rights, the press made a big story of the controversy. In time, this too died out, just as did the idea for developing Davies' play in another medium.

Hecht was now a figure of considerable fame as an artifact as well as writer and film worker. The process of recapitulating his past and being prodded to remember, occupied much of the time not taken up with miscellaneous film jobs. He had made his mark as a novelist and short story writer but was now more remembered than read. As a playwright his place was secure as a result of *The Front Page* rather than any of the more serious works by which he might have preferred to be known. As a film writer he remained a more important name than his current writing for the screen would tend to justify, and his place would be established only later by a process that continues. In the meantime he was busy with odds and ends of his past which was just beginning to be served up by others as well.

Jay Robert Nash, later a prominent writer on the history of organized crime, established in 1961 a Chicago paper called the *Literary Times* in oblique imitation of Hecht's *Chicago Literary Times*. Hecht was one of the authors interviewed at length in Nash's publication, whose existence was an indication of Hecht's ironic rise as a cult figure now that he was fading from more or less orthodox literary circles.

In 1964, still oblivious to some of the obvious contradictions of his five different lives, he spoke at Harvard University on the subject of his half-century aloofness from politics, statecraft and all similar "humanity-devouring" activities. All the while he was working on two projects that would finally symbolize the duality he lived out as both a popular and a self-indulgently elitist writer. The one was the book for a musical play loosely conjuring up the atmosphere of old Chicago. The other was the script of the film *Casino Royale*. This was a spoof of the James Bond films then popular but harkened back in some ways to the noisy comedies of the 1930s. It was the last film Hecht worked on, though it was not filmed and released until 1967.

He had recently passed a medical examination and was in good health for a man of seventy. However, on Saturday, April 18, 1964, he collapsed in his New York apartment while reading. He had suffered a heart attack, and all attempts at resuscitation failed. He was buried the following Monday after services at a New York

The Five Lives of Ben Hecht

synagogue. The obituaries were even longer and more generous than they usually are for old newspapermen. Fittingly, they were also full of contradictory adjectives.

The history of Hecht's reputation as a writer — that is, the way he was viewed when alive — inevitably gives way to the question of its future, or the usefulness of what he left behind. The situation is far rosier than he himself might have imagined, though also much different. Now that his films are undergoing revival and scrutiny (action he would have balked at, but with a wink), and now that his books are slowly coming into print again, many of the problems Hecht faced when alive still exist, but from the perspective of a different time, with different tastes and needs.

He was a writer who refused to be confined within a hierarchy of forms, and that fact got him into critical trouble almost from the start. The powers that be could nod at his newspaper background. So long as it did not constitute a school, such experience was an honourable enough beginning, one that had been shared by Howells and Mark Twain among others. They were also willing to forgive his dabbling in mystery stories and other supposedly substandard literary forms. They did feel, however, that he published much too promiscuously, even before he disgraced himself in their eyes by retiring to Hollywood. Yet the truth is that his dexterity was based in an admirable adaptability and dedication to purpose. The fact that one man could write, near the start of his career, for *Mother Earth*, Emma Goldman's anarchist magazine, and later for the Marx Brothers, indicates a strength and not a weakness.

Hecht was unfortunate not in his successors so much as in his contemporaries; at least, the differences between the two sets of people have tended to change the way he is viewed. He wrote when an epoch of fiction was ending and an epoch of journalism just beginning. His work, while a grand reflection of that nether world between the two, has found only a toehold in each. What's more, he wrote in an age of fierce individualism and is now being assessed in one of growing egalitarianism, when his contribution to collectivism (each motion picture a capitalist committee) becomes ever more important. He outlived his literary critics and predeceased his cinematic ones, with the result that he is in danger of being seen in terms of only the one discipline. Such a fate not only ignores fully half his work and importance, it also passes over all the many contradictions that make both halves, singly and together, so recognizably his own. The five Ben Hechts must be seen individually and then realigned before one can appreciate any Ben Hecht in particular.

He came out of several traditions at once. That fact produced some personal confusion but also the energy that fuelled his writing. He was first of all a Jew, though it was his recoiling from that fact, rather than his examination of it, that initially engaged him. Before his Zionism as during it, he was often denounced as an anti-Semite, but then so have a large number of Jewish-American writers, including such discrete figures as Philip Roth, Herman Wouk and Edward Dahlberg. Actually his attitude in the 1920s and 1930s, as the son of Ashkenazic Jews from the *shtetls*, is as much a part of the Jewish-American literary tradition as any other. He was the offspring of people who were both eager and anxious for his assimilation, knowing all the while that he would have to work out the problem for himself. It might appear at times that his discovery of his own heritage was a negative one (as he himself said), that it was founded in other people's anti-Semitism rather than his own Judaism. But a better reasoned notion is that the sudden shift from one extreme to the other was the only way he could resolve the conflict he doubltess felt very deeply — that of being thoroughly American and yet at base (he believed) so thoroughly only half-American.

It was only in his middle age, after World War Two and Palestine, that he began to feel comfortable with the circumstances of his roots. All the reminiscing he did as a Memoirist was to pave his future as well as to sort out his past. The future was simply that of a Jewish-American novelist-screenwriter who felt no pain at the hyphen, who was secure as the kind of outsider he somehow imagined he was. This is sometimes forgotten in readings of the majority of his work not concerned on the surface with the Jewish experience. For instance, Norman Jewison's 1969 film *Gaily, Gaily,* actually a garble of various tales and anecdotes by and about Hecht as a young reporter, simply ignores the fact of Hecht's Jewishness. In a movie remarkable for the director who later would make that laundered look at the ghetto, *Fiddler on the Roof,* Jewi-

The Five Lives of Ben Hecht

son changed the name Ben Hecht to Ben Harvey and awarded the part to no less a Presbyterian than Beau Bridges. The result came near to being incomprehensible.

At any rate, Hecht always considered himself an outsider, regardless whether such an attitude was justifed. At first his outsider status embarrassed him. Later it was made a point of defiant pride. Finally, toward the end, he was simply comfortable with it.

The other traditions from which he came were also outsider traditions. If newspapermen are the aristocrats of the outcast world, they are outcasts all the same. Hecht, privy to every stratum of society without being part of any, was thus provided with the excuse for exaggerating the need for independence to which, as an outcast, he was already resigned. He was also something of an outcast by virtue of his position as a midwesterner. Despite his allegiance to Mencken, and despite the fact that Mencken was, beneath all the rabblerousing, an embittered conservative, Hecht was something of a midwest radical. He was one of those characters always caught between populist sentiments and elitist ideals, so that he championed the underdog as long as the underdog was beset by stronger forces than the condescension and ridicule that Hecht himself, in a different mood, levelled at the common man.

All this has more to do with his art than with his politics, though it is also evident in the latter. *Count Bruga, A Guide for the Bedevilled* and *Perfidy* are not far from one another in style. In attitude, however, they reveal Hecht going from A to B and back to A again, with the last position informed by the other two. He was at his best with a clear target free of dangling subtleties, and the politics of Palestine and Israel were just as confusing to him as those of Germany had been in 1919. His politics were in the end simplistic. But for one to dismiss them as such, without learning how they came to be that way, is equally simplistic.

As early as the 1930s, Hecht was being listed in biographical dictionaries as "an intellectual maverick," which was fitting enough. All the conflicts of his life – about Jewishness, the newspaper life and other subjects besides – forced him into a position he never left and indeed kept reconfirming his belief in. He left the pack for good after the 1920s and became a kind of independent intellectual, which in the minds of those who confer respectability is not intellectual at all. Each booster shot of independence put him farther from the mainstream. The more mileage he placed between himself and his contemporaries, the more his own imaginative world was strengthened.

He was a critic of human frailties, including his own. Both knowingly and unwittingly, he was also an anarchist of emotions. That is why he is belatedly entering the clearly labelled pigeonhole he so long eluded. In our time parts of his contradictory nature are beginning to fade, leaving a classifiable residue. He was both optimistic and pessimistic about the future of the society he lived in but, on balance, an optimist about the future of such pessimism. He had in great quantity both sentimentality and cynicism. As the one grows less fashionable, the other becomes more necessary.

Hecht was a creator of special effects, though not in the sense of the film technician. He was more of a lay psychologist who set out with preconceived theories of human eccentricity which he believed could be proved merely by illustration. He had an unusual sense of the grotesque and dealt mainly with freaks whose deformity was of their own manufacture. He was concerned with both ordinary people in extraordinary situations and extraordinary people in more common ones. The latter was generally the case with all the Hechtian man material and indeed all the writing that was less reportage than exploration of his own isolation. In such cases he maintained a peculiar love-hate relationship with his own image, similar to the ones he maintained with Bodenheim, Sherwood Anderson or Hollywood. The dichotomy helps explain the ease with which he became the only big name literary figure of his generation to juggle film and literary work over a long period, making important contributions to each. It also puts in perspective the two basic types of writing he undertook: types which spanned all the media in which he worked and all the five lives he acted out.

Left to his own devices, Hecht became disconsolate when his work with eccentrics and miscreants revealed him to be an outsider. Left alone he became the intellectual gadfly and malcontent of *Erik Dorn*, *Gargoyles* and the early stories and plays. In that part of his writing he lived in a world of his own. The setting was a city full of harsh shadows, menacing rain, improbable buildings and crazy corruption and decay in which he pretended to revel for hollow amusement. His city was every bit as recognizable as Dickens' London or Balzac's Paris had been except that (despite the name Chicago) it was no city in particular but a sensibility and a state of mind: the modern urban experience. Nor was it a realistic city like the ones to come from James T. Farrell or Nelson Algren, for Hecht had little interest in the facts except inasmuch as they lent plausibility to his broodings. "There is hardly one in three of us who live in cities," he wrote at the end of *A Child of the Century,* "who is not sick with unused self." This could serve well as a statement of purpose for his early works, whether dramatic, melodramatic or comedic, in which urban alienation is the subject and the facts merely his concession to craft.

That was the Bohemian and Iconoclast and to some extent the Memoirist. The Sophisticate sometimes followed the same pattern, as with his interest in strange personalities and other sophisticates who were decadent in their opulence and waste. It also applies to that part of the Sophisticate obsessed with "miracles," by which Hecht meant the discovery of potential for unused self. In addition, there was a third part to the Sophisticate, which spilled into the other lives: that part which worked in collaboration with other writers.

When accompanied by MacArthur, or sometimes Fowler or Lederer, Hecht would move into a comedy of remembrance. At such times he was jovially cynical on the same themes about which otherwise he was deadly sober. Collaboration nearly always released him from artiness. If it also deprived him of a little of his originality at times, it created a group identity different from any other. With MacArthur or some other friend, he became young again in spirit and could laugh at his own earnestness, but not necessarily at the original reasons for it. *The Front Page* or *Soak the Rich* could only have been written in collaboration; *Notorious* and *Spellbound* only by himself alone.

If Hecht had at best only a large minority interest in his efforts with other directors, there can be no doubt that he was always the dominant partner in any sit-down collaboration with another writer. The resultant scripts, no matter how weak, were the better for his dominance. His comedies, even *The Front Page* and certainly some of the screenplays, were full of laughs to keep Hecht from crying at a society far less sensitive than himself. That is why some of them work as well as they do. He was writing about himself even when making fun of others.

What Hecht brought to American writing was a picture of the missing link between hero and anti-hero. He fell somewhere along the jerky but unbroken line between Natty Bumppo and Godfather Corleone. At some point the frontier had become the urban waste-land. It was at that crossroads that he lived and wrote, and the characters he created dwelt there too. In literature, that creation was the natural extension of what had been done by others before him. Hecht made it distinctly his own by bringing to it a different style, one made by fusing the decadents, impressionists and expressionists of Britain and the Continent with the American experience and the American language. In the new and essentially traditionless medium of the motion picture, however, it was virtually a new concept. It stuck.

His precise influence on film could be examined in much greater detail, from the fine points of his social attitudes, to his characteristic bits of business, to the overlapping dialogue of the kind one finds today in the movies of Robert Altman. Basically, however, his main contribution was his ability to personify, in his writings of all media and genres, thoroughly modern and American characters such as himself, so full of contradictions and so alienated from what they believe a meaningless society entitles them to.

From the 1920s onward he became less and less a figure of rarified high culture, but was able to convince ever growing numbers of the usefulness and integrity of the forms and styles in which he later worked. He was a figure at odds with his times, but one without whom they would not be quite the same times in our memory. He was a general practitioner in an age of specialists. He did not by any means debase traditional esthetic experiences, and he infused intelligence into the popular culture, making it more inventive, meaningful and important than it was before he arrived.

Appendix 1
A Hecht
Bibliography

All available bibliographies of Hecht's printed works are woefully out of date. For instance, he was dropped from Merle Johnson's *American First Editions* after 1936, along with other unworthies such as Ezra Pound. For the convenience of readers frequenting libraries and second-hand book stores I have therefore listed his books and booklets. They are arranged by year of publication and, within a particular year, by alphabet. I list all the English language editions I have discovered, including important reprints, but no translations into other languages. Only such plays are listed as were first published in editions for the general audience rather than in acting editions. Thus, because it first appeared in a trade edition, *The Front Page* is listed, followed by British editions but not the Samuel French edition for players. But *Twentieth Century*, which was announced for trade publication but eventually appeared only in a Samuel French version, is omitted.

The Hero of Santa Maria: A Ridiculous Tragedy in One Act, by Kenneth Sawyer Goodman and BH. New York: Frank Shay, 1920.

Erik Dorn. Novel. New York and London: G.P. Putnam's Sons, 1921. New York: Modern Library (Boni and Liveright), 1924, with an introduction by Burton Rascoe. Chicago: University of Chicago Press, 1963, with an introduction by Nelson Algren.

Fantazius Mallare: A Mysterious Oath. Pornography. Chicago:

193

Covici-McGee, 1922, with illustrations by Wallace Smith, limited to 2,025 signed and numbered copies. The undated pirate edition, in pale green cloth and lacking the tissue leaves preceding the illustrations, was probably produced in New York by Samuel Roth in the 1940s or 1950s.

Gargoyles. Novel. New York: Boni and Liveright, 1922.

1001 Afternoons in Chicago. Sketches and stories. Chicago: Covici-McGee, 1922, with a preface by Henry Justin Smith and illustrations by Herman Rosse. London: Grant Richards, 1923.

The Florentine Dagger: A Novel For Amateur Detectives. New York: Boni and Liveright, 1923, with a frontispiece by Wallace Smith. London: George H. Harrap, 1924. Cleveland: World Publishing, 1942.

Cutie, A Warm Mama. Satire, by BH and Maxwell Bodenheim. Chicago: Hechtshaw Press, 1924, supposedly limited to 200 copies but much more common than that would suggest. New York: Boar's Head Books (Samuel Roth), 1952, with a preface by Bodenheim.

Humpty Dumpty. Novel. New York: Boni and Liveright, 1924.

Broken Necks, and Other Stories. Girard, Kansas: Haldeman-Julius, 1925. Little Blue Book 699.

Tales of Chicago Streets. Stories. Girard, Kansas: Haldeman-Julius, 1925. Little Blue Book 698.

The Wonder Hat and Other One Act Plays, by Kenneth Sawyer Goodman and BH. New York and London: D. Appleton, 1925, with a prefatory note by Thomas Wood Stevens. Contains "The Hero of Santa Maria" and four others. The title play was published separately by the Stage Guild, Chicago, in 1938 and again in 1946.

Broken Necks. Stories and sketches. Chicago: Pascal Covici, 1926, with a preface by BH.

Bibliography

Count Bruga. Novel. New York: Boni and Liveright, 1926. Precedes the other 1926 edition published by Horace Liveright. Abridged, illustrated edition for the armed services – Royce Publishers, Chicago, 1944.

The Kingdom of Evil: A Continuation of the Journal of Fantazius Mallare. Pornography. Chicago: Pascal Covici, 1926, with illustrations by Anthony Angarola, limited to 2,000 signed and numbered copies. A cheap edition, in red cloth, was published by Pascal Covici later in 1926.

Infatuation, and Other Stories of Love's Misfits. Girard, Kansas: Haldeman-Julius, 1927. Little Blue Book 1166.

Jazz, and Other Stories of Young Love. Girard, Kansas: Haldeman-Julius, 1927. Little Blue Book 1165.

The Policewoman's Love-Hungry Daughter, And Other Stories of Chicago Life. Girard, Kansas: Haldeman-Julius, 1927. Little Blue Book 1163.

The Sinister Sex And Other Stories of Marriage. Girard, Kansas: Haldeman-Julius, 1927. Little Blue Book 1167.

The Unlovely Sin And Other Stories of Desire's Pawns. Girard, Kansas: Haldeman-Julius, 1927. Little Blue Book 1164.

Christmas Eve: A Morality Play. New York: Covici-Friede, 1928, limited to 111 signed and numbered copies for private distribution.

The Front Page. Play, by BH and Charles MacArthur. New York: Covici-Friede, 1928, with an introduction by Jed Harris. London: Grant Richards and Humphrey Toulmin, 1929. London: Cayme Press, 1929, with an epilogue for the British audience.

The Champion From Far Away. Stories. New York: Covici-Friede, 1931.

A Jew in Love. Novel. New York: Covici-Friede, 1931, as well as an edition limited to 150 signed and numbered copies. London: Fortune Press, 1934. Reprints – Triangle, New York, 1938.

The Great Magoo. Play, by BH and Gene Fowler. New York: Covici-Friede, 1933, with illustrations by Herman Rosse.

Actor's Blood. Stories. New York. Covici-Friede, 1936.

To Quito And Back. Play. New York: Covici-Friede, 1937.

A Book of Miracles. Novellas. New York: Viking Press, 1939. London: Nicholson and Watson, 1940. Reprints – Sun Dial Press, Garden City, NY, 1941.

1001 Afternoons in New York. Columns and sketches. New York: Viking Press, 1941, with illustrations by George Grosz. Probably preceded by a booklet of the same title published by the newspaper PM earlier in 1941. Abridged edition – Avon, New York, 1945, in the Avon Modern Short Story Monthly series.

Ben Hecht – 11 Selected Great Stories. New York: Avon, 1943, in the Modern Short Story Monthly series.

Concerning A Woman of Sin, And Other Stories. New York: Editions for the Armed Services, 1943. Except that this edition contains a preface by BH, it may otherwise be identical with a collection of the same title published in the Avon Modern Short Story Monthly series, 1947.

Miracle in the Rain. Story. New York: Knopf, 1943. Sydney, Australia: Peter Huston, 1946.

A Guide for the Bedevilled. Polemic. New York: Charles Scribner's 1944. Reprints – Garden City, Garden City, NY, 1945.

I Hate Actors! Novel. New York: Crown, 1944. Reprints – Bartholomew House, New York, 1946, under the title *Hollywood Mystery!*

Bibliography

The Collected Stories of Ben Hecht. New York: Crown, 1945, with a preface by BH. London: Nicholson and Watson, n.d. Reprints — Grosset & Dunlap, New York, n.d.

A Flag is Born. Play. New York: American League For a Free Palestine, 1946.

The Cat That Jumped Out of the Story. Children's story. Philadelphia: John C. Winston, 1947, with illustrations by Peggy Bacon.

A Child of the Century. Autobiography. New York: Simon and Schuster, 1954. Paperback reprints — Signet, New York, 1955, and Ballantine, New York, 1970. The last of these lacks some of the photographs found in the other two.

Charlie: The Improbable Life and Times of Charles MacArthur. Memoir. New York: Harper & Bros., 1957, with a preface by Helen Hayes MacArthur.

The Sensualists. Novel. New York: Julian Messner, 1959. London: Anthony Blond, 1960. Paperback reprints — Dell, New York, 1959 and 1964. Four Square, London, 1961. New English Library, London, 1969.

A Treasury of Ben Hecht. Stories and a miscellany. New York: Crown, 1959, with a preface by BH.

Perfidy. Polemic. New York: Julian Messner, 1961, with a preface by BH.

Gaily, Gaily. Memoir. Garden City, NY: Doubleday, 1963. London: Elek Books, 1964. The paperback reprint — Signet, New York, 1965 — was itself reprinted in 1969 with stills from the Norman Jewison film.

Concerning a Woman of Sin. Stories. London: Mayflower paperback, 1964.

In the Midst of Death. Stories. London: Mayflower paperback, 1964.

Letters From Bohemia. Memoir and correspondence. Garden City, NY: Doubleday, 1964. London: Hammond, Hammond, 1965.

Appendix 2
A Hecht
Filmography

At best any Hecht filmography will be incomplete and misleading. That much is guaranteed by the often unfair way in which Hollywood screen credits were awarded and the way in which Hecht himself worked. To be sure, a great many films in the following list bear very little trace of Hecht's hand. That there are many others to which he contributed, but which have not yet been ascribed to him, is almost as certain. Looking to Hecht for clues is often as exasperating as it is helpful. In *Theatre Magazine* in 1929, for instance, he wrote that up to that time he had sold six originals. If that statement is true, then some early films are still unaccounted for by researchers. In *Playboy* in 1960 he made a statement that can be interpreted as meaning that Erich von Stroheim was the first director with whom he worked on a talkie. If that was the case, then this is yet another puzzle. So far no other evidence has come to light indicating that they ever worked together. In the same article Hecht mentioned several scripts which for various reasons were never produced, including one written with Gene Fowler for W.C.Fields. Evidence of other unproduced scripts can be found elsewhere, but I have not attempted to list such scripts here. The following does cover, however, all his film credits as well as much uncredited work. It is more or less in harmony with the films he must have had in mind when, in the *Playboy* piece, he alluded to "the seventy movies I have written for Hollywood." The dates are those of release, not necessarily of production.

199

Double Trouble. 1915. Anita Loos in her autobiography states that BH supplied the idea for this Douglas Fairbanks vehicle.

Underworld. 1927. Directed by Josef von Sternberg. Story by BH. British title: *Paying the Penalty*.

The Big Noise. 1928. Directed by Allan Dwan. Co-scripted by BH (uncredited).

Unholy Night. 1929. Directed by Lionel Barrymore. Story by BH.

The Green Ghost. 1929. Directed by Lionel Barrymore. Story by BH.

Roadhouse Nights. 1930. Directed by Robert Henley. Story and screenplay by BH.

The Great Gabbo. 1930. Directed by James Cruze. Story by BH.

The Front Page. 1931. Directed by Lewis Milestone. Script by BH (uncredited) and Charles Lederer from the play by BH and Charles MacArthur.

Unholy Garden. 1931. Directed by George Fitzmaurice. Screenplay by BH and Charles MacArthur.

Scarface. 1932. Directed by Howard Hawks. Screenplay by BH.

Back Street. 1932. Directed by John M. Stahl. Screenplay (uncredited) by BH and Gene Fowler.

Hallelujah, I'm a Bum. 1933. Directed by Lewis Milestone. Story by BH. British title: *Hallelujah, I'm a Tramp*.

Topaze. 1933. Directed by Harry d'Abbadie d'Arrast. Co-scripted by BH (uncredited).

Turn Back the Clock. 1933. Directed by Edgar Selwyn. Co-scripted by BH.

Filmography

Design For Living. 1933. Directed by Ernst Lubitsch. Screenplay by BH.

Queen Christina. 1933. Directed by Rouben Mamoulian. Screenplay by BH and Gene Fowler (both uncredited).

Upper World. 1934. Directed by Roy Del Ruth. Story by BH.

Twentieth Century. 1934. Directed by Howard Hawks. Screenplay by BH and Charles MacArthur from their play of the same title, inspired by Charles Mulholland's play *Napoleon of Broadway*.

Shoot the Works. 1934. Directed by Wesley Ruggles. Script based on BH and Gene Fowler's play *The Great Magoo*.

Crime Without Passion. 1934. Directed by BH and Charles MacArthur. Screenplay by BH and Charles MacArthur from BH's short story of the same title.

Viva Villa! 1934. Directed by Howard Hawks and Jack Conway. Screenplay by BH.

The President Vanishes. 1934. Directed by William Wellman. Co-scripted by BH and Charles MacArthur (uncredited). British title: *The Strange Conspiracy*.

The Florentine Dagger. 1935. Directed by Robert Florey. Screenplay based on BH's novel of the same title.

Once in a Blue Moon. 1935. Directed by BH and Charles MacArthur. Screenplay by BH and Charles MacArthur.

The Scoundrel. 1935. Directed by BH and Charles MacArthur. Screenplay by BH and Charles MacArthur based on BH and Rose Caylor's play *All He Ever Loved*.

Barbary Coast. 1935. Directed by Howard Hawks. Screenplay by BH and Charles MacArthur.

Spring Tonic. 1935. Directed by Clyde Bruckman. Screenplay based on BH and Rose Caylor's play *Man-eating Tiger*.

201

Soak the Rich. 1936. Directed by BH and Charles MacArthur. Screenplay by BH and Charles MacArthur from their play of that title.

Nothing Sacred. 1937. Directed by William Wellman. Screenplay by BH from his play *Hazel Flagg*.

The Hurricane. 1937. Directed by John Ford and Stuart Heisler. Co-scripted by BH (uncredited).

The Goldwyn Follies. 1938. Directed by George Marshall. Screenplay by BH.

Let Freedom Ring. 1939. Directed by George Marshall. Screenplay by BH.

It's a Wonderful World. 1939. Directed by W.S.Van Dyke. Screenplay by BH.

Some Like It Hot. 1939. Directed by George Archainbaud. Screenplay based on BH and Gene Fowler's play *The Great Magoo*.

Lady of the Tropics. 1939. Directed by Jack Conway. Screenplay by BH.

Gunga Din. 1939. Directed by George Stevens. Screenplay by BH, Charles MacArthur, Joel Sayre and Fred Guiol, inspired by the Rudyard Kipling poem.

Wuthering Heights. 1939. Directed by William Wyler. Screenplay by BH and Charles MacArthur based on the novel by Emily Brontë.

Gone With the Wind. 1939. Directed by Victor Fleming. Co-scripted by BH (uncredited), based on the novel by Margaret Mitchell.

His Girl Friday. 1940. Directed by Howard Hawks. Screenplay by BH (uncredited) and Charles Lederer based on BH and Charles MacArthur's play *The Front Page*.

Filmography

Angels Over Broadway. 1940. Directed by BH and Lee Garmes. Screenplay by BH, inspired by a story by George Jessel.

Foreign Correspondent. 1940. Directed by Alfred Hitchcock. Co-scripted by BH (uncredited).

Comrade X. 1940 Directed by King Vidor. Screenplay by BH and Charles Lederer.

The Shop Around the Corner. 1940. Directed by Ernst Lubitsch. Co-scripted by BH (uncredited).

Lydia. 1941. Directed by Julien Duvivier. Co-scripted by BH.

Tales of Manhattan. 1942. Directed by Henry King. Co-scripted by BH.

China Girl. 1942. Directed by Henry Hathaway. Screenplay by BH. Produced by BH.

Roxie Hart. 1942. Directed by William Wellman. Co-scripted by BH (uncredited).

The Outlaw. 1943. Directed by Howard Hawks and Howard Hughes. Co-scripted by BH (uncredited).

Spellbound. 1945. Directed by Alfred Hitchcock. Screenplay by BH (credited) and Hitchcock.

Spectre of the Rose. 1946. Directed by BH and Lee Garmes. Screenplay by BH from his short story of that title.

Notorious. 1946. Directed by Alfred Hitchcock. Screenplay by BH.

Gilda. 1946. Directed by Charles Vidor. Co-scripted by BH (uncredited).

Her Husband's Affairs. 1947. Directed by S. Sylvan Simon. Screenplay by BH, Charles Lederer and I.A.L.Diamond.

Kiss of Death. 1947. Directed by Henry Hathaway. Screenplay by BH, Charles Lederer and I.A.L.Diamond.

Dishonored Lady. 1947. Directed by Robert Stevenson. Co-scripted by BH (uncredited).

Ride the Pink Horse. 1947. Directed by Robert Montgomery. Screenplay by BH and Charles Lederer.

The Paradine Case. 1947. Directed by Alfred Hitchcock. Co-scripted by BH (uncredited).

Miracle of the Bells. 1948. Directed by Irving Pichel. Co-scripted by BH.

Portrait of Jennie. 1948. Directed by William Dieterle.Co-scripted by BH (uncredited).

Rope. 1948. Directed by Alfred Hitchcock. Co-scripted by BH (uncredited).

Whirlpool. 1949. Directed by Otto Preminger. Co-scripted by BH (as "Lester Bartow").

Love Happy. 1949. Directed by David Miller. Co-scripted by BH (uncredited); the screen credit is to "Mac Benoff" which may mean BH and Charles MacArthur.

Where the Sidewalk Ends. 1950. Directed by Otto Preminger. Screenplay by BH.

Perfect Strangers. 1950. Directed by Bretaigne Windust. Screenplay based on BH and Charles MacArthur's play *Ladies and Gentlemen*, itself based on Ladislaud Bus-Feket's play *Twelve in a Box*.

The Secret of Convict Lake. 1951. Directed by Michael Gordon. Co-scripted by BH (uncredited).

Filmography

The Thing. 1951. Directed by Christian Nyby and Howard Hawks. Screenplay by BH and Charles Lederer (both uncredited).

Actors and Sin. 1952. Directed and produced by BH. Screenplay by BH from his short stories "Actor's Blood" and "Concerning a Woman of Sin."

The Greatest Show on Earth. 1952. Directed by Cecil B. De Mille. Co-scripted by BH (uncredited).

Monkey Business. 1952. Directed by Howard Hawks. Screenplay by BH, Charles Lederer and I.A.L.Diamond.

Roman Holiday. 1953. Directed by William Wyler. Co-scripted by BH (uncredited).

Living It Up. 1954. Directed by Norman Taurog. Screenplay based on BH's play *Hazel Flagg* and his screenplay *Nothing Sacred.*

Ulisse. 1955. Directed by Mario Camerini. Co-scripted by BH, inspired by Homer's epic. US and British title: *Ulysses.*

The Indian Fighter. 1955. Directed by André De Toth. Co-scripted by BH.

The Court Martial of Billy Mitchell. 1955. Directed by Otto Preminger. Co-scripted by BH (uncredited). British title: *One Man Mutiny.*

Miracle in the Rain. 1956. Directed by Rudolph Maté. Screenplay by BH from his book of that title.

The Iron Petticoat. 1956. Directed by Ralph Thomas. Screenplay by BH (uncredited).

Legend of the Lost. 1957. Directed by Henry Hathaway. Co-scripted by BH

A Farewell to Arms. 1957. Directed by Charles Vidor. Screenplay by BH based on the novel by Ernest Hemingway.

The Fiend Who Walked the West. 1958. Directed by Gordon Douglas. Screenplay based on BH and Charles Lederer's screenplay *Kiss of Death.*

Queen of Outer Space. 1958. Directed by Edward Bernds. BH is erroneously given credit for the story on which the screenplay is based.

John Paul Jones. 1959. Directed by John Farrow. Co-scripted by BH (uncredited).

Billy Rose's Jumbo. 1962. Directed by Charles Walters. Screenplay based on BH and Charles MacArthur's play *Jumbo.*

Mutiny on the Bounty. 1962. Directed by Lewis Milestone. Co-scripted by BH (uncredited).

Circus World. 1964. Directed by Henry Hathaway. Co-scripted by BH. British title: *The Magnificent Showman.*

Casino Royale. 1967. Directed by John Huston, Ken Hughes, Val Guest, Robert Parrish and Joseph McGrath. Co-scripted by BH (uncredited).

Gaily, Gaily. 1969. Directed by Norman Jewison. Screenplay by Abram S. Grinnes based on BH's books *Gaily, Gaily* and *A Child of the Century.* British title: *Chicago, Chicago.*

The Front Page. 1974. Directed by Billy Wilder. Screenplay by Billy Wilder and I.A.L. Diamond based on BH and Charles MacArthur's play.

Appendix 3
Sources

The following is less a list of sources referred to than of suggested reading. I have not felt obliged to cite the source of every fact used in the text, though I have annotated those I think most important. I have tried to compile, however, a selection of the most useful books concerning or mentioning Hecht or just reflecting particular periods or places in his life. Each year Hecht's name seems to turn up in more and more indexes – especially in books about film – so I have attempted to tip the scale here in favour of the older, noncinematic works. With a couple of exceptions, I have not listed reviews of his work in papers or periodicals but only those republished in books. Place of publication is New York City unless otherwise indicated.

Agee, James. *Agee on Film: Reviews and Comment by James Agee*. McDowell, Obolensky, 1958. One of two volumes, this contains reviews of *Spectre of the Rose* and *Kiss of Death*.

Allsop, Kenneth. *The Bootleggers: The Story of Chicago's Prohibition Era*. New Rochelle, NY: Arlington House, 1968. New edition.

Anderson, Margaret. *My Thirty Years' War*. Covici-Friede 1930. ed. *The Little Review Anthology*. Hermitage House, 1953.

Baker, Carlos. *Ernest Hemingway: A Life Story.* Scribner's, 1969. Source of Hemingway quote in Chapter One.

Barnes, Eric Wollencott. *The Man Who Lived Twice.* A biography of the playwright Edward Sheldon, a collaborator of MacArthur's.

Barris, Alex. *Stop the Presses! The Newspaperman in American Films.* A.S.Barnes, 1976.

Baxter, John. *The Cinema of Josef von Sternberg.* London and New York: A. Zwemmer and Barnes, 1971.

Beckerman, Bernard and Siegman, Howard, eds. *On Stage: Selected Theater Reviews from The New York Times, 1920-1970.* Arno, 1973. Contains unsigned review of *The Front Page,* 1928.

Behlmer, Rudy, ed. *Memo from: David O. Selznick.* Viking, 1972. A good source for Hecht screen credits.

Bellow, Saul. "The 1001 Afternoons of Ben Hecht." *New York Times Book Review,* June 13, 1954.

Bode, Carl. *Mencken.* Carbondale: Southern Illinois University Press, 1969. The foremost biography.

Bodenheim, Maxwell. *Minna and Myself.* Pagan Publishing, 1918. Bodenheim's first collection of verse, this contains "The Master Poisoner," the most infamous of the plays he wrote with Hecht.

  Duke Herring. Liveright, 1931. As easily obtainable in the paperback reprint, Checkerbooks, 1949.

Brent, Stuart. *The Seven Stairs.* Cambridge: Riverside Press, 1962.

Brogan, Louise. *Achievement in American Poetry.* Chicago: Henry Regnery, 1951. Insights into the way literature sprang from American newsrooms.

Sources

Brown, Geoff. "'Better Than Metro Isn't Good Enough!', Hecht and MacArthur's Own Movies." *Sight and Sound*, London, Summer 1975.

Brown, John Mason. *The Worlds of Robert E. Sherwood: Mirror to His Times*. Harper & Row, 1965. One of two volumes, source of Dorothy Parker anecdote in Chapter Eleven.

Butcher, Fanny. *Many Lives – One Love*. Harper & Row, 1972. The memoirs of the longtime book review editor of the Chicago *Tribune*, an observer of commercial Chicago writers as well as of the Renaissance group.

Carnevali, Emanuel. *The Autobiography of Emanuel Carnevali*. Compiled and prefaced by Kay Boyle. Horizon Press, 1967. Memoirs, assembled posthumously, of a poet involved in the Renaissance.

Casey, Robert J. *Such Interesting People*. Indianapolis: Bobbs-Merrill, 1943. The Chicago reporter's memoirs.

Churchill, Allen. *The Improper Bohemians*. E.P. Dutton, 1959, but most easily available in the Ace paperback edition, n.d. A popular history of artists in Greenwich Village, with material on Bodenheim both there and in the Chicago days with Hecht.

The Literary Decade. Englewood Cliffs, NJ: Prentice Hall, 1971. Publishing and literary folkways in the 1920s.

Park Row. Rinehart and Company, 1958. Anecdotal study of New York newspapering with obvious parallels with Chicago.

Cleaton, Irene and Allen. *Books & Battles: American Literature, 1920-1930*. Boston: Houghton Mifflin, 1937. Censorship.

Cohen, Mickey, as told to Nugent Peer. *Mickey Cohen: In My Own Words*. Englewood Cliffs, NJ: Prentice-Hall, 1975.

Colum, Padraic and Cabell, Margaret Freeman. *Between Friends: Letters of James Branch Cabell and Others.* Harcourt, Brace & World, 1962. Source of Ezra Pound epigraph to Chapter Three.

Corliss, Richard. *Talking Pictures: Screenwriters in the American Cinema 1927-1973.* Woodstock, NY: Overlook Press, 1974. The best criticism to date of Hecht as a screenwriter, with discussions of a few individual scripts and a good filmography. The material on Hecht appeared earlier in a paperback edited by Corliss, *The Hollywood Screenwriters* (Avon, 1972), itself a reprint of what appeared in *Film Comment* magazine.

Cowley, Malcolm, ed. *After the Genteel Tradition: American Writers 1910-1930.* Carbondale: Southern Illinois University Press, 1964. Revised edition. Contains "The James Branch Cabell Period" by Peter Monro Jack, which discusses Hecht's early fiction.

Exile's Return, A Literary Odyssey of the 1920s. Viking, 1951. Revised edition.

De Voe, E.T. "'A Soul in Gaudy Tatters': A Critical Biography of Maxwell Bodenheim." Doctoral dissertation. Pennsylvania State University, 1957, available from University Microfilms, Ann Arbor, Michigan. The pioneer study.

Dell, Floyd. *Homecoming.* Farrar & Rinehart, 1933.

Diehl, Digby. "New Monroe Book From Old Memoirs." Los Angeles *Times*, April 15, 1974.

Duffey, Bernard. *The Chicago Renaissance in American Letters.* Ann Arbor: Michigan State University Press, 1954.

Eyles, Allen. "Chicago, Chicago." *Focus on Film*, London, April 1970. A review of Jewison's film *Gaily, Gaily* with brief filmographies and biographies of Hecht and others.

Sources

Fiedler, Leslie. *The Collected Essays of Leslie Fiedler*. Stein and Day, 1971. Two Volumes. Consideration of Hecht in context of Jewish-American fiction.

Forgue, Guy J., ed. *Letters of H.L. Mencken*. Knopf, 1961.

Fowler, Gene. *Good Night, Sweet Prince: The Life & Times of John Barrymore*. Viking, 1944.

Minutes of the Last Meeting. Viking, 1954.

Skyline: A Reporter's Reminiscence of the 1920s. Viking, 1961.

Fowler, Will. *The Young Man From Denver*. Garden City: Doubleday, 1962. A biography of Gene Fowler by his son.

Friede, Donald. *The Mechanical Angel*. Knopf, 1948. Memoirs of one of Hecht's publishers.

Friedrich, Otto. *Before the Deluge: A Portrait of Berlin in the 1920s*. Harper & Row, 1972.

Gardner, Virginia. "A Literary Editor Remembers: Henry Blackman Sell." *Chicago History*, Fall 1974. Re: the review editor of the Chicago *Daily News*.

Gassner, John. *Dramatic Soundings*. Crown, 1968. Touches on Hecht the playwright.

Gazell, John Albert. "The High Tide of Chicago's Bohemias." *Journal of the Illinois State Historical Association*, Spring 1972. The sociology of the Renaissance.

Geduld, Harry M., ed. *Authors on Film*. Bloomington: Indiana University Press, 1972. Contains Sandburg's review of *The Cabinet of Dr. Caligari*.

Gilmer, Walker. *Horace Liveright: Publisher of the Twenties.* Davis Lewis, 1970. Less a biography than a corporate history.

Golden, Harry. *Carl Sandburg.* Cleveland: World, 1961.

The Right Time: An Autogiography. Putnam's, 1969.

Goldman, Emma. *Living My Life.* Knopf, 1931. More easily obtainable in paperback (Dover, 1970). Both are two volumes.

Goodwin, Michael and Wise, Naomi. "An Interview with Howard Hawks." *Take One,* Montreal, November-December 1971.

Graham, Sheilah. *The Garden of Allah.* Crown, 1970.

Guiles, Fred Lawrence. *Hanging on in Paradise.* McGraw-Hill, 1975. Hecht and MacArthur dominate this study of Hollywood screenwriters.

Norma Jean: The Life Story of Marilyn Monroe. McGraw-Hill, 1969.

Hahn, Emily. *Romantic Rebels: An Informal History of Bohemianism in America.* Boston: Houghton Mifflin, 1967.

Halper, Albert, ed. *The Chicago Crime Book.* Cleveland: World, 1967. The stories of Dion O'Banion, Carl Wanderer and others.

Hansen, Harry. *Midwest Portraits: A Book of Memories and Friendships.* Harcourt, Brace, 1923. Even though some Hansen considered important have now faded, this contemporary account, with an important chapter on Hecht, remains the best book on the Renaissance.

Harris, Warren G. *Gable and Lombard.* Simon and Schuster, 1974.

Sources

Hass, Joseph and Lovitz, Gene. *Carl Sandburg, A Pictorial Biography*. Putnam's, 1967.

Hayes, Helen. *On Reflection: An Autobiography*. Evans, 1968.

Hecht, Ben. "The Incomplete Life of Mickey Cohen." *Scanlan's*, March 1970.

Higham, Charles. *Hollywood Cameraman*. London: Thames and Hudson, 1970. Contains an interview with Lee Garmes.

Hoffman, Frederick; Allen, Charles; and Ulrich, Carolyn F. *The Little Magazine: A History and a Bibliography*. Princeton: Princeton University Press, 1947. A good source of information on Hecht's early publication in journals.

The Twenties: American Writing in the Postwar Decade. Collier Books, 1962. Revised paperback edition. Insightful, derogatory criticism of Hecht's early fiction.

Jessel, George. *So Help Me*. Random House, 1943. The entertainer's memoirs.

Kael, Pauline. *Deeper Into Movies*. Boston: Little, Brown, 1973. Contains review of Jewison's film *Gaily, Gaily*.

Kiss Kiss, Bang Bang. Boston: Little Brown, 1968.

Reeling. Boston: Little, Brown, 1976. Contains "Hard-boiled Valentine," a review of the Wilder version of *The Front Page*.

Kael; Mankiewicz, Herman; and Welles, Orson. *The Citizen Kane Book*. Boston: Little Brown, 1971. Contains Kael's essay "Raising Kane," which discusses the origins of Hollywood newspaper movies, especially *The Front Page*.

Kahn, E.J. Jr., *The World of Swope*. Simon and Schuster, 1963. A biography of the editor of the New York *World*.

Karsner, David. *Sixteen Authors to One.* Lewis Copeland, 1928. Contains essay on Hecht's early fiction.

Katz, Shlomo. "Ben Hecht's *Kampf.*" *Midstream: A Quarterly Jewish Review*, Winter 1962. An essay-review of *Perfidy*.

Kaufman, Beatrice and Hennessey, Joseph. *The Letters of Alexander Woollcott.* Viking, 1944.

Kerr, Walter. *Gods on the Gymnasium Floor and Other Theatrical Adventures.* Simon and Schuster, 1971. Contains review of the 1969 New York revival of *The Front Page*.

Kobler, John. *Capone: The Life and World of Al Capone.* Putnam's, 1971.

Kramer, Dale. *Chicago Renaissance: The Literary Life in the Midwest, 1900-1930.* Appleton-Century, 1966. A good source for the years until about 1916; the author is ignorant of Hecht's role.

Kroenberger, Louis. *No Whippings, No Gold Watches: The Saga of a Writer and His Jobs.* Boston: Little, Brown, 1970. An insider's view of PM.

Lambert, Gavin. GWTW: *The Making of Gone With the Wind.* Boston: Little, Brown, 1973.

Langer, Laurence. *The Magic Curtain.* Dutton, 1951. Autobiography of the founder of the Theatre Guild who knew Hecht as far back as the Renaissance.

Laqueur, Walter. *Weimar: A Cultural History.* Putnam's, 1974. Berlin life during Hecht's stay there.

Lasky, Jesse Jr. *Whatever Happened to Hollywood.* Funk & Wagnalls, 1975. Memoir by the screenwriter, son of the mogul of the same name.

Latham, Aaron. *Crazy Sundays: F. Scott Fitzgerald in Hollywood.* Viking, 1971.

Lawrence, Jerome. *Actor: The Life & Times of Paul Muni.* Putnam's, 1974.

Lee, James Melvin. *History of American Journalism.* Garden City: Garden City Publishing, 1923. Revised edition. Includes family trees of Chicago dailies.

Leonard, William T. *"The Scoundrel." Films in Review*, March 1975. An article on the making of the film and its aftermath.

Levant, Oscar. *The Unimportance of Being Oscar.* Putnam's, 1968.

Levin, Meyer. *In Search.* First published in Paris in 1950 and later in New York but most easily obtainable in paperback (Pocket Books, 1973). The autobiography of the novelist who knew Hecht during the Renaissance, succeeded him as feature writer on the *Daily News* and was later intimately involved with the Palestine crisis.

Lewis, Wyndham. *Blasting and Bombardiering.* London: Eyre and Spottiswode, 1937. Revised edition — London: Calder and Boyars, 1967. The autobiography of the British writer and artist who knew Hecht and whose novel *Tarr* influenced *Erik Dorn*.

Longstreet, Stephen. *Chicago 1860-1919.* David McKay, 1973. An excellent popular history for which Hecht was one of the primary sources.

Loos, Anita. *A Girl Like I.* Viking, 1966.

Lyle, John H. *The Dry and Lawless Years.* Englewood Cliffs, NJ: Prentice-Hall, 1960. The bootleg wars by one who was there as a Chicago judge.

McCarthy, Mary. *Sights and Spectacles, 1937-1958*. London: Heinemann, 1959. Contains "Two Bad Cases of Social Conscience," an important review of *To Quito and Back*.

McPhaul, John J. *Deadlines & Monkeyshines: The Fabled World of Chicago Journalism*. Englewood Cliffs, NJ: Prentice-Hall, 1962. The paperback, retitled *Chicago: City of Sin* (Beverley Hills: Book Company of America), lacks the index.

Manchester, William. *Disturber of the Peace: The Life of H.L.Mencken*. Harper & Brothers, 1951.

Maney, Richard. *Fanfare, the Confessions of a Press Agent*. Harper & Brothers, 1957. The memoirs of the press agent for the original stage productions of *The Front Page* and *Twentieth Century* and a good source of Hecht anecdotes.

Markey, Gene. *Literary Lights*. Knopf, 1923.

Meredith, Scott. *George S.Kaufman and His Friends*. Garden City: Doubleday, 1974. Much information about the original stage production of *The Front Page* but totally devoid of insight into the authors.

Mitgang, Herbert, ed. *The Letters of Carl Sandburg*. Harcourt, Brace, 1968.

Monroe, Marilyn. *My Story*. Stein and Day, 1974. Putative Hecht.

Moore, Jack B. *Maxwell Bodenheim*. Twayne Publishers, 1970.

Moore, William T. *Dateline Chicago: A Veteran Newsman Recalls Its Heyday*. Taplinger, 1973. Life on the *Herald-Examiner* by one who survived it.

Sources

Nash, Jay Robert. *Bloodletters and Badmen: A Narrative Encyclopedia of American Criminals from the Pilgrims to the Present*. Philadelphia: Lippincott, 1973. Good background on some of the villains Hecht knew and wrote about.

Nathan, George Jean. *Passing Judgments*. Knopf, 1935. Notes on Hecht and Fowler's *The Great Magoo*.

The Theatre in the Fifties. Knopf, 1953. Re: *Hazel Flagg*.

Oppenheimer, George, ed. *The Passionate Playgoer*. Viking, 1958. Hecht as playwright.

Perry, Albert. *Garrets and Pretenders, A History of Bohemianism in America*. Covici-Friede, 1933. The paperback (Dover, 1960) contains an epilogue by Harry T. Moore and is also available in cloth (Peter Smith). The pioneer study.

Postal, Bernard and Levy, Henry W. *And the Hills Shouted for Joy: The Day Israel Was Born*. McKay, 1973.

Putnam, George Palmer. *Wide Margins: A Publisher's Autobiography*. Harcourt, Brace, 1942

Putnam, Samuel. *Paris Was Our Mistress: Memoirs of a Lost & Found Generation*. Viking, 1947. Includes his life in Chicago during the Renaissance, before he left for Paris.

Rascoe, Burton. *Before I Forget*. Garden City: Doubleday, 1937. His memoirs. An important source for the Chicago years.

We Were Interrupted. Garden City: Doubleday, 1947. A continuation of the above.

Rexroth, Kenneth. *American Poetry in the Twentieth Century*.

Herder and Herder, 1971. The paperback (Seabury Press, 1973) is indexed. Passing critical comment on Hecht and Bodenheim; an excellent study.

An Autobiographical Novel. Garden City: Doubleday, 1966. No novel at all but an autobiography of his early years, with much detail about Chicago and the Renaissance. Alas, no index.

Robinson, Edward G. *All My Yesterdays: An Autobiography.* Hawthorn, 1973.

Rogers, Jason. *Newspaper Building.* Harper & Brothers, 1918. Financial case histories of a few newspapers, including the Chicago *Daily News.*

Rosenberg, Harold. *Discovering the Present: Three Decades in Art, Culture, and Politics.* Chicago: University of Chicago Press, 1973. Contains his important review of *A Guide for the Bedevilled*, "Man as Anti-Semite."

Sanders, Marion K. *Dorothy Thompson: A Legend in Her Time.* Boston: Houghton Mifflin, 1973.

Sarris, Andrew. *The American Cinema: Directors and Directions, 1929-1968.* Dutton, 1969. A paperback original.

The Films of Josef von Sternberg. Museum of Modern Art, 1966.

Sennett, Ted. *Lunatics and Lovers.* New Rochelle, NY: Arlington House, 1973. A study of 1930s screwball comedies.

Sherman, Stuart. *Critical Woodcuts.* Scribner's, 1926. A conservative, anti-Mencken critic of the 1920s; includes his review-essay "Ben Hecht and the Supermen."

Simon, John. *Movies Into Film: Film Criticism 1967-1970.* Dial Press, 1971.

Sources

Smith, Henry Justin. *Deadlines*. Chicago: Covici-McGee, 1923. *Josslyn*, Chicago: Covici-McGee, 1924. Two fictional works about life on Chicago newspapers, in which Hecht appears in fictional composites. The two were reprinted in one volume as *Extra! Extra! Deadlines and Josslyn* (Chicago: Sterling North, 1934) in an edition of 2,000 signed and number copies, with a preface by Burton Rascoe.

Snyder, Louise L. and Morris, Richard B. *A Treasury of Great Reporting*. Simon and Schuster, 1962. Revised edition paperback.

Sobol, Louis. *The Longest Street*. Crown, 1968. Contains anecdotes of Hecht, Bodenheim and Fowler by the Broadway columnist.

Starrett, Vincent. *Born in a Bookshop: Chapters From the Chicago Renascence*. Norman: University of Oklahoma Press, 1965. Despite the subtitle, a full autobiography, not just a memoir of the Renaissance. Quite reliable.

Stevenson, Elizabeth. *Babbitts and Bohemians*. Macmillan, 1967. In paperback (Collier Books, 1970) as *The American 1920s: Babbitts and Bohemians*.

Swanberg, W.A. *Dreiser*. Scribner's, 1965.

Targ, William. *Indecent Pleasures: The Life and Colorful Times of William Targ*. Macmillan, 1975. Part memoir, part reflections, by the New York publisher who was a bookseller and literary publisher in Chicago at the tail end of the Renaissance.

Teichmann, Howard. *George S. Kaufman: An Intimate Portrait*. Antheneum, 1972.

Smart Aleck: the Wit, World and Life of Alexander Woollcott. Morrow, 1976.

Thomas, Bob. *Marlon: Portrait of the Rebel as an Artist*. Random House, 1973. Biography of Marlon Brando.

Selznick. Garden City: Doubleday, 1970.

Thalberg: Life and Legend. Garden City: Doubleday, 1969.

Thurber, James. *The Years With Ross*. Boston: Little, Brown, 1959.

Von Eckhardt, Wolf and Gilman, Sander L. *Bertolt Brecht's Berlin*. Garden City: Doubleday, 1975.

Von Sternberg, Josef. *Fun in a Chinese Laundry*. Macmillan, 1965.

Waldau, Roy S. *Vintage Years of the Theatre Guild 1928-1939*. Cleveland: Case Western Reserve University Press, 1972. Re: *To Quito and Back*.

Weinberg, Herman G. *The Lubitsch Touch: A Critical Study*. Dutton, 1971. Revised paperback edition.

Wheelock, John Hall. *Editor to Author: The Letters of Maxwell E. Perkins*. Scribner's, 1950. Source of quotation in Chapter Eight.

Wolf, Dan and Fancher, Edwin. *The Village Voice Reader*. Grove Press, 1962. Contains an interview with Hecht on the occasion of *Winkelberg*.

Woollcott, Alexander. *Long, Long Ago*. Viking, 1943. Contains a profile of MacArthur.

Ziff, Larzer. *The American 1890s: Life and Times of a Lost Generation*. Viking, 1966. An excellent study with discussion of events in the Midwest leading to the Renaissance.

Index

221

Index

223

Index

Index

227